WELLINGTON AT WATERLOO

by Jac Weller

By the same author
Wellington in the Peninsula
Wellington in India
On Wellington

Greenhill Books, London
Stackpole Books, Pennsylvania

Greenhill Books

This edition of *Wellington at Waterloo* first published 1998 by Greenhill Books,
Lionel Leventhal Limited, Park House, 1 Russell Gardens, London NW11 9NN
and
Stackpole Books, 5067 Ritter Road, Mechanicsburg, PA 17055, USA

British Library Cataloguing in Publication Data
Weller, Jac
Wellington at Waterloo. – (Greenhill military paperback)
1. Waterloo, Battle of, 1815
I. Title
940.2'7

ISBN 1-85367-339-0

Library of Congress Cataloging-in-Publication Data available

Publishing History
Wellington at Waterloo was first published in 1967 (Longmans, London) and
reprinted in 1992 by Greenhill Books exactly as the original edition, with the
addition of a new Foreword by the author. It is reproduced now in paperback
exactly as the first Greenhill edition.

Printed in Great Britain

To
'the best of all instruments, British infantry'
Wellington to his brother 19 June 1815

Contents

Illustrations

All photographs, except no.1, are by the author

Maps, etc.

Foreword
to the New Edition

It isn't often that a writer gets to see republication of one of his books more than thirty years later. As a man approaches eighty, he is surely less vain and I hope more truthful. What little credit there may have been to me for writing my three books on Wellington should have been shared with my wife, Cornelia. As an undergraduate more than half a century ago, I was a mechanical engineer and a football player. Cornelia was the historian. Even though the earlier writing was done in my name, it should always have been joint. More specifically, we wrote *Wellington In Confederate Grey* for *The British Army Review* (August and December 1990) under our joint names.

Looking back to when we were smarter and had more stamina, we believe our particular and personal approach to writing about the Duke and Waterloo may be summed up by our five objectives:

First, we never wanted to remember too clearly ourselves what was happening 'on the other side of the hill'. We tried to let the reader know no more than Wellington himself knew at any particular time. Any reasonably studious field officer would win over the great captains if he had complete intelligence about his enemy continuously. Napoleon's lack of interest in his enemies is in contrast to Wellington's painstaking procedures. Information is vital, but for authors to reveal it too soon depreciates the ability of their protagonist.

Second, we have never written about a battle that we had not walked over and carefully studied topographically. In this My Little Wife has been of extreme value. She has handled reservations and rented vehicles. She has bought maps and sat in uncomfortable British Museum seats. In our younger days, we both walked from Hougoumont to Mount Saint Jean and even from La Belle Alliance to Waterloo. We bought or borrowed, including from the New York Public Library, all we thought might be of value, but we did our work also on site, especially at Waterloo, some of it in the dead of winter.

Third, we have used photography throughout our Wellington study. The Waterloo pictures taken from the air and included in this book helped us to visualise the scene of the battle. We hope they are equally useful to our readers. Waterloo, like Gettysburg, is amorphous on the ground, but is almost instantly comprehensible from the air if you have done your homework.

Fourth, the Wellers cannot claim brilliance for their writing, or for unusual insights into complicated characters. We have, however, worked hard. For instance, we have fired more than 300 pounds of lead through several variations of Baker rifles and Brown Bess muskets at ranges up to 300 yards. We hope we have absorbed something from our wonderful friendship with the 'Seventh Duke', the most gracious human being we have ever known. Lord and Lady Longford are also unique. To these three, the 'Great Duke' was still 'present' at Apsley House and at Stratford Saye.

Finally, we realise that we wrote about Wellington from an Anglo-Saxon point of view. We have had friendly criticism from a classmate with German persuasions. We remember especially a Belgian Army officer that knew every foot not only of the battlefield, but of the entire campaign area.

Without the Duke on 18 June 1815 the Emperor and France would have been restored to power. As Sir John Kincaid said, the Rifle Brigade had no fear for the outcome of the battle so long as nothing happened to Arthur Wellesley. A US general officer, who was our cherished friend for many years, glorified Napoleon. He said, moreover, 'Every time we put the Battle of Waterloo through a computer properly programmed, the French win.'

Wellington's total victory was gained, of course, with the help of many others high and low, but among them all the most important may have been the English, Scottish, Welsh and Irish infantry soldiers fighting with their Brown Bess muskets and bayonets. Wellington was 'Nosey' to most of them, but he never lost a battle nor the life of a man who he could reasonably have saved.

As the wounded sergeant of the 29th said in the field hospital after Albuera, 'If you had commanded us, My Lord, there wouldn't be so many of us here.' Beresford and Hill were good at their jobs, as was Paget (Anglesey) who would have taken over at Waterloo, but thank God nobody hit the Duke.

Princeton, New Jersey
1991

Preface

Waterloo and Gettysburg are the most widely studied battles of the Western world. Waterloo has been described briefly, at medium length, and interminably, in English, French, German, and some other languages. What excuse is there for another book?

First, because the pattern set by Napoleon at St Helena has been followed, even by British writers. To some extent at least, every book that I have seen on Waterloo deals with hypothetical situations which did not occur. Writers have said in many different ways, 'If General Blank had moved to his right as he ought to have done, rather than to his left as he did do, he would have become Queen of the May', or something similar and nearly as ridiculous. After an exhaustive reading of Waterloo literature, I flinch like a recruit firing a service rifle for the first time when I come upon a sentence which begins with either 'if' or 'had'. Some authors have so much of this sort of thing in their books that there is little space left to describe what did happen.

Observations giving alternatives and criticisms certainly have a place in military history. I feel, however, that this sort of thing is often over-done. It may be appropriate in Staff College seminars and in books written principally for readers at that level, but armchair strategists, at their leisure, in possession of all facts, but with no problems of practical command, can figure out ways to beat all the great captains. Their solutions don't have to stand the test of real battle, and are really unimportant. There is room, I hope, for one book written primarily for young officers and others who want to know what did happen, with as few additional words as possible about what I think ought to have happened.

My second reason for writing about Waterloo is that most previous accounts have described the battle from an omniscient point of view. Most authors have told their readers what was happening on both sides throughout the entire campaign. A clear picture can be created by telling what the French, the Prussians, and the Anglo-Dutch did continuously, but this approach is often unfortunate. It tends to diminish the stature of even the greatest commanders and is not meaningful for young officers who want to profit from the past. I have striven to give them no more information than Wellington had at any particular time. They will be fortunate if they know as much of their future enemies.

This approach does not, of course, originate from me; I believe Douglas Freeman developed it first. It has disadvantages; you will not be told any more of Grouchy on 18 June than Wellington knew at the time. I hope, however, that my account of Waterloo will bear a greater relevance to the practical problems of directing an army in battle. These have changed less in 150 years than many would expect. In spite of enormous technological changes, the military situation on 1 June 1815 had certain similarities to our own today. France, like Russia in 1966, was the strongest land power in Europe and could be defeated only by a coalition of less totalitarian Allies. Wellington had to await an attack unpredictable as to time and direction and use troops not perfectly assimilated into a unified army to defeat it.

My third reason for writing this book is that most of those at present available have been written about grand strategy, or about the human experience of men doing the fighting. We have excellent accounts of what happened from governmental, down to about divisional level. We also have vivid descriptions of what was happening to individuals and going on in their minds. But we do not have a great deal in the area between brigades and platoons. I have endeavoured to bridge this gap.

My tactical descriptions have presented many difficulties; Waterloo is not a simple battle. Disagreements in the original sources as to positions, times, formations and the like are legion. I have usually been able to solve these problems, at least to my own satisfaction; I have included in the footnotes the principal opposed opinions. I humbly admit, however, that some of my tactical conclusions are not based as solidly on unconflicting original material as I could wish. We know more of the uniforms worn by the contending armies than we do about their offensive and defensive formations. For instance, no one can ever be sure how the French Imperial Guard was formed at the crisis of the battle, nor how and by what units it was defeated.

My fourth reason is that more recent military history helps to explain what happened in Belgium in 1815. We can better understand Napoleon's objectives, his brilliantly conceived strategy, his initial success, and his ultimate complete failure because of Lee and Gettysburg, or the 1944 German campaign of the Bulge. It is easier to plan than to execute; a dangerous offensive on a large scale usually goes well at first. When it fails, there are frequently many convincing 'ifs' which obscure what actually happened. But it is eternally important to those who may be attacked unexpectedly to know how a great commander of the past weathered the almost inevitable initial reverses and then beat the enemy completely.

In Part One of this work, I have endeavoured to describe what actually took place, with the emphasis usually on what Wellington did himself. Part Two contains three moderately technical chapters and three chapters devoted to mistakes and criticisms, one each given to Wellington, the French, and the Prussians. This has led to some unavoidable repetition, but has kept unwanted author's comments in Part One to a minimum.

My study of the battlefield of Waterloo began with an eight-day visit in 1953; my reading about Wellington started many years earlier. Over this long period, so many people have been of assistance. To mention some and not others seems unfair, but it cannot be helped. I never knew the full name of the

Belgian innkeeper who showed and told me much of actual battlefield relics, and he died before my second visit in 1957. Other Belgians have welcomed me to their homes and farms and told stories of what happened there in June 1815.

On a different level, I am deeply and humbly indebted to Commandant Émile Dehond of the Belgian Staff College for so much material aid and guidance, and to Lieutenant-Colonel Stan McClellan, U.S. Army, who brought us together. I appreciate also what Dick Dilworth and Ralph Nunziato did in arranging for me to see the campaign and battlefield area from the air slowly and at low level. Keith Neal and Major Hollies-Smith have helped me with small arms and other material of this era; Mr A. N. Kennard of the Tower of London and Mr Dalkin of the Rotunda at Woolwich have answered questions authoritatively and shown me personally all their remarkable Waterloo relics. I am grateful for the help and suggestions of Major G. Tylden and Major Dawney of the Society for Army Historical Research. Brigadier F. J. Siggers kindly gave me permission to search in the Woolwich Library; Mr O'Connor helped me find vital, but unpublished, material there in the Dickson papers concerning Waterloo.

I appreciate also the kindness and consideration of many British officers, active and retired. Jim Thwaites, Gywnne Davies and many others have shown me what their predecessors were like, those company and field officers in the British foot regiments who never lost to Bonaparte. I thank also Field-Marshal Sir Francis Festing and our fellow members of the Rowland Club for their comments and encouragement.

I must also extend my special thanks to Brigadier C. N. Barclay, editor of *The Army Quarterly and Defence Journal* and an eminent military historian, and to Brigadier Peter Young, Reader in Military History at Sandhurst. Brigadier Barclay gave me full answers to several questions that had been puzzling me for months. Brigadier Young read this work in typescript and offered numerous suggestions which were gratefully accepted. I must apologise to him and others for not following two of these. I stand by my belief that Napoleon's army at Waterloo was uniquely remarkable for its number of veterans, although in many instances their organisation was new.

More important and more embarrassing for me as an American, Brigadier Young has suggested that I have been too severe a critic of the British heavy cavalry. I can but set down honestly the results of my research; to change them would be unfair to the light cavalry and the ever efficient British infantry. I was encouraged by what some British authorities have told me and written on this subject. The British heavy cavalry regiments were composed of brave and strong men, but some at least went out of control. They are said to have done the same when in tanks attacking Rommel in the desert more than a century and a quarter later. A glorious fault, but still a fault.

I must again mention Dudley Johnson of Princeton and Gordon Craig of Leland-Stanford without whom I would probably never have started in this field. I appreciate also Ian Robertson's interest and his guidance in the past. More thanks are due to My Little Wife, Dorothy Connelly, Helen Nason and Mildred Christopher. Between them, they did so much that I could not possibly have accomplished myself.

I am grateful to the following for permission to reproduce copyright material: Macmillan & Co. Ltd for extracts from *The Hundred Days* by Anthony Brett-James and from *The History of the British Army* by the Rt. Hon. H. W. Fortescue; John Menzies & Co. Ltd for an extract from *Life of a Regiment* by Lt.-Col. C. Greenhill Gardyne, and Routledge and Kegan Paul Ltd for an extract from *Napoleon and Waterloo* by Major A. F. Becke.

¶ *Author's note.* I have used only one unusual abbreviation, namely PLHS for the Papelotte, La Haye, Smohain area on the Waterloo battlefield.

WELLINGTON
AT
WATERLOO

WELLINGTON AT WATERLOO

by Jac Weller

Greenhill Books, London
Stackpole Books, Pennsylvania

PART ONE

I

A Brief Interval of Peace

On 12 April 1814, Wellington received official notification of Napoleon's first abdication at Paris six days earlier. The war was soon over and Wellington's Peninsular Army, one of the most skilful ever put together, was disbanded. Anglo-Saxons have a unique facility for doing these things quickly, perhaps too quickly.

The ex-Commander-in-Chief was out of a military job, but the British Cabinet could always find something for the man who kept them in power for so long. After briefly superintending the demobilisation of his army, he set out on 30 April for Paris to undertake the duties of British Ambassador to the French; he arrived on 4 May and was immediately caught up in the festivities of the capital. Louis XVIII, the restored Bourbon king of France, had as his official guests the Tsar of Russia, the King of Prussia, the Emperor of Austria, and many other dignitaries.

Wellington did not begin his diplomatic duties immediately: Viscount Castlereagh, British Foreign Secretary, was present in Paris and continued to handle matters of this type. He and Wellington were often together and rode one day in civilian clothes to watch a foreign military parade pass the windows of the Tuileries. The crowned heads of Europe were comfortably inside, but expended more effort in craning their necks to get a look at Wellington than in examining the Russian Cossacks and other unusual troops in the parade.

Bad news from Spain reached Paris before Wellington had been there a week. Ferdinand VII, after long captivity in France and some secret negotiations which finally led to his release by Napoleon, had returned to Spain in an evil humour. If something was not done

3

quickly, he would probably plunge his unfortunate country into another civil war.[1] Wellington was the only man in Europe who could prevent this. He agreed to undertake a special mission to Madrid to persuade both the king and his political enemies to be moderate in their acts and plans and left Paris on 10 May 1814.

The trip to Madrid was made along the old road that Wellington knew so well. He passed the Bidassoa within sight of the shrimpers' fords which his army had used only a few months before. San Sebastian still showed the scars of its long siege, although British money was being spent to repair the damage their artillery had caused. Wellington passed through Vitoria and the valley of the Zadorra, the scene of his greatest offensive victory. His coach ran fast through the gorge where Hill's forces began the battle which probably changed the fate of Europe.[2]

Once in Central Spain, Wellington had more to do than remember Salamanca where his great counterstroke had crushed '40,000 Frenchmen in 40 minutes'.[3] The 3rd and 4th Spanish Armies were between Burgos and Madrid and of questionable loyalty to their new monarch. Wellington was still nominally Commander-in-Chief of all Spanish Armies and stopped at each headquarters long enough to persuade the principal officers of both not to create an open break with central authority in Madrid. He explained the lateness of his arrival at the capital – he entered on the 24th rather than on the 22nd as planned – by saying that his coach had broken down.

Everyone in Spain from the king to indigent waifs in the street hailed Wellington as their personal deliverer. He was confirmed in all his Spanish honours. Ferdinand was sincerely grateful for the achievements of the great Englishman during the war. On the other hand, the king and his ministers had embarked on political plans that were dear to their hearts; they did not want criticism from any foreigner. The

[1] This story, as well as the Spanish king himself, is complicated and unpleasant; see *Oman*, VII, 297–8, 300–7 and 423–7.

Refer to the Bibliography, pp. 246 ff., for details of short titles used in the footnotes.

[2] News of Wellington's victory at Vitoria, fought on 21 June 1813, strengthened the Northern European coalition against Napoleon so that the Armistice of Plasswitz, signed on 4 June, was ended on 11 August and Austria entered the finally victorious war against the French Emperor. Napoleon's successes at Lutzen (2 May 1813) and Bautzen (20–21 May 1813) might have kept him on his throne, but for Wellington's much more complete victory far to the south.

[3] The Salamanca shift from the defensive to the offensive is a classic in military history; see *Weller*, 206–26.

democratic Cortes had already been abolished and many of the princi-
pal Spanish Liberals imprisoned. Ferdinand obviously wished to restore
Spain to what it had been politically before the French Revolution.
He was determined to do this, even though he caused bloodshed.

Wellington thought Ferdinand not quite such a fool as others who
have left reasonably disinterested opinions of the new monarch. He
soon discovered, however, recent secret understandings between
Ferdinand's ministers and France. Spain seems to have been pledged to
side with France against Britain.[1] This situation is inexplicable, if it
were not for the various agreements reached at Valençay between
Ferdinand VII and Talleyrand before the king was released by Napoleon. The Emperor was gone, but Talleyrand was still powerful.
There may also have been a religious basis for this Spanish preference
for France, another Catholic country. Priests were of importance in
Ferdinand's Government; the Inquisition had been re-established,
although in a milder form.

Wellington remained in Madrid for only twelve days, but made
considerable progress in persuading both factions to be reasonable.
Ferdinand and his ministers were reminded of reality and told where a
severe, revengeful political policy was likely to lead them and their
country. The Liberals who had been arrested by the Government were
released. The Liberal element in the army agreed to do its military
duty and avoid the horrors of civil war, at least temporarily.

Wellington approached the matter of friendship between France and
Spain diplomatically. He refrained from mentioning gratitude to
Britain for recent wartime aid in his discussions of the relative abilities
of France and his own country to be a useful friend to Spain. But he
did point out the military, economic, and commercial power of Great
Britain. There was still a subsidy due to Spain of £800,000 for 1814;
Wellington told the Government that this would not be paid unless
Britain was satisfied that Ferdinand was not moving backwards into
eighteenth-century despotism.

While in Madrid, Wellington was notified that he had been created
a British Duke. This was no great surprise, even to Wellington himself.
What was astonishing, however, was that his Government voted him
£400,000 in money. The Tories proposed £300,000, but the Opposition raised the amount. Further, Britain finally decided to bring

---

[1] Wellington to Castlereagh, Madrid, 1 June 1814; *Dispatches*, XII, 37–40, especially:
'It is quite obvious to me that unless we can turn them entirely from these schemes, or can
attain their objects for them, they will throw themselves into the arms of the French . . .'

Wellington home. He began the long trip from Madrid on 5 June, but broke his journey for five days at Bordeaux to take final leave of his troops. His General Order issued in Bordeaux on 14 June 1814 is worthy of being quoted in full.

1. The Commander of the Forces, being upon the point of returning to England, again takes this opportunity of congratulating the army upon the recent events which have restored peace to their country and to the world.

2. The share which the British Army has had in producing these events, and the high character with which the army will quit this country, must be equally satisfactory to every individual belonging to it, as they are to the Commander of the Forces; and he trusts that the troops will continue the same good conduct to the last.

3. The Commander of the Forces once more requests the army to accept his thanks.

4. Although circumstances may alter the relations in which he has stood towards them, so much to his satisfaction, he assures them that he shall never cease to feel the warmest interest in their welfare and honour; and that he will be at all times happy to be of any service to those to whose conduct, discipline, and gallantry, their country is so much indebted.[1]

Wellington stopped briefly at Paris to make arrangements for British cavalry and artillery to march across France to Calais. He arrived at Dover on 23 June 1814 after a continuous absence of five years and two months. When he had last seen those shores in April 1809, Napoleon had dominated all of Continental Europe save for a few small states and a part of Portugal. The new Duke had done much to change the former Emperor's fortunes in the intervening time.

Wellington was wildly acclaimed in Dover, along the road to London, and in London itself. He was unique in the experience of all living Britons, a victorious military commander who returned home triumphant. He took his place in the House of Lords on 28 June 1814 as a baron, viscount, earl, marquis, and duke. He received the formal thanks of the House of Commons on 1 July and attended a banquet given by the Lord Mayor of London in his honour on 9 July. On all three occasions, he thanked those present and the nation that he had served so long and dutifully by stressing the bravery and efficiency of his officers and men.[2]

---

[1] *Dispatches*, XII, 62.

[2] *Alexander*, II, 341, says, 'In returning thanks, he feelingly alluded to the pride and gratification which he felt in such testimonies of public approbation of his services, and to his grateful sense of support which he had received from his officers and the valour of his troops.'

Wellington spent only five weeks in Britain; his time was taken up with social, political, and public functions. His two sons who had been infants when he saw them last and his Duchess played a less important part in his life than is normal. It would appear from contemporary evidence that the marriage was unfortunate, but Wellington resolutely never admitted this to himself or anyone else.[1]

The Duke left Britain for Paris on 8 August 1814 to begin his duties as Ambassador to France. On his way, he joined the Prince of Orange, the heir to the throne of the Netherlands, in a survey of the fortifications and defensive arrangements between that country (which now included Belgium) and France. The young Prince, aged twenty-two, had been on Wellington's staff in the Peninsula and had some pretensions to military knowledge. The Duke was also accompanied by topographical engineers and spent a fortnight in careful military reconnaissance of the border territory from the Channel to the Ardennes. The French had destroyed all the old fortifications north of their border except those at Nieuport, Ostend, and Antwerp which they had preserved to defend their own port facilities in these places. Wellington recommended that a number of small fortified towns be restored to reasonable military efficiency rather than that a few larger places of greater strength be constructed. He suggested specifically the renovation of the works at Menin, Ypres, Tournai, Courtrai, and Mons. He also proposed that Oudenarde, Ghent and Brussels be fortified.

The Duke made another military observation during this tour that was to prove of great value later on. He recognised the inherent strength for his type of defensive battle of the position south of Waterloo which he occupied ten months later and had a map of it prepared.[2] Wellington's military eye picked up immediately the good features, such as the lateral ridge across the road south of Mont Saint Jean and the communication behind it to the north, but this was only one of several similar positions examined and found suitable in the area between the French border and Brussels. The Waterloo position covered adequately the approaches from Charleroi and Genappe, but would have been useless if a French army advanced along some other route.

[1] See *Gleig's Reminiscences*, 274–7 and *passim*, for one of the best contemporary explanations.

[2] This map is reproduced in *Yonge*, facing p. 565, but is disappointing. It is hardly more than a hurried sketch and full of errors; La Haye Sainte is on the wrong side of the Genappe road. The original was on display at Wellington Barracks in June 1965.

The Duke also observed during his short stay in Belgium that the people there, though contented as Austrian subjects until 1792, had then apparently totally transferred their allegiance to France. Their loyalty to Napoleon was greater than that of the inhabitants of some parts of France itself. Even so early as the summer of 1814, it was clear to someone of the Duke's experience that their pleasure in the union with the Netherlands and their fondness for the House of Orange was limited. Belgian troops had fought valiantly for France; they would be of questionable value in the event of their being called on to fight against their old comrades. Belgians would probably remain subjects of the Netherlands only so long as they were forced to do so by the presence of foreign bayonets.

On 24 August 1814 the Duke presented his credentials to Louis XVIII. He remained in the French capital for precisely five months and handled all his various functions as Ambassador, including the care of British civilians, the fostering of British commercial and business enterprises and the collecting of money owed to British banking institutions from before the French Revolution, among many others, in an unobtrusive but efficient manner. He urged the French Government to join his own country in several anti-slavery measures that were popular in Britain at that time, including the prohibition of the slave trade. Louis XVIII was at first willing to outlaw it entirely, but found himself unable to do so. Practically no one in France appreciated the fact that Britain was largely unselfish in her desire to stop the horrible abuses of European military power in Africa where thousands of Negroes were taken into custody, packed like sardines into foul sailing ships, and carried long distances over tropical seas to be sold into lives of hard labour in the New World. The general idea in France seems to have been that Britain already had her possessions well stocked with slaves and did not need any new ones. British commercial interests were thought now to oppose the trade in order to prevent colonial rivals from obtaining the most important single ingredient for producing sugar, cheap controllable labour.

Wellington's principal job in Paris soon became, however, the keeping of the new king on his throne. France was not in good shape economically: industry, commerce, and finance all needed to be remodelled in accordance with the new situation. The nation no longer included the vast areas added over the past twenty years by Napoleon's victories. The flow of raw materials and products of all types from the conquered enemies of France had ceased. There was widespread unemployment and discontent, particularly among the officers and men who had served in the French Army and had become used to a privileged existence, both in their own country and in French military stations beyond her borders.

Wellington was soon deeply involved with these problems and was of considerable assistance to the French Government. There was nothing he could do, however, about bettering the public image of the restored Bourbon king. Louis XVIII was pleasant, kindly, and reasonably intelligent, but so fat that he moved with difficulty. He suffered terribly when compared with the Emperor as the French liked best to remember him, a lithe, lean, muscular man mounted on a superb horse. In spite of everything that Wellington and Britain did, the new French Monarchy became less and less popular. Wellington pointed out in some detail in his day-to-day letters to various people the conflicts in Paris between the Royalists and the pro-Bonapartists and indicated the possibility of Napoleon's restoration.[1]

The Duke's personal position in the French capital changed greatly. In May 1814, he was received as a military hero who had not only befriended the French people, but also restored to them their rightful Bourbon monarch. Most Frenchmen were at that time glad to be rid of Napoleon who had bathed Europe in blood for years and had finally been utterly defeated. But public memories are short; the French soon forgot the bad sides of life under the Empire and remembered only Napoleon's magnificent victories. They began to resent the presence in their capital of the man who had done most to bring to a close the period of France's greatest achievements. The opponents of Louis XVIII's Government also accused Britain and Wellington of placing the now unpopular monarch on the French throne and keeping him there.

The Duke received threatening letters; veiled threats of physical assault appeared in newspapers.[2] The Tory Ministry was seriously concerned; they had earlier considered him as a new overall Commander-in-Chief in America. They could still send him there, for the war with the United States was not yet over. But the Duke realised that the conflict in the New World held insoluble problems for both

---

[1] *Dispatches*, XII, *passim*.

[2] The famous Paris attempt on the Duke's life whose perpetrator was immediately acquitted by a French court and received a legacy from Napoleon – actually never paid – did not occur until 1818, but there was a lot of talk of violence in the autumn and winter of 1814–15.

sides and was never enthusiastic about an American command. In spite of his many and varied capabilities, an army appointment which did not include control of the navy would probably have been indecisive. He pointed out candidly that if a new war should start in Europe, Britain and her Allies would need him immediately, not five or six months later. He wrote from Paris on 9 November 1814, 'You cannot, in my opinion, at this moment decide upon sending me to America. In case of the occurrence of anything in Europe, there is nobody but myself in whom either yourselves or the country, or your Allies, would feel any confidence.'[1]

He objected also to leaving Paris as if forced to do so by fear of personal injury; if he was sent somewhere else, it had to be to a post commensurate with the Duke's value to Britain and his abilities. The British Government found him such a position. Viscount Castlereagh was representing Britain at the Congress of Vienna which was attempting to set up new national boundaries and distribute the spoils made available by the recent defeat of France, but he was needed for the opening of Parliament in London. What could be more natural than for Wellington to take his place? No Englishman was so much respected internationally, and he did not lack diplomatic experience.

The Duke left Paris on 24 January 1815 and arrived in Vienna on 3 February. He found that the victors in the recent war were near to a new one among themselves. Castlereagh, Metternich of Austria, and Talleyrand of France had negotiated a secret treaty between themselves which pledged mutual support against Russia and Prussia if the latter pressed their respective claims for Poland and Saxony to the point of war. Prussia also wanted and ultimately received the South German Rhineland, even though at that time most of it was more French than German.

Amongst the inhabitants of the left bank of the Rhine we found a kind of stolid indifference prevailing towards Germany, her language and customs. All interests had turned to France: commercial relations were almost wholly broken off with Germany: the line of custom-houses on the Rhine, and the difficulties of crossing that river, contributed to this result. Between Mainz and Wesel there were no pontoon bridges. The French Government had carefully separated the province from Germany, in order to transform it more surely and quickly into French departments.[2]

---

[1] *Supplementary Dispatches.* IX, 425. It would take the time mentioned for a message to cross the Atlantic and Wellington to return under normal weather conditions.

[2] *Müffling's Passages*, 204.

Wellington immediately assumed a leading role at the Congress of Vienna. The conflict of territorial interests on the Continent was extreme; only Britain had no desire for additional territory and considered that the inhabitants of a country should be consulted about their future allegiance. But in spite of some violent squabbles, the assembly was one of the most festive ever held. Petrie brilliantly writes that Wellington

was at this time forty-five years old, and the assembled monarchs and statesmen whom he met in Vienna were mostly of his own age; which is to say that they were, judged by modern standards, young men. Alexander I of Russia was only thirty-seven; Metternich was forty-one; Frederick William III of Prussia was forty-four; Castlereagh was forty-five; while Nesselrode was but thirty-four. These were the men who took the lead at the Congress of Vienna, and it is perhaps not entirely fanciful to suggest that in their comparative youth may be the explanation not only of the festivities by which the conference was marked, but also of the fact that they were able to devise a settlement which lasted for forty-five years.[1]

Wellington's fairly austere personal habits did not prevent him from taking full advantage of his numerous opportunities to talk to professional soldiers about the recent protracted period of war and the tactics and strategy of Napoleon himself. The Duke already personally knew many of the French marshals and several of the German commanders including Blücher. While in Vienna, he made the acquaintance of most of the Austrians and Russians as well.

After thirty-two days in Vienna, Wellington received from Lord Burghersh, British Minister at Florence, a confidential dispatch which revealed that Napoleon had left Elba. He says of this:

I received here on the 7th instant a dispatch from Lord Burghersh, of the 1st, giving an account that Buonaparte had quitted the island of Elba, with all his civil and military officers, and about 1,200 troops, on the 26th of February. I immediately communicated this account to the Emperors of Austria and Russia, and to the King of Prussia, and to the Ministers of the different Powers, and I found among all one prevailing sentiment, of a determination to unite their efforts to support the system established by the peace of Paris.[2]

The Duke is supposed to have immediately called in his own quarters a meeting of the heads of government to consider the situation. His guests who only hours before had been antagonistic suddenly found

[1] *Petrie*, 183.
[2] *Dispatches*, XII, 266.

that their differences were of small importance compared to this mutual danger. Britain, Austria, Russia, and Prussia were again firm friends; the treaty of Chaumont was reaffirmed.[1]

News from France went from bad to worse. Napoleon triumphed over the armies of Louis XVIII practically without firing a shot. Few soldiers from privates to marshals took their recent oaths of allegiance to the Bourbon king seriously. When the Emperor appeared in person, the army went over to him practically to a man. Wellington finally on 27 March 1815 received the news of the impending flight from Paris of Louis XVIII which meant, of course, that Napoleon would again be Emperor of the French.[2]

During the three weeks following the news of Napoleon's initial movements, the new coalition against France became a solid reality. Acting with limited authority, Wellington re-negotiated the original treaty of Chaumont and produced a new instrument which granted a subsidy to Austria, Russia and Prussia totalling five million sterling. He also pledged Britain to furnish an army of 150,000 of her own troops, or make appropriate payments to the smaller allies who could supply any deficiency in this total. All countries which had fought against Napoleon and France in the recent successful war were invited to subscribe to this treaty and participate in renewing hostilities and in the British bounty.

During these negotiations, the Tsar of Russia offered Wellington a place on a four-man council that would have ultimate responsibility for all military operations; a position never described in detail. The Duke refused and mentioned in his correspondence that he would prefer to carry a musket.[3] Preparations for the coming campaigns were begun by all the new allies, while plans matured rapidly in Vienna for a joint offensive.

Parts of the Austrian forces were already in northern Italy and were soon actively engaged against Murat, King of Naples and Napoleon's brother-in-law. Murat had survived the fall of the First Empire because he had become one of the allies against Napoleon. He now, however, prematurely chose to side with him and attacked the Papal States with obvious hostile intentions against the Austrian territories in north-

---

[1] The original Treaty of Chaumont was negotiated on 9 March 1814 by Britain, Austria, Russia and Prussia and was, of course, directed against the First Empire.

[2] The news came from Fitzroy Somerset in Paris, *Dispatches*, XII, 284.

[3] *Dispatches*, XII, 268, Wellington to Castlereagh, says, 'As I should have neither character nor occupation in such a situation, I should prefer to carry a musket.'

ern Italy. He and his Neapolitan army were utterly defeated before Napoleon could come to his aid.

The northern allies co-ordinated their plans for attacks between the Alps and the Channel. An Austrian army was first to hold and then advance across the southern Rhine while a Prussian force was to be concentrated south of the northern Rhine and west of the Ardennes. An Anglo-Dutch army was to operate west of the Prussians. A large Russian army was to cross Poland and Germany and arrive in the vicinity of Mainz early in the summer. When all these were assembled and ready for action, they would begin separate but mutually supporting drives into France with a total strength of over 600,000 men. (See Map 1.)

Wellington would, of course, return to a military command. As he did not want the nebulous post offered him by the Tsar, he would naturally take over the small Anglo-Dutch Army temporarily under the Prince of Orange. The Duke left Vienna on 29 March 1815 and arrived in Brussels on 5 April, assuming immediately his new duties.

II

Organisation, Tactics and Strategy of the Contending Armies

Many soldiers and most officers of field rank and higher who participated in the Waterloo Campaign had seen a great deal of active service. Even though the conflict was short, it was fought in accordance with experience gained over one of the most extended periods of war in all history. There were three different systems, the French, the Prussian, and the British. The first two had many similarities because of close contact between them over many years.[1] The French tactics and strategy at Waterloo were those used by Napoleon to defeat all his Continental enemies. The Prussians did as they had done at Leipzig and thereafter until the Emperor's first abdication in 1814. Wellington basically used his Peninsular methods modified to fit a heterogeneous army and what he learned of Napoleon's own battle manœuvres.

The three ways of making war evolved logically from the practice of each nation in 1789; their military experience thereafter and the character of their commanders were also important. The organisation, strategy, and tactics of Napoleon and his war machine owed more to the Bourbon armies of the eighteenth century than is generally realised.[2] But the old system was modified by experience in the wars which followed the French Revolution. The Prussians began with the tactics and strategy of Frederick the Great, but changed them as defeat followed defeat. Wellington evolved a system of his own, but based

---

[1] A much reduced Prussia was the nominal ally of France after the Peace of Tilsit in 1807, but the tendency to copy a successful opponent was probably a stronger factor in shaping the Prussian military system.

[2] *Liddell Hart*, 27–100, traces this admirably.

it on the virtues of the eighteenth-century British Army, study, and a lot of practical experience in the field. The campaign and battle of Waterloo will be clearer if we discuss first how the three major armies were accustomed to operate.

FRANCE AND NAPOLEON

The French won the battles which followed their Reign of Terror because they usually had more men and an advantage in patriotic spirit. Many French commanders at various levels were professional soldiers, but their forces as a whole had little military experience and poor equipment. Infantrymen were generally recently conscripted and had virtually no basic training; their weapons were deficient in number and of low quality. French field-artillery units usually had poor weapons and only a few trained gunners. French cavalry was practically non-existent. These deficiencies were not insurmountable; the new techniques of war evolved by French military theorists earlier in the century[1] could be employed to some extent even with semi-trained soldiers. Valour, common sense, and personal initiative at all levels were also important.

The formal lines of battle presented by the Continental armies opposed to Republican France proved to be their own undoing. French commanders sent forward against them swarms of skirmishers, or tirailleurs, who maintained no rigid alignment, but took advantage of cover. Even though disorganised, individual courage enabled them to approach close to the enemy line and direct aimed fire at it. The idea of skirmishers did not, of course, originate with French Republican commanders: light infantry tactics had been known for a long time.[2] But the French now placed up to 25 per cent of their total force in these irregular lines which frequently extended across their entire battlefront. The tirailleurs swept away the skirmishers of the enemy, if any, and then attacked their main lines. Numerous casualties were inflicted; confusion often resulted. Mere returning the fire of the tirailleurs by line formations was ineffective because individual Frenchmen who took full advantage of any available cover presented such small targets.

[1] Notably Saxe, Bourcet and Guibert.

[2] Military operations in North America during the eighteenth century show the value of rangers and riflemen; see particularly *Fuller's British Light Infantry*. There are also contemporary treatises about these tactics, particularly by German professional soldiers.

During the few minutes that the tirailleurs engaged the entire enemy front, French commanders would send forward one or more heavy columns to strike selected points. Infantrymen in these needed a minimum of training. Only the front and outside men on the flanks could fire their muskets effectively. Columns advancing with patriotic determination on narrow fronts against sections of enemy lines already disorganised by the tirailleurs were extremely formidable. Shock was opposed to firepower; the bayonets of the columns were arrayed against the muskets of the lines. Artillery accompanied these attacks and opened from the flanks at such short range that skill in aiming and the quality of the pieces themselves were not important. Properly brought into action – against enemies other than England – the columns and close-range artillery always won.

In the Revolutionary battles and later throughout the Empire, French infantry in column often broke enemy lines without taking their muskets from their shoulders.[1] They were not actually exerting shock for no fighting took place. The power applied by columns was psychological, but it was just as effective. If disorganising fear could bè induced into the minds of the enemy immediately in front of the head of a French column, physical shock was unnecessary. If enemy front lines could be penetrated, the French usually won the mêlées which followed because of their superiority in numbers and personal valour. Where the enemies of France had two battle lines fairly close together, the second was involved in the downfall of the first. If the second line was too far back, it was unable to participate in the initial fight and was defeated in a second similar action.

After Bonaparte's 1796 Italian campaign and especially after his return from Egypt in 1799, the French Army improved in many professional details. The tirailleurs were better organised, armed and trained. They were better able to disrupt the enemy battle line and conceal the final intentions of Napoleon's columns. Long-range artillery fire also helped in this respect and will be discussed presently.

Cavalry was reintroduced into the French Armies in the proportions common earlier in the eighteenth century. By stages, an extremely efficient cavalry composed of three distinct types was developed. Light cavalry was for reconnaissance and screening. Heavy cavalry was for use on the battlefield, to deliver shock attacks. Dragoons functioned at first as mounted infantry, but soon became true cavalry. They were

[1] *Jomini's Art*, 297–8.

intermediate between the light and heavy types and could act as either. Most of the French cavalry which Wellington met in the Peninsula were dragoons.[1]

Most important of all in the minds of many military tacticians, French artillery was improved in efficiency and material. Weapons were standardised and provided in ample numbers.[2] Personnel was well trained and disciplined. Napoleon used a larger proportion of heavy field-guns than any other modern commander. He used them not only to reinforce his tirailleurs in disorganising the entire enemy front, but also to concentrate fire on the points to be attacked by his infantry columns. The French light artillery was also improved; it still dashed forward beside the columns and went into action at even shorter range, often at below 100 yards. Multiple ball charges were extremely effective in enfilade from the flank against an enemy line at close range.

The organisation of French Armies changed more rapidly than their tactics and soon became unique in war as it had been known. Napoleon created an articulated military machine capable of spreading over a large area, moving quickly and precisely according to complicated orders from a central source, and then concentrating for battle. He gained a strategic mobility unattainable with the old centralised armies.[3] Division-sized units with some autonomy had been known in armies since the Roman legions, but Napoleon increased their independence and created separate, unified, self-contained corps which were to be the basis of much of his winning strategy.

A French corps at full strength contained about 25,000 infantry, cavalry, artillery, and engineers plus some military and civilian support units. A corps frequently consisted of four infantry divisions, a cavalry division, and from five to eight batteries of artillery. Even though French divisions could operate away from their corps, this was not usually considered desirable when large forces were assembled in one area. Napoleon compensated for his own rather sedentary attitude to

---

[1] Heavy cavalry was used by Napoleon in the first Spanish campaigns, but was found difficult to maintain, and unsuited to the terrain, and was mostly withdrawn in 1809.

[2] This standardisation under Marmont did not go as far as it might have; Part Two, Chapter II, of this work discusses contemporary artillery in some detail.

[3] We should not overlook Napoleon's indebtedness to Bourcet, particularly for the plan followed in the Italian campaign of 1796.

army direction by giving his corps commanders a great deal of initiative in executing general instructions.[1]

There was one significant exception to the French organisation into divisions and corps. The Imperial Guard which contained infantry, cavalry and artillery was not a corps: divisions in this *élite* body of troops were different from those found elsewhere. Napoleon's Guard was composed of all the various types of soldiers which he found to be of greatest value. He assembled them together loosely and retained battle control of most of this force personally.[2]

The breakdown of French line divisions into their immediately smaller component parts was not always uniform. There were usually two brigades per division in both infantry and cavalry. An infantry brigade, however, could contain from two to six battalions depending upon individual strength and other factors.[3] At Waterloo, battalions were composed of six companies each, about 90 men strong. A cavalry brigade might have two regiments, each of about three squadrons of about 120 men.

A company of French infantry when formed for battle was three ranks deep and about 30 men broad. This was the basic company formation and seldom varied. But the final appearance of battalions, brigades and divisions depended upon the different arrangements of companies. A battalion in column could have a front of one or two companies, that is about 30 or 60 files.[4] This would have given a depth of 18 or 9 ranks.[5] The distance between ranks in the same company

---

[1] *Marmont*, 49–50, believed Napoleon advanced too rapidly to supreme command to be at home with the actual tactical control of troops. He says, 'Simply an officer of artillery, up to the moment when he was placed at the head of armies, he had never commanded either a regiment, a brigade, a division, or an army corps. Brigadier-General Chanez, former sergeant of the Gardes Françaises, commanding officer of Paris during the winter of 1795–96, taught General Bonaparte infantry manœuvres when he was general-in-chief of the army of the interior.'

[2] *Anatomy of Glory* is a first-rate study of the Imperial Guard.

[3] Napoleon did not like uniformity above battalion level, since an enemy would have been able to compute French strength quickly and accurately as soon as he knew what units there were opposing him.

[4] A company formation of six ranks and about fifteen files was also sometimes used and would have led to a battalion column formed on a half company front thirty-six ranks deep.

[5] A battalion's light company of tirailleurs was sometimes detached as skirmishers, but these figures do not take this into account. At Waterloo, entire battalions were used as triailleurs more often than individual companies.

was 30–32 inches, but the companies in column were usually about 68, 34, or 17 feet apart – full, half, or quarter distance.[1] All companies could also form a 'close' column with 30–32 inches between successive companies, but this was not usually done intentionally.

A brigade could be formed into column either by having the battalion columns one behind the other, or in line parallel to each other. Similarly, a division could have its brigades one behind the other, or side by side. Another column arrangement was used at Waterloo: entire battalions were formed into three rank lines – all companies in a single line – and these battalions placed one behind another.[2] This formation will be dealt with exhaustively later on.

French artillery was organised into brigades, but this word is misleading. A brigade meant a battery in the modern sense. In the French horse artillery, the guns, caissons and other equipment were all horse-drawn; all gunners were mounted. These units were generally assigned to cavalry. In the foot artillery, horses were still used to draw all matériel, but the gunners marched or occasionally rode limbers and carriages for short distances. Brigades of foot artillery were composed of six guns and two howitzers. Similar horse-artillery units had four guns and two howitzers.

To turn to Napoleonic strategy. Throughout his long military career, Napoleon endeavoured always to surprise his enemies, particularly at the beginning of a campaign. Strategically, he did the unexpected. He used dispersion, rapid movement and battlefield concentration to keep his opponents off balance. In his great Italian campaign of 1796, he moved rapidly and began fighting astride enemy communications. By striking at unexpected places, he won with relatively light weapons. He was always a master of strategic surprise. His casualties in his early campaigns were moderate because he was able to employ some tactical surprise as well.

As Napoleon's military resources increased, he began to rely more on power than on surprise, once on the field of battle. He was usually able to keep the strategic initiative by out-thinking his opponents and making full use of the remarkable French strategic mobility based upon

---

[1] This full distance was based upon the space required to form into line by a simple ninety-degree wheel of each company.

[2] Oman in *Wellington's Army*, 89, says that this was unique to Waterloo, but *Jomini's Art*, 205, reads, 'In the later wars of Napoleon, twelve battalions were sometimes deployed and closed one upon the other, forming thirty-six ranks closely packed together.'

his corps organisation. No opposing commander could ever anticipate where the Emperor would move and from what point he would strike. His actual tactical strokes, however, became more massive. This was particularly true after 1809 and in his northern European campaigns. French Armies under the marshals in Spain continued to try to fight in the old way.

Of what did this tactical massiveness consist? It was more a new emphasis than a new organisation. The same cavalry, artillery and infantry were deployed on narrower fronts and fought even more stubbornly for limited objectives. But there were some technical changes too. Napoleon increased the ratio of heavy cavalry. He kept it all in the Cavalry Reserve, usually close to his headquarters, and used it for shock charges at critical times on the field of battle. Normal cavalry functions such as reconnaissance and outpost duties were handled by other units.

Napoleon's artillery was always well handled, as numerous as possible and important in his battle plans. With the passage of time, however, he began to rely even more on concentrations of fire by several batteries on a single point. His new guns were larger in bore and weighed more than his old ones; the percentage of heavier pieces also increased.[1] Napoleon concentrated them even more and used particularly his Imperial Guard's 12-pounders and 6-inch howitzers in preparing the way for his massive cavalry and infantry attacks.[2]

Napoleon's conception of an offensive battle also changed with the years. Early in his career, he beat inept commanders and poorly organised armies by confusing them utterly and then striking hard at an unexpected place. This system did not work indefinitely: opponents learned through defeat and made their dispositions so that tactical surprise by the French was more difficult to achieve. Napoleon's later victories came only after hard fighting. But he still had the patriotism, increasing population and material resources of France to rely on. The Emperor began to send forward dedicated Frenchmen of all three arms not to conquer immediately, but to wear down the enemy in bloody, almost even combat. He weakened his enemies by repeated attacks by troops 'of the line'; he used no more fresh troops than necessary. When his enemies were approaching the limit of their endurance, if possible

---

[1] The older Gribauval light howitzers appear to have disappeared entirely.

[2] *Becke*, 114-15, quotes Napoleon as saying, 'It is the Artillery of my Guard which decides most of my battles, because I can bring it into action whenever and wherever I wish.' He referred to his Guard 12-pounders as his '*jeunes filles*'.

after most of their reserves had been committed, Napoleon would suddenly throw the Guard infantry and light artillery forward in a final victorious movement. This hammering type of battle plan became more or less standardised during the last years of the Empire. It was effective, but costly.

Before leaving the French Army, we should consider one aspect of their staff organisation. Napoleon developed a system of control for his army unlike that of any previous commander. French corps were normally commanded by a marshal. Napoleon allowed them tactical freedom, but directed their strategic movements, usually through Marshal Berthier, the Imperial Chief of Staff. Even when present with a corps, Napoleon exercised an overall direction only. He allowed his subordinates to make decisions as to formations and other details. This system produced many victories, but it had its weaknesses. A marshal who did not understand an overall concept could jeopardise its success by carrying out his part badly.

BLÜCHER, GNEISENAU AND PRUSSIA

The Prussian Army in the reign of Frederick the Great had a reputation second to none. The French victory at Valmy in 1792 changed this considerably; Prussia was finally defeated completely in the campaign of Jena in 1806. The formal way of giving battle with infantry and artillery in two lines supported by cavalry on the flanks and in reserve just did not work against French mobile power. A new national army based upon conscription was formed, somewhat after the French type. The Prussian military reformers were more interested in strategy than in organisation and tactics. A group of younger officers headed by Scharnhorst and Gneisenau began to gain control; these were intensely patriotic, but also intellectual. They opposed some old Prussian traditions, and carefully studied the campaigns of Napoleon.

On the other hand, the best Prussian soldier of the Napoleonic era was Blücher, a man of seventy-two at the time of Waterloo. He had served under Frederick, but was not brainy. His greatest military virtues were steadfast courage, dash, fire and an intuitive grasp of how to handle an army in battle. He was only a fair organiser and lacked the powerful, resourceful intellect of many great military leaders. In 1813 and again in 1814, however, he was the best of the Allied commanders in northern Europe. He was to prove his right to high command in the Waterloo campaign.

Blücher realised his own shortcomings; Gneisenau and Müffling played leading parts in the campaigns of Leipzig and northern France.[1] Gneisenau was again to be Blücher's Chief of Staff; he was a fine planner and organiser, but lacked the old man's knack of battle direction and leadership. Blücher had a personal dominance and an intuitive battle sense which made him a great commander in spite of several defeats.

The Prussian Army was organised after the French plan into separate corps, each of which contained infantry, cavalry and artillery. There were no Prussian divisions, but this is of little significance since their brigades were about the size of French divisions. The Prussian corps lacked, however, the subordination to central authority which made those of Napoleon so formidable. They moved more ponderously and tended to be separate armies, rather than a single integrated army composed of more than one corps.

Prussian infantry, cavalry and artillery had taken the outward appearance of the French and had similar organisation. The Prussian artillery was as heavy as the French after the new models began to be introduced in 1812, but not so nimble or so easily controlled. Prussian cavalry was 'lighter' on the average than that of the French. Prussian horsemen were good at screening and reconnaissance, but could not be relied on to stand a shock charge by an equal number of French cuirassiers. All mounted units and batteries were assigned to corps; there was no artillery or cavalry reserve for use at critical times in battle.

Infantry was the main arm of all armies of the Napoleonic period, including that of the Prussians. Personnel and training left something to be desired; conscription was not popular everywhere. Blücher, Müffling and Gneisenau knew exactly how Wellington had used British infantry in line to defeat French infantry in column in the Peninsula, but felt that Prussian infantry would not stand, if so deployed. Even though many Prussians were extremely patriotic, others were not. Some units lacked the discipline, training and stamina to retain their morale when deployed in line.[2]

---

[1] *Cotton*, 262–3, says, 'When Blücher was at Oxford in 1814 he received an intimation that the heads of the University intended to confer upon him the dignity of a Doctor. Blücher, who never dreamed of becoming one of the learned, could not refrain from laughter, and remarked, "Well, if I am to be a doctor, they cannot do less than make Gneisenau an apothecary; we both work together. It is he who has to make up the pills which I administer."'

[2] *Müffling's Passages*, 216, says, '"Our infantry does not possess," I told Wellington, "the same bodily strength or powers of endurance as yours. The greater mass of our troops are too young and inexperienced."'

The strategic concepts of the Blücher–Gneisenau team were predominantly offensive in nature. All Europe realised that Blücher preferred to attack. His offensives were generally, however, heavy rather than mobile and imaginative. Even with Gneisenau as Chief of Staff, a Prussian army was not so easily handled as a French army, nor so capable of complicated manœuvre. Some of Napoleon's very finest work was against Blücher early in 1814 when the Emperor won at Champaubert, Vauxchamps and Montmirail. But Blücher persevered and retrieved all that he had lost at Laon and Montmartre.[1] A Prussian army commanded by Blücher could rally after initial defeat, and persevere; it often scrambled, clawed and bit its way to success. A Prussian victory was likely to be based on perseverance rather than strategic or tactical brilliance.

WELLINGTON AND BRITAIN

Wellington commanded a battalion in the Duke of York's unsuccessful campaign in Flanders in 1794–95. As he said, he learned a good deal about how not to conduct military operations, but he handled his own command flawlessly in one minor action, and was in charge of a brigade for several weeks. He acquired a lot of useful knowledge about soldiering in Belgium and the Netherlands.[2]

Wellington's next active duty was in India. He was extremely successful at fighting, logistics and getting the most from the ever-confused political combinations of that strange land, and became a major-general in 1802, at the age of thirty-three. He learned to care for troops under the most trying conditions and commanded in all kinds of situations. He knew intimately cavalry, infantry and artillery. He conducted a remarkable campaign against the Mahrattas which included the battle of Assaye where he defeated a European-trained army of some 40,000 with a force of less than 7,000 of his own and captured 98 enemy guns. Years after Waterloo, the Duke was to say that Assaye was his finest professional accomplishment.[3]

Wellington returned to Britain in 1805. He was a knight now and had a good military reputation based partly on his flawless and imaginative

[1] *Ellesmere's Essays* 149, says, 'Defeat he suffered often; however, few victories have been more fairly won than the great battle of the Katzbach.'

[2] *Guedalla*, 43–7, gives a remarkably clear and concise picture of this phase of Wellington's military life.

[3] *Chad*, 20, says, '"Pray, Duke, what is the best thing you ever did in the fighting line?" The Duke was silent for about ten seconds and then answered, "Assaye".'

handling of cavalry. But Indian reputations were not rare in Britain; he was still a relatively junior major-general, although thoroughly trained in his profession. He spent the next three years in command of several different brigades and won a minor victory in Denmark, but he was a politician also and Chief Secretary for Ireland from April 1807.[1] He kept this job when he first went to Portugal in the summer of 1808.[2]

Six years of victorious war in Portugal, Spain and Southern France (1808–14) gave Wellington a unique opportunity to develop his military methods, his army and himself. He controlled everything including civilian governments and developed a remarkable system of transportation, supply and army health. More important, he perfected his tactics, organisation and strategy in an unbroken series of victories.

Let us consider tactics first. Wellington inherited infantry that was noted for steadfast qualities in action; it had demonstrated an ability to stand in a two-deep line and defeat a more numerous French column at the minor action of Maida in 1806.[3] But this appears to have happened almost by accident; the Duke developed the idea and standardised it. The British Army between Marlborough and Wellington had its share of failures, but the latter made his infantry into the best in the world by careful attention to organisation, training and equipment. It gained also the priceless confidence which comes with continuous victories.

The basic infantry unit of the British Army was the battalion; regiments, even then, were not used as field-organisation units. A battalion was divided into ten companies, two of which were the 'flank' companies. These two, the Grenadier and the Light (skirmishing) company, had slightly different uniforms and training, but all infantry-men carried the same weapons. The eight line companies were identical and were periodically made uniform in strength. Wellington did not take the flank companies away from his battalions as some British commanders before him had done.

---

[1] The Danish victory was at Kioge on 29 August 1807. Wellington had taken a brigade to North Germany in December 1805, but brought it home in February 1806 without firing a shot in anger.

[2] Wellington resigned as Chief Secretary when he returned to the Peninsula in April 1809.

[3] Maida was of small importance; both sides together numbered less than 12,000 men. See *Oman's Studies*, 37–69.

British infantry battalions averaged about 500 men in the field, although some were much larger. A 500-man battalion would have had a skirmishing force of about 50 men. A French battalion of the same size would have had one-sixth – one of its six companies – functioning as tirailleurs. The French would have had a numerical advantage of about 90 to 50 in the skirmish line. Wellington arranged for at least a numerical equality in his skirmish lines in the Peninsula by assigning light units to all Allied brigades.[1] Many of these were armed with rifles which gave them an additional advantage. In battle after battle, the French tirailleurs were defeated before they could fire on Allied main lines.

Wellington also protected his line infantry from French artillery by posting it on reverse slopes. In that era, targets not visible to the enemy gunners were hit only by accident and never taken under fire. Once the main French infantry columns came forward, however, Wellington had his own infantry advance a short distance in line, halt and open fire. Every musket in a two-deep Allied line could be fired effectively; most of those in column could not. The lines always won because their firepower would stop the columns which could not, or would not, advance over their own dead. The French light artillery which did come forward beside their infantry columns was frequently put out of action by Allied riflemen before it fired a single round.

Wellington's influence on British artillery was not so great as on infantry. He made no effort to increase the size and number of his field-pieces after the French fashion. In the Peninsula, his artillery units mostly had 6-pounders and light 5·5-inch howitzers; the French were always superior in weight of metal and number of pieces.[2] Further, Wellington seldom concentrated his artillery fire. His guns were not for counter-battery work, but to support his individual infantry units, particularly against the French columns.

Wellington was disappointed throughout his European military career in his cavalry. Even though he had handled mounted troops well in India, he made little use of them in battle in the Peninsula.

---

[1] The mechanics of achieving this skirmish line increase varied. Sometimes a strong rifle company was assigned to brigade headquarters; other brigades would have an organic light infantry battalion. Portuguese Caçadores were always light infantry and often armed with rifles.

[2] Wellington mentioned in his *Dispatches* the Allied need for more powerful pieces and more of them, yet his Vitoria-Pyrenees campaigns were fought with only one battery per division. Some 9-pounder guns which were available were not assigned in the Peninsula.

The main cause was the cavalry itself. British horsemen were fine physically, brave and superbly mounted, but they lacked field training, active service experience and officers of professional competence. The great historian of the Peninsula says:

We have Wellington's authority for the fact that he hesitated to mass great bodies of horse, because he doubted the tactical skill of his officers, and the power of the regiments to manœuvre. 'I considered our cavalry', he wrote ten years after the war was over, 'so inferior to the French from want of order, that although one squadron was a match for two French, I did not like to see four British opposed to four French. As numbers increase, order becomes more necessary. Our men could gallop, but could not preserve their order.' Foy, in his excellent history of the Spanish War, emits an opinion in words curiously similar to those of Wellington, stating that for practical purposes the English troopers were inferior to the French on account of their headlong impetuosity and want of power to manœuvre. When two such authorities agree, there must clearly have been some solid foundation for their verdict.[1]

All authorities seem to agree that British cavalry units could not be controlled once they were launched in a charge; the officers were the worst offenders. The only significant exception to this was at Salamanca. The British General Le Marchant handled his heavy cavalry with real competence and aided greatly in achieving a magnificent victory, but he was killed before the battle was over.

In the Peninsula, Wellington won essentially with his infantry; cavalry and artillery were usually subordinate to it. He supported all his units flawlessly; his system of transportation and supply were such that he was able to move large armies over hundreds of miles without loss of combat efficiency. Ammunition of all types, adequate food in ample variety for those times, a full ration of spirits, tents, blankets, greatcoats, medical supplies and many other items were available when required in spite of primitive roads, ox carts, pack mules and native drivers.

Wellington's army organisation was simple compared to Napoleon's. The Duke set up autonomous divisions in 1809 and kept them until Toulouse, but he did not have formal, permanent corps. Several divisions were sometimes placed under the command of Sir Rowland Hill, and less frequently under Sir Thomas Graham and Sir William Beresford.[2] But these arrangements were used principally when

[1] *Oman*, I, 119. See also *Stanhope*, 149.

[2] Hill's 'corps' varied in size over several years, but almost always included at least one division besides his own.

Wellington could not command all his divisions in person because of the distances involved. When possible, he preferred to give orders himself directly to his division or even lower-echelon commanders, or to write them short, definite instructions for simple movements.

Wellington did not delegate command responsibility, save when forced to do so. He did not encourage initiative because over many years he found that subordinates were less likely to make good decisions than he was himself. On battlefield after battlefield, he demonstrated an uncanny ability to be at the right place at the right time. At Salamanca, he personally sent into action every single Allied division. This method of control required, however, not only the ability to foresee where he would be needed, but also many expensive horses, superb practical horsemanship and in himself the hard physical condition of a steeplechase jockey.[1]

When distance and terrain precluded this personal supervision as in the Pyrenees, Wellington still did not direct his army through a Chief of Staff, such as Berthier or Gneisenau. He did not even have an officer of high rank to translate his wishes into a system of explicit orders for subordinate commanders. He did make full use of the talents of QMG Sir George Murray when he was available, but could manage with others of lesser ability when necessary.[2]

In strategy, Wellington was far more straightforward and less of a gambler than Napoleon but he probably possessed an intellect fully equal to Napoleon's on military matters. These two have had few equals in military history in seeing clearly all aspects of large military problems. The Duke could not risk defeat, nor even a victory if losses would be unacceptably high; the Emperor could afford enormous casualties, but often had to win quickly so he could get back to Paris. These considerations led to what appeared to be slow, methodical defensive procedures for Wellington as opposed to rapid strokes of offensive genius, sometimes unrewarding, for the Emperor. But the Duke could also attack with speed, power and co-ordination, and did so on several occasions.

One of the two great modern British military historians says:

[1] Wellington has been accused of having a 'poor seat'; he was perhaps not a pretty rider. But he could probably move faster and farther than any other senior commander in European history. *Maxwell*, II, 28, says that on 16 June 1815, 'The Duke had ridden from Brussels 5 miles beyond Quatre Bras, 29 miles, then 7 miles to Ligny and back, 43 miles in all, before the battle began, and remained in the saddle till nightfall.'

[2] See *Harry Smith*, I, 142–3, for how Wellington and Murray worked together. But even here Wellington went personally into every detail.

Because Wellington possessed the faculty of combining foresight with common sense, his imagination seldom ran away with his reason. His armies usually were numerically inferior to his opponent's, he was compelled to be prudent. Yet it is a great mistake to assume, as many have done and as Napoleon himself did, that he was no more than a cautious general. Though a master of defensive warfare, he could, when conditions were favourable, be audacious in the extreme. His Fabian tactics were common sense: when conditions demanded prudence, he was prudent, and when they did not, he could strike like a thunderbolt.[1]

Wellington understood the employment of sea power, political support for armies, centrally directed guerilla activities, military intelligence and field subsistence as few commanders have. He was a professional soldier of rare ability based on thorough training and experience. He had abounding patience, a quality which Napoleon lacked.

Wellington saw no fundamental difference between offensive and defensive war. If he was more powerful than his enemy, he normally took the offensive. If he was not, he made up for it by using terrain, the transportation difficulties of his enemies and the many and various troubles that French Armies always had in supplying themselves. He considered every practical move the enemy could make and distributed his forces accordingly. He was most feared because of his defensive ability, but he was far from a 'one-way' player. As I have already mentioned, his Vitoria campaign was an offensive masterpiece which depended upon victory and sustained mobility according to a brilliantly conceived plan.[2] Whether in offensive or defensive, Wellington always avoided defeat and directed all critical operations himself.

After Toulouse and the first abdication the Duke studied carefully the later strategy and tactics of Napoleon and the French Army. As was mentioned in the preceding chapter, Wellington had ample opportunities to discuss with northern European commanders the military operations of recent years. Few believed that Napoleon was totally removed from the European military picture as long as he was only banished to Elba.

Wellington had no admiration for Napoleon as a man, but he did not underrate him as a soldier. He was particularly impressed with the

[1] *Fuller's Decisive Battles*, II, 493.

[2] Wellington moved more than 400 miles against armies which had a combined strength superior to his own between 29 May and 30 June 1813. He travelled with enough speed and by such devious routes that the French commanders failed to achieve a concentration in spite of giving up most of Spain in their efforts to do so. See particularly *Weller*, 251–73.

Emperor's 1814 campaign in France and said, 'I have studied it very much. Bonaparte beat the Austrians, Prussians, and Russians – different armies – always with the same troops. I have had experience enough to know how very exact a man must be in his calculations and how very skilful in his manœuvres to be able to do that.'[1]

But he also understood the growing dependence of the Emperor on tactical mass. The Duke must have evolved procedures to neutralise and ultimately defeat a numerous and powerful French field-artillery, Napoleon's heavy shock cavalry and full corps-size French infantry columns. He probably also pondered about the pounding attacks in series which Napoleon delivered at critical points to weaken his opposition, sometimes for hours on end, before finally sending forward the Imperial Guard to win the victory. To discover what Wellington's counter-tactics were we must await the discussion of the fated meeting of these two great commanders in battle.

[1] *Stanhope*, 12.

III

Wellington, Britain and the Allies to 15 June 1815

Wellington was not pleased with what he found in Brussels on 5 April 1815. He was accustomed to situations which required his unusual talents for organising and integrating, but the present one was to be his greatest challenge. His victories in India, Portugal, Spain and Southern France had been made possible by a careful build-up of all strengths available including Britain's commerce and economy, her control of the sea and military strength, local production and man-power, and favourable relations with all Allies at all levels. He still had many advantages, but he was pitted against time, a rapidly re-surgent France led by Napoleon, and political apathy both in Britain and in Belgium. His army early in April was hardly worthy of the name.

We will briefly run through his principal difficulties. Belgium was not content to be a part of the Netherlands. It had been French for a generation; French was the principal language. The legal, commer-cial, agricultural and financial systems were more French than Dutch. Belgian civilians were divided in their sentiments, but nearly all expected Napoleon to win.

The Anglo-Dutch Army in early April consisted mainly of Sir Thomas Graham's force, which had unsuccessfully attacked Bergen on 8 March 1814, with, in addition, some Dutch-Belgian units com-posed about equally of veterans who had served in French armies and young recruits. The entire army had been commanded by the young Prince of Orange until the Duke arrived. The British portion of this force was made up of six regiments of cavalry, twenty-five battalions of infantry, and some miscellaneous artillery, about 14,000 in all. Some units which had served under Graham were poorly armed, disciplined and trained.[1] The Dutch-Belgian forces were a real problem. The House of Orange was following a policy of forwarding the interest of officers who had held high rank in Napoleon's armies; many soldiers still wore French uniforms.

This situation appears illogical: France was the potential enemy of the Netherlands and her newly acquired territory. But Wellington wrote of the Netherlands Government, 'One of their first measures has been the removal of almost all the German officers from the Belgian regiments, men on whom most reliance could have been placed. These were replaced by officers who had risen under Buonaparte, and are admirers of his system and government. Some of the German officers included in the first general proscription have been restored, but such only as had been employed under Buonaparte.'[2] Perhaps the reason was that 'the head of the Ministry of War was General Janssens, who, having fought unsuccessfully against the British both at the Cape and in Java, would hardly have been human if he had felt kindly towards them; and the officers of almost every department under him were known to be at heart partisans of the revolution and of France.'[3] The British Government specifically ordered Wellington not to hand over the command of either Antwerp or Ostend to a Netherlands officer.[4]

The King of the Netherlands was difficult. Wellington was soon embroiled in all kinds of controversy and threatened to have nothing more to do with him until he mended his ways. The King with good grace appointed Wellington C.-in-C. of his forces and Field-Marshal in the Netherlands service, but things were not perfect thereafter. The Duke had to keep the Prince of Orange in a high command, even though the young man was to prove himself unable to handle efficiently a single battalion. Even worse, young Prince Frederick of the Netherlands, a boy of eighteen, would have to be at least nominally the commanding general of a division of Netherlands troops. The presence of these two princes with high rank and other rivalries caused Wellington serious trouble. Peninsular division commanders with years of

---

[1] Notable exceptions were three Guards battalions, 2/1st, 2/Coldstreamers, and 2/3rd, which had all been with Graham. These plus the 3/1st Guards of Peninsular fame were to form Cooke's Guards Division; see *Aubrey-Fletcher*, 354–5.

[2] *Supplementary Dispatches*, X, 182.

[3] *Fortescue*, X, 243.

[4] *Supplementary Dispatches*, X, 215.

active service would not tolerate being commanded by callow youths.[1]

There were also problems as regards subsistence, fortifications and staff. Early in April, those who could supply food and other necessaries to the Anglo–Dutch Army were reluctant to do so because they were not sure they would be paid for them. The Prussians in the area to the east were taking what they required, making only vague arrangements for payment. The Belgian border fortresses were not much better than when Wellington had inspected them the previous summer. The staff assembled by the Prince of Orange was wretchedly inefficient. Discipline and training were lax in many units; physical condition was poor in most.

To make matters worse, news from home and from France was mostly bad. There were riots in London against unpopular Corn Laws; those in command in Ireland dared not relinquish regular soldiers from their service there unless the militia was called out. Many veteran battalions were in America and the date of their return was uncertain, even though the war was over. Numerous accounts from Paris told of phenomenal military progress. Napoleon was busy organising and equipping; parts of his Empire were almost as enthusiastic as in 1794. The Emperor would have a field army of 600,000 men by the end of the summer.

The scheme the Allies made in Vienna to invade France in May or early June with three army groups was almost certainly optimistic. The Anglo–Dutch under Wellington and the Prussians under Blücher who together were to compose the western force would probably be ready. But they could advance into France only if an Austrian Army under Schwarzenberg also attacked along a route much farther east. The Austrians were going to be late and the Russian Army under Barclay de Tolly which was to move into France between the first two, through Saarbrücken towards Nancy, was now sure to be even later.

A delayed Allied offensive meant that the French might attack first. Napoleon had done this often in the past and usually succeeded. If the Emperor did choose this course, Wellington and Blücher in Belgium were the most likely target because of the terrain, the lack of border fortresses and unified command, and the sympathies of the population. All Allied commanders, especially Wellington, realised this danger and the power and ability of a veteran French Army to take full advantage of it. They had all lived through the era of Napoleon's

[1] Picton in particular; *Cole*, II, 74, says, 'Picton required the assurance that he should be employed under the Duke and no other general officer of superior rank to himself.'

offensive victories; only Wellington had not been personally involved in them. The Duke and Blücher had to be ready to fight defensively.

We have stated the problems briefly; now let us see what the Duke did about them. With characteristic energy and his never-failing logic, Wellington began improving things one by one. His most important initial efforts were directed at increasing the size and quality of his British and Hanoverian force. Veteran Peninsular infantry would soon be arriving from America; he made sure that they would immediately be forwarded to Belgium. Cavalry was soon on its way, for not much had gone overseas. The Ministry in London was willing to do almost anything for the Duke, but would not call out the militia. Perhaps they had no legal right to do so until war was formally declared, but their reluctance is hard to understand. 'The British Navy had begun to take French prizes in the Channel and on the Atlantic seaboard before the end of March. The Prince of Orange had arrested French prisoners who were on their way to France from Russia; and the Continental Powers had cut off all regular communications between France and the world without. All of these were hostile acts, and it is therefore difficult to understand why Ministers should have boggled at the wording of the Militia Statutes.'[1]

Once appeals for help had been dispatched to London, the Duke began reorganising the army he had. First, the Hanoverians. Some King's German Legion units had been halted in Belgium on their way to Hanover to be disbanded, when news of Napoleon's flight from Elba arrived there. These consisted of five strong regiments of cavalry, eight weak battalions of infantry and three and a half batteries of artillery. There were also now some other Hanoverian troops in Belgium, twenty-five battalions of infantry both militia and regular, some militia cavalry and some incomplete batteries of artillery. Wellington would have liked to draft militia infantry into the KGL battalions, but the Hanoverian Government would not give its permission. Instead, he reduced KGL battalions from ten to six companies and put the extra officers and NCOs into Hanoverian militia units. A somewhat similar amalgamation took place between the Hanoverian and KGL artillery. The Hanoverian militia cavalry appears to have been so poor that no real effort was made to improve it by combination with other troops.

The Dutch-Belgians presented a tougher military problem, but had to be used; without them the Duke's army would be too small.

[1] *Fortescue*, X, 237.

Wellington's solution was to combine good and bad, not only to promote combat efficiency but to prevent desertion. The reorganisation of his entire force which took place on 11 April 1815, only six days after he arrived, must have been in his mind for some time. It was a masterpiece.

In every British Division except the First, foreigners were blended with red-coats. Alten's and Clinton's had each one brigade of British, one of the Legion, and one of Hanoverians; Picton's and Colville's had each two brigades of British and one of Hanoverians. Even so, however, the subtlety of mixture is not yet wholly expressed. In Cooke's division of Guards the three young battalions were stiffened by one old one from the Peninsula. In Alten's, where all the British were young, the battalions of the Legion were veterans and the Hanoverians were regulars; in Colville's, where the British were both old and young, the Hanoverians were both regulars and militia; in Clinton's where the British as well as the troops of the Legion were old, the Hanoverians were all militia.[1]

For the first time, the Duke used three permanent corps, rather than mostly independent divisions, in his army organisation. The Prince of Orange commanded the First, Lord Hill the Second, and Wellington himself the Third which was called the Reserve. The First and Second Corps each had two British divisions and about two Dutch-Belgian divisions; the Reserve would eventually have two British divisions, the Brunswick 'corps', and Kruse's Nassauers.[2] This mixing of forces and, to some extent at least, varying numerical strengths would ultimately produce three Allied corps of approximately equal fighting strength. These corps included all infantry and artillery in the army, but cavalry only in the Duke of Brunswick's command. British-Hanoverian cavalry formed a separate force as initially did the Dutch-Belgian cavalry.

Both the strength and the efficiency of Wellington's army increased during April and May. It had been 40,000 on 4 April, but was more than 60,000 by the end of the month. Discipline and drill were improved because of hard work; morale rose also throughout the army. Slowly, the Duke's quiet confidence passed down, throughout his own units at least. Peninsular veterans and newer soldiers too recalled Salamanca and Vitoria.

Wellington's relations with the Allies under his command are not

[1] Ibid., X, 247.

[2] The British divisions in the Reserve were those of Picton and Cole. Picton arrived in Brussels on 15 June 1815; Cole was still in Britain getting married on that day. Picton's Division was at full strength, but Cole's was represented by Lambert's Brigade only, and it had just arrived from America.

entirely clear. There was never any question as regards the personal dominance of the British commander; all subordinates accepted him without question as C.-in-C.[1] The troops also felt the Duke's hand in small things like pay, food and drink, which all became more regular. But drill manœuvres were a long way from the British standard. The Dutch-Belgians remained more French than British.

Wellington personally never worked more efficiently than he did in the spring of 1815. Even while reorganising and training, he was dealing with other things too. His Dispatches, Supplementary Dispatches, General Orders and correspondence of other types show the extent and variety of his tasks. He was constantly advising the Government at home and other people in high positions both in Britain and elsewhere. He was thinking, making decisions and seeing that they were carried out in connection with trenches, camp kettles, greatcoats, muskets and ammunition, and artillery. 'Everything was thrown upon him; and, as holder in some degree of the English purse-strings, he was treated by his German colleagues of all professions, Blücher perhaps excepted, with a kind of jealous servility. It was no easy course that was given him to steer; and indeed his functions during this campaign, as in the Peninsula, were perhaps even more diplomatic than military.'[2]

Even though the original Allied plan was to invade France, Wellington thought also of defence. The fortifications at Nieuport, Ostend and Antwerp were improved and the places garrisoned. Thousands of civilians and soldiers set to work on the defences of Ypres, Menin, Tournai, Courtrai and Mons. The places were soon sufficiently restored to resist a *coup de main* and suitably garrisoned. A central fortification at Oudenarde was also constructed to allow the Duke to cross the Scheldt at this point in either direction as required. Ghent was refortified; some efforts appear to have been made to construct earthworks around Brussels.

The problem of proper disposition of troops in order to withstand an attack was even more important than fortifications. The terrain in this part of Belgium was well suited to manœuvres of the French type because of the flatness of the land and an extensive system of good roads. Wellington realised that an efficient defence depended fully as much on Blücher and his Prussians as on that of the Anglo-Dutch.

[1] *Petrie*, 195.
[2] *Fortescue*, X, 259.

The Emperor could undoubtedly gather a field army stronger than Wellington's or Blücher's alone. If Napoleon could attack either one or the other separately, the French were bound to win. Close co-operation between the two Allied commanders and their armies was as essential in defence as if the Duke and Blücher had been carrying out their original Vienna offensive plans.

Wellington, Blücher and their two staffs met at Tirlemont on 3 May 1815. This meeting produced no formal statement of intent, nor even recorded plans. From various sources, however, we are able to determine much of what was decided. Perhaps the most important agreement between the two commanders was on full and unselfish personal co-operation. So long as they remained in Belgium, the two armies would occupy positions closer together than they had before that time. They would canton themselves on either side of the old Roman road from Bavay to Maastricht, then still in use throughout its length.[1] Each army was to control diligently and with adequate forces a long stretch of border east and west of their dividing line.[2] When they did advance into France, Wellington would go by way of Mons and Cambrai while Blücher would go through Charleroi and Maubeuge.

The two commanders also probably agreed to weaken their outer flanks and position the bulk of their strength in the central area in front of Ghent and Brussels. This meant taking a calculated risk on Wellington's right west of the Scheldt and on Blücher's left in the Ardennes, but the full significance of a capture by the French of Brussels, or even of Ghent, was obvious to all. Each army would support the other as soon as possible. A Prussian concentration at Sombreffe and an Anglo-Dutch concentration at Nivelles seems to have been discussed and agreed upon, if the French advanced either through Charleroi or through Mons. Napoleon's fondness for attacking Allies approximately where their armies joined was well known.

These decisions must have been reached with some feeling of un-easiness. Napoleon had also shown a facility for opening a campaign by moving on the communications of a hostile army, or the communications of one of two co-operating armies. The Prussians with their headquarters at Namur were based on Cologne on the Rhine.

[1] *Müffling's Passages*, 224, says that this 'strategic line of demarcation', i.e. along the Roman road, was the only concrete decision reached at this conference. He also says that there were minutes, but these have been lost. See also *Ropes*, 72.

[2] Binche was the town where the Anglo-Dutch and Prussian cavalry outposts came together. It appears to have been occupied by the Prussians, although original records are not unanimous on this point.

The British were dependent upon Ostend. Antwerp offered facilities for larger vessels, but involved considerable trouble for sailing ships trying to navigate the Rhine river system so far inland. Both commanders must have realised the unpleasant possibilities of a lightning attack by the French on Liège which would cut the Prussian Army off from Prussia, or an attack west of the Lys which would deprive Wellington of his best communications with Britain, but neither move, if successful, could be so immediately significant, politically as well as militarily, as a French victory in the centre.

Wellington, Blücher, and their staffs also discussed communications between their headquarters; representatives of each army were attached to the commander of the other. Baron Müffling, a lieutenant-general in the Prussian Army, came to join the Duke accompanied by a large staff. Colonel Hardinge with a smaller organisation continued to represent Wellington with the Prussians. Immediately after the Tirlemont meeting, Blucher issued orders to General Ziethen who commanded the First Prussian Corps at Charleroi to forward at once any intelligence of enemy movements to Müffling and Wellington at Brussels. Intelligence of any major movements of either army was to be communicated immediately to the other through these representatives.

Perhaps the Tirlemont conference was not so efficiently recorded as those of Britain and the U.S. in World War II, but the general principles upon which the two armies would base their future operations were definite and clear in the minds of all. If the French should attack, the initial positions of all Allied units were of extreme importance. These would have been determined at this conference and did not change as the armies grew in May and early June. Let us examine the Prussians first. (See Map 2, p. 226.) The Prussian Army consisted of four corps, each containing infantry, cavalry and artillery, but there was no central reserve. Blücher's headquarters was at Namur roughly equidistant between the centres of his two forward corps which were at Charleroi (Ziethen, First) and Ciney (Thielemann, Third). The Second under Pirch was north of Namur so it could move quickly forward to reinforce either Ziethen or Thielemann. The Fourth under Bülow was in reserve around Liège.[1]

Secondly, the Anglo-Dutch Army. (See again Map 2.) The First Corps was to the east, or left, next to the Prussians; the Second Corps to the west, or right, extending slightly beyond the Scheldt and Lys.

---

[1] Bülow's Corps was not expected to move forward into France with the Blücher-Gneisenau team, perhaps because Bülow was senior to Gneisenau.

There was a moderately heavy cavalry cordon in front of both corps just behind the French border, but the rest of Wellington's horsemen were comfortably quartered in the valley of the Dender to the right rear and between the two forward corps. The Reserve Corps was in and around Brussels. The individual divisions, and even brigades and battalions, of each corps were quartered in other towns and villages in these areas in order to facilitate healthy living. Even Wellington preferred to billet soldiers with civilian families and in dry, airy barns to having them live in tents, save in midsummer. This usually meant dispersing even a battalion over several hundred yards.

We should look briefly at Wellington's staff and subordinate commanders. As mentioned, these were at first not good. The Duke of York as Commander-in-Chief of the British Army controlled its personnel and, to some extent, other aspects including organisation and equipment, but not operations which came under the Government. The Duke of York was the brother of the Prince Regent – both were sons of George III, still alive, but mentally defective – and jealously guarded all appointments, commissions and details of organisation. Both he and the Prince Regent had some admirable qualities. In spite of the scandals connected with his administration, the Duke of York made many beneficial changes.[1] But neither of the royal brothers really liked Wellington; he was not their sort of heavy-drinking dinner companion. His first-class physical condition, his logical thinking on all subjects and his extreme professional competence were obvious, but perhaps not appealing. Men who are in complete control of themselves are seldom popular with those who are not.

Years later Wellington was to say:

I can't say that I owe my successes to any favour or confidence from the Horse Guards; they never showed me any, from the first day I had a command to this hour. In the first place, they thought very little of any one who had served in India. An Indian victory was not only no ground of confidence, but it was actually a cause of suspicion. Then because I was in Parliament, and connected with people in office, I was a politician, and a politician never can be a soldier. Moreover they looked upon me with a kind of jealousy, because I was a lord's son, 'a sprig of nobility,' who came into the army more for ornament than use.[2]

The Duke of York gave Sir John Moore a free hand with regard to his subordinates; Wellington was told pointedly that he had no

---

[1] See particularly *Glover, passim.*
[2] *Croker*, I, 342–3.

authority whatever in this connection.[1] He complained long, however, and to the verge of insubordination, about his inability to get the men he wanted for his army, and ended with most of them. His Chief Staff Officer, after he had managed to get rid of Sir Hudson Lowe, was Sir William De Lancey, the second most able man for that position from the Peninsula.[2] The best, Sir George Murray, was still in America. The Adjutant-General was Sir Edward Barnes, a capable Peninsular veteran. The Duke finally fought the Waterloo campaign with an immediate staff of thirty-three, of whom thirty-one had at least some Peninsular experience.

The real cause of this controversy was probably the Earl of Uxbridge, the Lord Paget of the Peninsular War. He was a firm personal friend of the two royal brothers and was forced upon Wellington as his cavalry commander in spite of the fact that Uxbridge had run away with the fascinating, but supposedly happily married wife of Wellington's younger brother.[3] Uxbridge was older than Wellington; they had never served together. The new chief of British cavalry had been an able leader of a few regiments under Sir John Moore in 1808, but had not been on active service since. Sir Stapleton Cotton, Wellington's chief of cavalry in the Peninsula and now Lord Combermere, was kept away from the Anglo-Dutch Army under various pretexts, so there was no possibility of the Duke shifting commanders and shelving someone he probably did not want.[4]

---

[1] Duke of York to Wellington, 28 March 1815, *Supplementary Dispatches*, X, 1; 'The power of appointing to commissions is not vested in you; you will be pleased to recommend to me such officers as may appear to you most deserving of promotion, stating the special reasons where such recommendations are not in the usual channel of seniority.'

[2] Actually the title was then Quartermaster-General; *Creevey Papers*, I, 289, quotes Wellington as saying, 'As for Lowe, he is a damned fool. When I came to Brussels from Vienna in 1815, I presently found the damned fellow would instruct me in the equipment of the army, always producing the Prussians to me as models. I was obliged to tell him I had commanded a much larger army in the field than any Prussian general, and that I was not to learn from their service how to equip an army. I thought this would have stopped him, but shortly afterwards he was at me again about the equipment of the Prussians. I was obliged to write home and complain; the Government were kind enough to take him away from me.'

[3] See particularly *Anglesey*, 89–96, and *passim*. See also 156 which says, '"Paget has brought about a complete reconciliation between the P. and the D. of Y.", wrote old Lady Uxbridge to Arthur Paget, "and they both thanked him most cordially for having effected it."'

[4] There is no record of any personal animosity between Wellington and Uxbridge; they appear to have been firm friends for many years after the battle.

Wellington was also dependent to some extent upon the Master General of Ordnance, Lord Mulgrave. His department was completely independent of the Duke of York and responsible only to the Crown and to the Government. Lord Mulgrave controlled the artillery, engineers, weapons, and ammunition of the British Army and did all in his power to help Wellington. Matériel of all types arrived in large quantities. For the first time in his military life, the Duke was supplied with many more field pieces than he could possibly use and was given a choice of two sizes of guns, the old 6-pounders used so successfully in the Peninsula and new 9-pounders which were more powerful, particularly with canister.[1]

The British Waterloo artillery was by far the best in personnel and materiel that Wellington ever commanded. In this arm, he had all the officers he wanted most, more than enough guns and an abundance of ammunition. There was even a rocket battery under Captain Whinyates that was highly thought of by some officers and had served in Northern Europe, including Leipzig, during the wars that led to the defeat of the First Empire.[2] Three batteries of 18-pounders had been provided for siege use; a pontoon train was taking shape and two companies of British sappers and miners were actually with the army.

As May passed into June, the Anglo-Dutch infantry and artillery improved in every way. Veteran British units joined; the Hanoverian militia profited by the thirty-two cadres of company officers and NCOs from the KGL. All units including those of the Allies were drilling, manœuvring and being inspected. British and KGL units at least were having considerable target practice.[3] Physical condition and discipline were improving. The spirit of the British, KGL and Hanoverian units was excellent. The Dutch-Belgians remained a problem. They too improved in appearance and drill but the loyalty of some of

[1] Mulgrave to Wellington, *Supplementary Dispatches*, X, 18: 'As you may wish to equip your horse brigades with nine-pounders, I have ordered spare nine-pounder guns to be sent. You may have the option of using either sixes or nines.'

[2] Particularly at Leipzig, 16–19 October 1813, but see *Mercer*, 91–92, for the Duke's opinion. He 'looked upon rockets as nonsense'.

[3] This point is sometimes disputed, but see *General Orders*, 395; *Surtees*, 41–42; *Leach*, 408; *Brett-James*, 75; *Regulations for Riflemen*, 13–14. *Marbot*, 423, says, 'The English were the only troops who were perfectly practised in the use of small arms, whence their firing was far more accurate than that of any other infantry.'

these units was at best doubtful.[1] The composite organisation of the Anglo-Dutch Army would not allow good opportunities for desertion, but Wellington cannot have relied greatly on their fighting power.

The Duke's cavalry was also a worry. There was no question that man for man and horse for horse the British mounted arm during the Waterloo campaign was superb. It continued, however, to lack the professional excellence, the controllability and the combat experience of his KGL units. Uxbridge certainly knew how to make his force look well on parade, but there was one British brigade commander from the Peninsula who thought he went too much for show.[2] The Dutch-Belgian cavalry was not only of doubtful loyalty, but also deficient in horsemanship. Wellington did not combine Dutch-Belgian cavalry with British-KGL units, probably because of the objections of the Prince of Orange. He may also have lacked confidence in the result.

As regards the matter of military intelligence, nations have seldom fought a war in which both sides knew so much about the other. Wellington, Blücher and many of their subordinates had been in Paris for varying lengths of time during the past year. Louis XVIII was then residing in Ghent and had taken with him a skeleton French Army ready and able to give details of what they had left behind them in March and the changes made since.[3]

Napoleon was known to have about 200,000 veteran professional soldiers; National Guards and recruits of all sorts were increasing his total force week by week. As early as the end of April, Wellington and Blücher realised that Napoleon was beginning to concentrate his best troops in Northern France. His maximum disposable field force, however, was not expected to be much greater than about 125,000 men, because of other frontier defences and internal strife. The Emperor

---

[1] *Napoleon*, 63, says, 'We had good sources of information in the Belgian Army.' He implies, *passim*, that many Belgians were ready to desert. *Creasy*, 384, says, 'The Belgian regiments had been tampered with; Napoleon had well-founded hopes of seeing them quit the Duke of Wellington in a body.'

[2] *Vivian*, 258.

[3] This force was not a part of Wellington's command and did not fight; *Mercer's Journal*, 84, says, 'This curious corps presented a most grotesque appearance – cuirassiers, hussars, grenadiers à *cheval*, and chasseurs, dragoons and lancers, officers and privates, with a few of the new *garde de corps*, were indiscriminately mingled in the ranks. One file were colonels, the next privates, and so on, and all wearing their proper uniforms and mounted on their proper horses, so that these were of all sizes and colours.'

had to retain some troops on the Spanish and Italian borders and protect the area between the Alps and the Ardennes. Late in May, La Vendée was still in open military insurrection. Almost daily intelligence reached Brussels of militarily significant information from Paris.

Wellington realised that Bonaparte undoubtedly knew as much or more about the strength, organisation, and disposition of the Allies. Dozens of Belgian and Dutch officers were communicating regularly with the enemy; military men on the staff of Louis XVIII were undoubtedly doing their share of reporting what they saw and found out. But this did not worry the Duke greatly, for no secrets of this nature could have been kept anyway in the midst of the Belgian civilian population.

Early in June, Wellington was receiving a mass of information about the movements of French Armies south of the border both through Sir William Dörnberg, cavalry commander at Mons, and Lieutenant-Colonel Colquhoun Grant of Peninsular fame who appears to have been operating inside France.[1] Amateur and professional spies reported Napoleon to be in several different places at the same time. There was certainly a great deal of movement of military units just behind the French border from Lille west of the Scheldt all the way to Givet on the Meuse. The artificial peace on land which still existed prevented proper cavalry reconnaissance.

Something was obviously about to happen; Napoleon would probably attack, but the point or points where the French would advance were still unpredictable. As already mentioned, there appeared to be little likelihood of the French advancing either west of the Lys or across the barren country of the Ardennes. But they could easily come along metalled roads by at least three routes to be discussed presently.

The Anglo-Dutch Army under Wellington numbered approximately 92,000 men on the eve of the opening of hostilities. It was still cantoned as described earlier in this chapter and shown in Map 2; it was constituted as shown in 'Strengths of the Contending Forces' (see Appendix, p. 237). The Prussian dispositions and strengths can be determined in the same way. To summarise Wellington's disposition of his army, he had his two independent corps side by side, each in rough box formations of four divisions. There was a cavalry screen in front, but

---

[1] There were two Colquhoun Grants. One was in command of a brigade of cavalry and a favourite of the Duke of York and the Prince Regent; the other was the intelligence officer.

the main cavalry strength was to the rear in a separate cavalry command positioned between the two infantry-artillery corps. The Duke's Reserve Corps was farther back still and slightly to the left, or east of centre, nearer the Prussians. The territory west of the Scheldt and Lys was to some extent vulnerable, but there were cavalry patrols, the fortifications of Ypres and Nieuport, and the redoubts on both sides of the Scheldt at Oudenarde which would allow the Anglo-Dutch Army to counter a French attack close to the Channel. Anything between the Scheldt and the Roman road, however, could be met directly. Wellington planned a concentration of all his field forces at or near Nivelles in the event of a French attack on Blücher's army.

The Duke's staff at this time was able to write out and transmit his orders to every single command unit in the entire force in a total elapsed time of six hours or less. In the event of a French attack, the entire force could concentrate on either flank in forty-eight hours; two-thirds of it could be assembled to oppose any border crossing in Wellington's area twenty-two hours after news of the event arrived at Brussels.

French activity as reported to the Duke on and after 10 June 1815 confirmed his original conclusion that the French would not advance to the west of the Scheldt and Lys, nor across the Ardennes. A major attack on Brussels, however, could be launched by Napoleon along three main routes. (See Map 2 again.) First, the French could come through Mons. This was the main route from Paris to Brussels at that time as it is today.[1] This route was the most direct, by good roads from the border to the Belgian capital, ten miles shorter than by way of Charleroi. Further, an attack here was really on the 'hinge of the line', where Blücher's troops joined Wellington's. But Mons was partially refortified.

The second likely route was through Tournai and to either side of it. This would allow the widest choice of good roads and open flat country for manœuvres. Tournai and some other places on the Scheldt were fortified, but the French could cross that river well inside France. The third route, the one actually chosen, was through Charleroi. The paved roads leading from the concentration centres of Maubeuge, Beaumont and Philippeville had been torn up by the French as far as the Belgian border early in the Hundred Days.

Attacks along the first two routes were the primary responsibility

[1] *Wood*, 47; *Müffling's Passages*, 233, says, 'The main road of traffic between the one capital, Paris, and the other capital, Brussels, runs by Mons.'

of the Anglo-Dutch Army, although the Mons attack would have soon involved the Prussians. An advance through Charleroi would be primarily against the Prussians. No one could predict beforehand which of the three routes Napoleon would choose, if he did finally attack at all. But Wellington was understandably more concerned with the Mons and the Tournai routes. He had confidence in Hill, but what about the Prince of Orange? He must have realised that a French attack through Mons would strike an Anglo-Dutch corps commanded by a young man of twenty-three who had no experience of commanding a large force in combat. Moreover, Orange's army lacked the advantage of a river like the Sambre across the Charleroi route and the Scheldt partially across the Tournai route. On the other hand, a French attack through Tournai would endanger the Duke's best communications with Britain; the Prussians would take at least two days to move that far west.

If the French did attack Charleroi, Wellington would support the Prussians as quickly as possible but after taking other possibilities into consideration. Napoleon had often in the past launched diversionary attacks to conceal his main thrust. The Duke would begin his concentration immediately he received intelligence of a major French attack in any area, but he had to move cautiously not only because of French guile, but also because his army as a whole was poor at manœuvre and not entirely dependable.

1. Wellington with the Sword of State, by Sir Thomas Lawrence. This was the favourite likeness of the Duke and his family.

2. The crossroads at Quatre Bras. In the left background is Materne Lake. The sun is directly on the house taken by the 92nd with Barnes at their head. The enclosed farm, north east of the crossroads, is original.

3. Quatre Bras. The foreground was once covered by Bossu wood. On the Genappe–Charleroi road, left to right: Quatre Bras, the house taken by the 92nd (now somewhat enlarged), the Duke of Brunswick monument and Gemioncourt. In the centre background is Materne Lake.

4. Materne Lake, the Nivelles–Namur road and Thy. The house left of the lake is modern. Piraumont is all but obscured by the trees, centre right. The church tower, centre background, is in Marbais. The Bois de Cherris which stood north of the road—approximately above the top left corner of the lake in this picture—has disappeared.

5. The intersection of the Genappe and Nivelles roads in Mont St Jean with the Lion monument in the right background.

6. The farm of Le Grand Pierrepont south west of Quatre Bras. It was taken by the French early in the battle of 16 June but was retaken by the 'English' towards the end of the action.

7. Gemioncourt from the Genappe–Charleroi road.

8. Inside the biggest farm at Piraumont (both this farm and the adjacent village are referred to as Piraumont).

9. Lairalle from the north.

10. A section of the old Roman road no longer in use between the battlefields of Quatre Bras and Ligny. The buildings on the centre horizon are modern; those on the far right are Villers–Perwin. Marbais is to the right and Wagnelee to the left, both out of the picture.

11. Ligny Church which changed hands several times on 16 June.

12. The bridge across the Dyle downstream from Genappe which was used by both armies. This was the standard minor road width in 1815.

IV

Napoleon Attacks the Prussians

Wellington rose early on 15 June 1815 as was his invariable custom. His organisation was beginning to function more efficiently; there were still many tasks before him and much correspondence, but he now had more time to think. His army was better and stronger than it had been and properly deployed, but intelligence from all sources was disquieting. By now Napoleon was surely with the French Army just across the border. There were rumours of activity west of the Scheldt, but more credible reports of a concentration around Maubeuge were also coming in. The Duke could take no active counter-measures until the French began something definite. The Anglo-Dutch Army was as well disposed as it could be until the enemy crossed the border in force at some point.

All remained quiet in Brussels until between 3 and 4 p.m., but then three reports arrived in quick succession. These consisted of a dispatch from Ziethen in Charleroi,[1] a dispatch from Blücher in Namur and an eyewitness report by the Prince of Orange. All were late and incomplete, but all agreed that the Prussian First Corps around Charleroi had been attacked. The initial area of combat was south of the Sambre, in the vicinity of Lobbes, Thuin and Binche. Charleroi was certainly threatened, but so was Mons.

The attack on the Prussians south of the Sambre started shortly after dawn, before 5 a.m. The first message to arrive appears to have come

---

[1] Some secondary sources deny that Ziethen sent a message, or at least that it arrived: *Robinson*, III, 666. There is also the partially substantiated story that Ziethen's messenger was 'the fattest man in the Prussian army' and took eleven hours to cover the distance: *Maxwell*, II, 8.

directly from Blücher at Namur which involved a dispatch rider's trip from Charleroi to Namur (28 miles), the drafting of a new dispatch, and then another ride to Brussels (42 miles) over poor roads. The direct distance from Charleroi to Brussels was only 32 miles on good roads, a three-hour ride for a capable messenger on a good horse. Wellington might have known of the initial French attack as soon as Blücher, before 9 a.m. at the latest, if Ziethen had followed instructions and/or the messenger sent had carried out his assignment properly. Why did he hear nothing until after 3 p.m.?

Many writers have expended tens of thousands of words on the question of this communications breakdown; no completely satisfactory explanation has ever been found. Houssaye claimed that Wellington did receive a dispatch from Ziethen at 8 a.m., but chose later to deny it.[1] There is not one shred of evidence for such a view in all the dozens of memoirs which survive. Wellington's whole life and character argue against it. Besides, it is not logical; he would have reacted immediately if he had known that the French had begun an attack anywhere.

The breakdown in communication between the Prussian and the Anglo-Dutch Armies really started the day before. On the night of 13 June, the reflection of the French bivouac fires in the sky – the camps were behind hills – plus other intelligence was sufficient to alert the Prussians to a real concentration of the French Army south of them.[2] Gneisenau on his own responsibility issued orders for the Second, Third, and Fourth Prussian Corps to move on Sombreffe. He passed on, however, to Müffling and Wellington neither intelligence of his actual movements, nor the reasons for them. His messages to the Second Corps (Thielemann) and to the Third Corps (Pirch) were terse and to the point, since he was senior to both commanders. His orders to Bülow of the Fourth Corps, his superior, were so respectful as to be ambiguous and misleading; this formation was far away at Liège and did not move until the morning of the 15th.

The intelligence which Wellington did receive in mid-afternoon of the 15th only included news of a French attack shortly after dawn and did not give details of strength, nor, most important of all to Wellington, of the approximate east and west limits of the French offensive area. The Prince of Orange reported that even though none of his

---

[1] *Houssaye*, 81, based on Von Ollech.

[2] *Jomini*, 116, says that a drummer of the Old Guard deserted and gave the Prussians information about French plans.

troops had been engaged, the town of Binche had been occupied by the French after the Prussians had been driven out. He had seen no fighting, but the sound of it was audible at Braine le Comte. The French and Prussians were skirmishing vigorously, but there was nothing to indicate the position and direction of Bonaparte's main attack. What had occurred might be merely a feint to conceal some other French advance which the Emperor might press much more strongly.

Wellington issued his first set of preparatory orders mainly for a concentration of all divisions at their division assembly points; these went out some time after 5 p.m.[1] The Duke did not order any general movements beyond these concentration points because so far he did not know precisely in which direction his army should move. He did indicate, however, some changes in his plans not apparent in his organisation and cantonment arrangements. He did not contemplate handling his army by corps in the French style; the Prince of Orange was not given a true operational command, and received independent authority only with regard to the two Dutch-Belgian divisions of his corps about Nivelles and Quatre Bras with permission to bring up one British division to their aid. Hill was treated more leniently and was instructed to transmit orders to the Dutch-Belgians under him; 500 men were to remain in the defensive works at Oudenarde on both sides of the Scheldt.

Wellington's real problem was to determine which of the three likely lines of advance – through Charleroi, Mons or Tournai, as shown on Map 2 – the French were using; a combination of two or even three of these was also possible. News from Mons was vital. The Duke was unwilling to make dispositions of his forces to help the Prussians stop the Charleroi attack that would prevent him from countering an advance along either or both the routes that were his primary responsibility. If he could be reasonably sure Napoleon was advancing with his entire force in the Charleroi area only, he could concentrate near the Roman road.

Towards midnight, Wellington told Müffling, 'I have got news from Mons, from General Dörnberg, who reports that Napoleon has turned towards Charleroi with all his forces, and that there is no longer any enemy in front of him. Orders for the concentration of my army at Nivelles and Quatre Bras are already dispatched.'[2] These orders are

[1] See *Ropes*, 77, and *Dispatches*, XII 472–3 for details.
[2] *Müffling's Passages*, 230.

often known as the second set and probably went out between 10 and 11 p.m.[1] Deliveries were in some instances delayed by the messengers missing their way in the darkness. Not all command units were notified within six hours; some appear to have moved without orders even as late as 8 a.m. on the 16th. But all did move.

The Duke must quickly have analysed the situation on the evening of the 15th. If the French were attacking by one route only, through Charleroi, the Anglo-Dutch Army could risk moving east. If there had been French forces south of Mons, Dörnberg with his cavalry patrols now extending well across the border would know about them. If Napoleon was planning to use not only the Charleroi attack route, but also one of the other two, the French would have had to keep some kind of connecting link between their armies. Since there was no connecting link, there was little chance that the Emperor was doing anything other than attacking with his whole effective force in the Charleroi area.

These deductions were confirmed by further dispatches received by Müffling from Prussian headquarters. Earlier intelligence had reported a French attack, but had given no details as to strength; those arriving later were clearer. The French advance across the Sambre on both sides of Charleroi indicated the use of a large force, so large that a feint-and-strike-elsewhere operation was hardly possible. The Prussian Army was concentrating in the area around Sombreffe to meet a threatened French attack from Fleurus.

Too much has been made of the focal point of the Anglo-Dutch concentration, whether it was to be at Nivelles or Quatre Bras. The entire army was to move towards its left or east flank. The only divisions immediately concerned with a distinction between these two places were the two Dutch-Belgian divisions under the Prince of Orange, commanded by Chassé and Perponcher, particularly the latter which was stationed in and about both Nivelles and Quatre Bras. To all other Anglo-Dutch units, a movement on Nivelles was also one towards Quatre Bras; they were only seven miles apart.

Wellington actually attended the Duchess of Richmond's ball on the night of the 15th, along with many of his officers of higher rank. This can have caused him no real inconvenience, for his powers of concentration regardless of surroundings were well developed. Further, he habitually took over any available facilities for aiding himself and his staff to accomplish their duties. The concentration of officers was

[1] See *Robinson*, III, 702–9, for an analysis of these two sets of orders.

certainly no disadvantage; he was able to give directions to several. The cancelling of the ball was unthinkable because of the encouragement it would have given to the Francophil Belgians.

The Duke appears to have been in bed shortly before 2 a.m., arisen about 5.30 a.m., breakfasted (tea and toast) and undertook routine duties. He left Brussels on horseback shortly after 7 a.m. His Reserve Corps, the part of the army directly under his personal command, had left Brussels soon after dawn – sunrise at this time of year and in this area was about 3.50 a.m. – with Picton's Division in the lead. It was to move south as far as Mont Saint Jean where the road forks and await further orders. The right-hand branch leads to Nivelles and the left-hand branch to Quatre Bras via Genappe. The Duke himself passed them on the road and pushed on fast for Quatre Bras. He arrived there about 10 a.m.

At Quatre Bras, a hamlet located at the junction of the Nivelles-Namur and Charleroi-Brussels roads, Wellington found the military situation satisfactory. It was obviously important to hold this position in order to keep open easy communications with the Prussians who were concentrating just south of Sombreffe, a village about eight miles east of Quatre Bras and also on the Nivelles–Namur road. Prince Bernhard of Saxe-Weimar who commanded a brigade of Nassau troops in the pay of the Netherlands, a part of Perponcher's Second Dutch-Belgian Division, had fought an action against the French near Frasnes the evening before and held them well south of Quatre Bras. Saxe-Weimar had about 4,400 infantry with eight guns against 1,800 French cavalry with no artillery. Losses were trifling since the French did not attack in earnest, and the crossroads had been held.[1]

Even more important, Perponcher's Division had been concentrated at Quatre Bras on the morning of 15 June rather than at its concentration point, Nivelles. The Prince of Orange, his Chief of Staff, General Constant Rebecque, and Perponcher all deserve credit in this connection. But a decision of this kind is one that any good subordinate commander should make. The first set of orders had specifically allowed some initiative to the Prince of Orange who arrived at Quatre Bras from the ball at about 6 a.m. After Saxe-Weimar's fight on the evening of the 15th, Perponcher and Rebecque could hardly retreat from a weaker enemy so as to open a gap between the armies of Wellington and Blücher. Little harm could come from concentrating

[1] *James*, 75, citing *de Bas*, 539, says the Nassauers lost only a total of forty men including some prisoners. Bernhard had some Prussian cavalry helping him for a few hours.

a single division some seven miles west of Nivelles, as the entire Anglo-Dutch Army was known to be marching towards it. Every responsible Allied subordinate commander must have realised that contact had to be maintained between the Anglo-Dutch Army and the Prussians. Napoleon might easily defeat either Wellington or Blücher, if he could fight them one at a time.

By 10 a.m. on the 16th, Perponcher's Division was all in position south of Quatre Bras. Its units were spread out rather widely in a rough arc of a circle with Quatre Bras as its centre. They occupied several large farms and one small village. Wellington inspected and approved the positions of these Dutch-Belgian troops. The enemy did not appear to be either particularly strong or offensively inclined at the moment. The Duke sent orders to his Reserve Corps which had stopped at Mont Saint Jean to move on Quatre Bras by the Genappe road, sent a report to Blücher giving the positions of the various units of the Anglo-Dutch Army,[1] and sent staff officers west towards Nivelles to bring forward to Quatre Bras those Anglo-Dutch directed to Nivelles in the second set of orders, as soon as they arrived there.

For the moment at least, there was little for Wellington to do at the crossroads. The only Anglo-Dutch troops actually in position were those already deployed under the Prince of Orange, about 8,000 men in all. Reinforcements were on the way from the north and west, but would not arrive for at least three hours. The Duke, accompanied by some of his staff, rode across the old Roman road to visit Blücher. The meeting took place at the Bussy windmill near the village of Brye. The two commanders quickly brought each other up to date on recent developments in their respective armies. Ziethen's First Prussian Corps had fought a sound rear-guard action the day before and been pushed back over the Sambre.[2] The Germans appear to have lost some 1,500 men, but the French had also suffered casualties, had failed to win a decisive victory and had lost valuable time. Blücher now had his First, Second and Third Corps in position in front of Sombreffe. They were holding several villages including Ligny which gave its name to the battle soon to be fought there. There was also a stream of the same name which gave some advantage to the defence. The Prussian position was indifferent and practically featureless from a military standpoint.

[1] This order gave some erroneous information, but will be discussed in detail in Part Two, Chapter II, 'Wellington's Mistakes'.

[2] *Fortescue*, X, 289, says that Wellington had already learned much of this from Prussian stragglers at Quatre Bras earlier in the day.

It was also poorly taken up. The Prussian infantry in columns were in the open and exposed to French artillery fire.[1]

Wellington explained quickly his own plans for a concentration at Quatre Bras and the fact that the French might attack him there. Gneisenau apparently asked Wellington to detach a portion of his force to reinforce the Prussians at Ligny. Wellington refused to divide his army, but suggested instead that he attack the French south of Quatre Bras, drive them in and fall on the French left flank and rear. The Prussians thought that the time required to do this would be excessive; they asked instead that the Duke come to their assistance. He finally promised to move from Quatre Bras towards Sombreffe by the Nivelles–Namur road with his entire disposable force 'provided I am not attacked'.[2]

After the conference, Wellington returned quickly to Quatre Bras, arriving shortly before 3 p.m. The entire disposition of the French forces to the south had changed; Wellington realised immediately that an attack was imminent. This was soon delivered by infantry, cavalry and artillery. The Dutch-Belgians were probably not greatly out-numbered and initially held positions of considerable strength. They were perhaps over-extended, but the farms of Petit and Grand Pierre-pont on the west of the Charleroi road, and Gemioncourt, Lairalle and Piraumont (actually a village) on the east, were of considerable strength. See Map 3 for the arrangement of these places and other features of this battlefield.[3]

So far, the Dutch-Belgian commanders had done an excellent job; they had concentrated imaginatively and handled their troops flawlessly. They had prevented a French force from occupying Quatre Bras on the evening of the 15th and had skirmished effectively during the early hours of the 16th. They had infantry and artillery well settled into defensive positions which they should have been able to hold for a considerable time against the French attack as now delivered. When it came to actual combat, however, the Prince of Orange's men were not willing to meet the French. They gave up their positions without a determined effort to hold them and retired almost in panic. Only in Bossu wood which then extended for a mile roughly parallel to and on the west side of the Charleroi road south of Quatre Bras did they

---

[1] The Ligny battlefield is discussed in Part Two, Chapter VI, 'Topography'.

[2] These words are used in most accounts of this meeting, including those of *Müffling* and *Dörnberg* who were present.

[3] The Quatre Bras battlefield is also discussed in Part Two, Chapter VI, 'Topography'.

do any serious fighting. Bernhard's brigade of Nassauers, after losing the Pierreponts, showed real spirit among the trees and undergrowth. Fortunately, Picton's fine division was beginning to arrive from Mont Saint Jean by the Genappe road. What happened after 3 p.m. properly belongs to Wellington's battle at Quatre Bras and will be told in the next chapter.

was some 300 yards south of this vital road and would cover Quatre Bras admirably on the east. But before the Rifles could get close to the place, a strong force of French infantry moved into it. An attack across open fields on a more numerous enemy behind stone walls was not attempted. The riflemen did occupy, however, the Bois de Cherris extending north of the road and the road itself north of Piraumont, and pushed their flank east along the road so as to occupy a small group of buildings known as the hamlet of Thyle. They were soon engaged in a long and bitter fire fight with more numerous French tirailleurs who advanced from Piraumont, but save for one brief interval to be described presently, they retained complete possession of the road. The next five hours of fighting amply demonstrated the superiority of rifles over muskets when the former were handled skilfully by men who were both well trained and well practised with their weapons. The 1/95th was neither outflanked nor outfought, but did have the support of a Brunswick battalion which arrived after about thirty minutes.

This relative immobility of Wellington's eastern flank, based not only on the fine fighting qualities of the 1/95th and those who aided them throughout the afternoon, but also on favourable terrain, gave him a strong pivot on which to swing the rest of the line. This he soon organised. The Piraumont-Thyle area was separated from the battle-field west of it by some low ground, a dam and the artificial Materne lake. A somewhat similar feature on the west was the already mentioned Bossu wood. Gemioncourt brook rose in the wood, then flowed east across the Charleroi road, past Gemioncourt farm and through a small marsh into Materne lake. It was never much of a military obstacle, save next to the lake. The distance from Bossu wood to Materne lake was about 1,500 yards. Both boundary areas saw serious fighting, but the battle was really decided in the open between the two. The north-to-south distance between Quatre Bras and the level of Lairalle and the Pierreponts was about 2,500 yards, so that the serious fighting in the open occurred within a rough rectangle less than a mile wide and less than a mile and a half long.

The French took two-thirds of this area while Picton's Division was arriving by the Genappe road. As has already been mentioned, Saxe-Weimar's Brigade was holding Bossu wood and appears to have done a fair job of fighting under difficult conditions.[1] In order to gain time

---

[1] *Boulger*, 16, says that these soldiers were armed with French muskets (two battalions) and with rifles of four calibres (two battalions); they had initially only ten cartridges per man.

for a proper deployment of Picton's main force, Wellington ordered Perponcher's other brigade under Bylandt to re-take Gemioncourt. He sent forward the 1/28th, the second British battalion to arrive, to support the Netherlanders in their attack with the additional instructions that if this group of farm buildings could be captured, the 28th was to become its garrison. These massive buildings were characteristic of Belgian farms at that time. They included the principal and subordinate dwellings, large barns, sheds and other buildings all arranged around a courtyard. These farms were of strong brick and stone construction; most of them are still in use today. They were solid enough in most cases to be impervious to the fire of the field-artillery of that era and could be entered only through strong wooden gates.

Bylandt's Brigade did not come close to taking Gemioncourt. They did, however, gain some time. Wellington deployed the brigades of Pack and Kempt along the Namur road from Quatre Bras to the artificial lake. Kempt's Brigade, less the 95th and the 28th, was to the east; the 1/79th was posted by the Duke personally well south of the road and about level with the western edge of Materne lake. The 1/32nd was in close support on the right, half way back to the road. The four battalions of Pack's Brigade were extended in line along the road itself with the 1/92nd at or near Quatre Bras, and the 1/42nd next to them on the east; the 2/44th and the 3/1st were between the 1/42nd and the 32nd.[1] Wellington placed Picton's Hanoverian Brigade under Best in a supporting second line north of the road. Initially the divisional artillery was stationed with one battery on each flank; Roger's was on the left between the 79th and 95th and Rettberg's (KGL) was on the right in front of the 92nd next to Quatre Bras.

Wellington appears to have made a short reconnaissance east of Materne lake; he was pleased with the progress made by the Rifles, but made a mental note to send them some support as soon as possible. He returned to the 1/79th and saw that the French were either continuing their original infantry attack supported by artillery and cavalry, or mounting a new one. Three heavy columns, probably full brigades, were moving north between Materne lake and the Charleroi road. One of these would cross the Gemioncourt brook just to the east of the farm; another would cross it close to the lake. The third was intermediate between the other two. At least one more similar column

---

[1] No amount of research can establish the exact relative positions of these battalions (including the 1/28th when it returned) thoughout the action; original authorities just do not agree.

was moving north on the west side of the Charleroi road. In addition, a mass of French troops could be seen even farther west in the general vicinity of Bossu wood moving north to support those already fighting against Saxe-Weimar's Nassauers. The situation was near desperate; Ney appeared to have at least three infantry divisions plus artillery and cavalry in proportion. No Allied cavalry was available; the single Prussian squadron which had been useful earlier had now disappeared from the field.[1] Perponcher's Division left much to be desired; Bylandt's Brigade had not even closed to musketry range in their counter-attack on Gemioncourt. In effect the Duke had little more than one division to fight three.

Even as he surveyed the scene, some of Roger's gunners within yards of him were hit by the fire of French sharpshooters. A long irregular line of tirailleurs had moved north between the Charleroi road and the artificial lake, concealed throughout most of its progress by standing crops of rye five to six feet tall. To await a French attack against such odds might lead to disaster; the Duke decided to attack them instead. He ordered the 1/79th to move forward in line and prevent the French from passing the lake. He then rode to the west and ordered the 32nd to do the same thing. Successively, each British battalion moved out in line. The entire movement of the two brigades was an almost perfect example of an echelon attack, left in front, extending over about three-quarters of a mile.[2]

The 79th encountered the enemy first. It brushed back the tirailleurs easily and met a French infantry brigade in column just north of the head of the lake. The British line appears to have surprised the much larger French column, perhaps because of hedges and crops.[3] As in the Peninsula, the British line used its superior firepower and won easily. The other British battalions effectively defeated with fire all other enemy columns between the lake and the Charleroi road. When the French retreated, however, Picton's infantry which had advanced to or across the brook, was clearly revealed to the French batteries and received a heavy fire. The French artillery was superior to that of the Allies both in number of pieces and weight of metal. The Dutch-

[1] These were Prussians of the 2nd Silesian Hussars who had joined their own army, *Boulger*, 48–52.

[2] The 1/92nd probably did not take part in this advance because of its responsibility for the crossroads.

[3] *Gardner*, 69, and others say that there were hedges along Gemioncourt brook in this area.

Belgian batteries of Perponcher's Division did not operate effectively after their first retreat. Some of these guns were probably captured by the French.[1]

As Wellington reached the crossroads after sending forward each battalion in turn, he met the head of the Duke of Brunswick's 'corps' which was just arriving by the Genappe road. He dispatched the vanguard infantry battalion of this unit east along the Namur road to support the 95th Rifles. He deployed the rest of Brunswick's infantry, which arrived at this time, west of the Charleroi road to help Saxe-Weimar's Nassauers who were losing heavily in the Bossu area and being pushed back by veteran French tirailleurs.

Picton's British brigades had now retired somewhat to avoid French artillery fire, but remained in front of the Nivelles–Namur road. Wellington ordered the Duke of Brunswick to attack with his cavalry down the Charleroi road and to the west of it in the open between the road and the woods. Brunswick charged at the head of his regiment of hussars, but appears not to have accomplished much. The Brunswickers were not up to smashing into French infantry which quickly formed squares. Their commander did manage, however, to rally and re-form his cavalry to some extent and to take possession of a large house or small farm some 200 yards south of Quatre Bras to the east of the Charleroi road. He fell mortally wounded a few moments later while trying to get a stable line of resistance established in this area:

The Prince of Orange heard of Brunswick's death and came up to complete the rallying of the hussars; he added the Brunswick lancer regiment to them along with most of Van Merlen's Dutch-Belgian cavalry brigade which had just arrived from Nivelles, and led them all, apparently in a two-line formation, a considerable distance south on either side of the Charleroi road. The Allied cavalry was confronted at about Gemioncourt by most of a French light cavalry brigade. Even though more numerous, the Dutch-Belgian and perhaps the Brunswick horsemen refused to charge the French cavalry. The French squadrons came forward, but the Allies broke before contact and streamed back towards Quatre Bras in the area between the Charleroi road and Bossu wood.

Wellington personally endeavoured to rally this cavalry just south of Quatre Bras, but soon found himself almost surrounded by French

---

[1] *Boulger*, 58, says, 'three taken and four damaged', but others concede only one or two taken and do not mention damaged pieces. Ney claimed to have taken only one gun.

lancers and hussars. The 92nd was in an L-shaped line in ditches at the crossroads with the long bar towards Namur and the short one towards Genappe. The Duke called to the Highlanders to put down their bayonets and crouch low while he put his horse to the jump and cleared them easily. The French light cavalry was received by the 92nd with steady half-company volleys and repulsed with ease, but a number of them squeezed the 92nd's right flank and the Brunswick infantry posted near the north-east corner of Bossu wood. These enemy troopers were subjected to a heavy fire, suffered serious casualties, turned about and retired the way they came.

Other portions of this same French light cavalry went through gaps between the 92nd and the 42nd and between the 42nd and the 44th. These horsemen were so intermingled with the retreating Allied cavalry that they escaped being fired upon by the British infantry. Once through the line, however, French lancers attacked the flank and rear of the 42nd and 44th. Colonel Macara of the 42nd endeavoured to have his men form square; they could not complete this manœuvre before the French lancers were into the temporarily exposed Highlanders.[1] But the 42nd did close their square by main strength and killed every French cavalryman caught inside; their regular rolling fire soon defeated those outside. Serious casualties, including their colonel and two other field-officers, were sustained, however, in these few seconds of disorganisation.[2]

The 44th might have suffered even more severely than the 42nd, for it had less time to prepare for the wheeling charges of the French cavalry which poured through gaps on either flank. But the Colonel of the 44th made no effort to charge his formation. He ordered his rear rank to face about and await the French with loaded muskets. The lancers tried to charge home, but were received with a volley. Contact was actually made in the middle of the line where some gallant Frenchmen tried to capture the regimental colours.

A French lancer severely wounded Ensign Christie, who carried one of them, by a thrust of his lance, which, entering the left eye, penetrated to the lower jaw. The Frenchman then endeavoured to seize the Standard, but the brave Christie, notwithstanding the agony of his wound, with a presence of mind almost unequalled, flung himself upon it – not to save himself, but to preserve

---

[1] *Siborne*, 158–9, says that the square was nearly formed, but that the two flank companies were not quite closed together in the rear.

[2] *Batty*, 53, says, 'Colonel Macara, of the 42nd, was severely wounded, and whilst some of his men were conveying him to the rear, a party of the French cavalry rode up and killed him and his faithful attendants', probably with lances.

the honour of his Regiment. As the Colour fluttered in its fall, the Frenchman tore off a portion of the silk with the point of his lance; but he was not permitted to bear even the fragment beyond the ranks. Both shot and bayoneted by the nearest of the soldiers of the 44th, he was borne to the earth, paying with his life for his display of unavailing bravery.[1]

The French cavalry which survived swept back through the gaps between the British battalions and received the fire of the first rank of the 44th as they retreated.

Wellington again endeavoured to rally the Dutch-Belgian and Brunswick cavalry. Some squadrons of the former had their confidence sufficiently restored to take a position to the east of the Genappe road behind Best's Hanoverian infantry. In appearance at least, these units were supporting the Allied troops in front of them, although they were not again to face the French in the open field. The Brunswickers were somewhat more dependable and were formed just south of the Nivelles road between Quatre Bras and Bossu wood, probably in and behind a small orchard.

Saxe-Weimar's troops in the wood were sustaining heavy casualties and were beginning to lose their morale, but the Brunswick infantry which had been exposed to the French for a lesser time was still holding on. Pack's four battalions and Kempt's three – the 1/95th was too far east – were beginning to suffer from French artillery fire which had opened again after the retreat of their cavalry. The British infantry had no reverse slope to occupy because Wellington had not been able to choose a position beforehand. Any retreat would allow the French to cut the all important Nivelles–Namur road. So long as these battalions could remain in line, they did not suffer too greatly; the tall rye gave some protection, while the narrow ditch on the north side of the road also appears to have helped. They could lie down when no enemy was close. But most of these battalions were now in square and vulnerable to artillery fire because they could not tell when the French cavalry might come forward again.

Wellington was personally engaged in reorganising his artillery: there appear to have been only five batteries all told, two British, one Brunswick and the remains of two Dutch-Belgian. As we have seen, the Duke did not believe in using his artillery for counter-battery work, but needed every piece to fire canister into advancing French masses when they did appear. He did not have long to wait. Ney launched some 800 cuirassiers in a relatively compact mass charging north on

[1] *Siborne,* 161.

V

Quatre Bras

Wellington took over the battle which developed when the French attacked the forces commanded by the Prince of Orange south of Quatre Bras. The start was not propitious, for most of the Dutch-Belgian units were already retreating in disorder. Even worse from the Duke's point of view, he was forced to fight for a military objective, the Nivelles–Namur road, in order to maintain contact with the Prussians and could not choose a position for himself. The flat land in this area was not adaptable to his normal type of defensive tactics. His disposable forces were weaker in numbers and quality than those of the enemy. But he wasted no time in idle wishes or recriminations. He had a job to do with what he had at hand, so he proceeded to do it.

Before the French who were commanded by Marshal Ney could get within musket-shot of the vital road, Picton's Division began to arrive at Quatre Bras. It consisted of Kempt's and Pack's strong brigades of British Peninsular veterans and Best's Hanoverian Brigade.[1] Wellington took charge of these and the Duke of Brunswick's command that followed close behind and began to produce order from chaos.

The 1/95th Rifles was the lead battalion of Picton's command. The Duke sent them off to the left around Quatre Bras and down the Namur road with instructions to retake and hold the village of Piraumont which had formed the east flank of the Dutch-Belgian position when the French began their attack. This straggling group of buildings

---

[1] Organisation tables show Picton as having Vincke's Hanoverian Brigade in his division, but Best's from Cole's incomplete Division took its place at Quatre Bras. Both were under Picton at the beginning of Waterloo, but Best's was more closely associated with the brigades of Pack and Kempt towards the end of the battle.

either side of the Charleroi road.[1] They drove in the British skirmishers quickly; actually, the 42nd and the 44th knew about the attack only when their skirmishers ran in. Wellington was again with the 92nd and had a clearer view of what was happening. He kept these Highlanders in a four-deep line, but probably abandoned the L-shape for they appear to have been on both sides of the Genappe road.

The 92nd took the brunt of this attack and behaved admirably. Nearly all the cuirassiers charged towards them, but Wellington personally directed the first volley. The 92nd held its fire until the French cavalry was no more than thirty yards away; it stopped them in their tracks, a rearing mass of killed, wounded and panic-ridden horses and men. The rolling half-company volleys did the rest. The 92nd and to some extent the 42nd and 44th, which were formed in square to the east, were not so sorely tried by the heavy horsemen and their sabres as they had been by the lighter French cavalry armed with lances.[2]

The formation of attack used by the cuirassiers extended no more than a quarter of the distance between Bossu wood and the lake; they charged down the Charleroi road and to either side of it almost as if into the open end of a V. The Brunswickers lined the edge of the rear section of Bossu wood; the 42nd and 44th in square were in front of the east flank of the 92nd. Many cuirassiers including their commander, Kellermann, had their horses shot under them. Some were killed by bullets which passed through their breastplates; this armour was generally pistol-proof, but never musket-proof at close range.[3] A few cuirassiers penetrated past the right flank of the 92nd and into Quatre Bras, but these found themselves in a cul-de-sac, lost their nerve, and retreated. Other groups passed between the 92nd, the 42nd and perhaps the 44th, and crossed the Namur road, but they were soon defeated by Best's Hanoverian Brigade. The Brunswick cavalry just to the west of Quatre Bras seems also to have fought some of these cuirassiers. The French horsemen were soon in a headlong retreat which took them entirely out of the battle area.[4]

[1] These were one of Kellermann's four brigades, but he led them personally. He is said to have ordered them forward as soon as possible so they would not have time to see the odds against them: *Fortescue*, X, 308.

[2] See Part Two, Chapter V, 'Cavalry Attacks on Infantry Squares', for details of actions of this type.

[3] See Part Two, Chapter I, 'Ordnance', for details of cavalry and infantry weapons.

[4] *Wood*, 93, says that some of these cuirassiers did not draw rein until they reached the vicinity of Frasnes.

Even though the French cuirassiers accomplished nothing significant against Wellington's infantry, they did do some damage to the British and Brunswick skirmishers who were caught in the open and to artillerymen who were not able to reach safety after firing their pieces for the last time. Once the enemy cavalry was clear of the Allied infantry, the French artillery reopened fire. Some of Ney's guns were now in position north of Gemioncourt less than 500 yards away. The tall rye in front of Pack's Brigade was sufficiently trampled down by men and horses for three of his four battalions to be clearly visible to the gunners. Under the protection of their artillery, the French tirailleurs took advantage of the natural reluctance of the British skirmishers to leave the protection of the squares after their late harrowing experience with the cuirassiers. These sharpshooters crawled forward and harried Wellington's main line for almost the first time in the Duke's long career of fighting the French. There was little he could do about it. He had no effective cavalry of his own; the French horsemen were close and in some cases concealed by folds of ground and still-standing crops. Had he deployed Picton's infantry into line and advanced to drive off the tirailleurs, the French cavalry might have come on suddenly and inflicted irreparable damage.

Wellington was fortunate that this artillery and sharpshooter ordeal came to an end fairly quickly, although if it had not he would probably have thought of a move to counter it. The French cavalry reappeared, this time cuirassiers, lancers and hussars together. A double line of attack extended all the way from the Charleroi road to the marshy ground west of Materne lake, but again the brunt of the attack fell on Pack's Brigade. The first onset was stopped easily: Pack was sufficiently well supported by Kempt on the west, Best's Hanoverians on the north and the Brunswickers to the east, so that his four battalions held their formations. The 92nd appears to have remained in a quadruple line, but to have moved to the south side of the Nivelles–Namur road; the 42nd, 44th, and 3/1st (until now only lightly engaged) were in square. The French cavalry retired a short distance after their first unsuccessful charge to allow their artillery and tirailleurs to get at the British infantry again.

This second ordeal was even worse than the first. The 92nd, 42nd and 44th were nearly out of ammunition. The light companies of these three battalions tried to keep off the tirailleurs, expended every cartridge and had to retire. The tirailleurs were less than a hundred yards away and were inflicting serious loss on the heavy line of the 92nd and the squares of the 42nd and 44th. These three battalions dared not expend their few remaining cartridges in shooting at elusive tirailleurs.

Promptly, Wellington ordered Picton to take the 28th from Kempt, join it to the Royals (3/1st) of Pack's Brigade and move the two in close column to the assistance of Pack's three sorely tried battalions just east of Quatre Bras. Picton accomplished this difficult manœuvre brilliantly. Disregarding normal British combat procedures, he led both battalions into a solid, well-disciplined mass on a two-company front between the 92nd in line and the 42nd in square. He drove back the French tirailleurs by the deterrent of a precipitate bayonet attack, and occupied a slightly elevated position south and a little west of the gap between the 92nd and 42nd. Before the French cavalry could effectively attack this seemingly exposed column, Picton formed his two battalions into a single square. Within a minute, he defeated an extemporised but all-out attack by the French horsemen in the immediate area. Half-company volleys were sent in the direction of any tirailleurs who came within effective range.

While Picton was moving the 1st and 28th, Wellington himself appears to have ridden east to the 32nd and 79th and moved them much closer to the 44th. All seven battalions could now support each other with fire. They were formed in a chequered arrangement east from the Charleroi road. The French cavalry soon gave up milling around close to the new British formation, four battalions of which had plenty of ammunition, and retired for the third time.

The French artillery reopened in earnest; the tirailleurs came forward again to do their close-range work, mostly from a prone position. But now the British light companies were more concentrated and advanced gallantly to meet again their old enemies of the Peninsula. Wellington brought forward one of Best's Hanoverian battalions from the second line to extend the first to the east, and made what dispositions he could to shelter the individual battalions from artillery fire. But the military situation was still desperate. Picton's Division had already suffered severe casualties: some of the battalions were below two-thirds of their original strength. In spite of some sharing of ammunition between battalions and perhaps a little replenishment, all were now running low.[1] Wellington's good-quality artillery and

---

[1] British and Hanoverian infantry carried 60-cartridge ammunition pouches; each man had an additional 60 rounds in his knapsack, but the latter may not have been taken into battle.

infantry was only one third of Ney's artillery and infantry of similar quality. There were also between 3,000 and 4,000 first-rate French cavalry, both heavy and light, whereas the Duke did not have a single horseman willing to charge in the open against real opposition. The Dutch-Belgians (cavalry, infantry and artillery) were leaving the field. Even the Brunswick infantry in Bossu wood was showing signs of disorganisation; they were now holding only the extreme northern end of it.[1]

The French cavalry came forward again, cuirassiers, lancers and hussars. They caught the Hanoverian battalion which Wellington had just brought into the first line in open order, perhaps because the rye in this area was not yet trampled down. The rank and file of this force were militia and could not stand; they were ridden down so that many did not reach the Namur road in their frantic flight. But the pursuing French cavalry ran into another Hanoverian battalion which Wellington had personally aligned in the ditch just south of the road; a volley emptied some saddles. The attack was not pressed home, in part because some of Van Merlen's Dutch-Belgian cavalry was arrayed to the north in what appeared to be a steady formation.

The fighting between the French cavalry and the British infantry closer to Quatre Bras was even more severe than before. The 92nd had now so little ammunition left that it was completely unable to deliver its usual fire. Most of the French horsemen had already charged these squares and the quadruple line three times, and had learned to respect them. They no longer tried to charge home, but used firearms at close range instead. Those who still had lances were using them for thrusting or even throwing javelin-fashion. Casualties were inflicted on both sides, however, for the infantry still had enough ammunition to fire platoon volleys at really profitable targets.

An even more serious situation was developing to the east. The French infantry operating around Materne lake was now able to push back the 95th Rifles and the Brunswickers from the hamlet of Thyle, perhaps because Wellington had been forced to draw most of Kempt's Brigade west. The Rifles and the Brunswickers would have been separated from the Allied centre if they had not retired to the Bois de Cherris. They were soon hotly engaged there and were having trouble holding this small wood.

This was probably the low point in Wellington's most uncharacteristic battle. As has been said, his serious problems came from a poor

[1] The Brunswick cavalry appears to have been north-west of the crossroads by this time.

position which he had to defend in order to hold open communications with Blücher and from the inescapable fact that he had an inferior force. But reinforcements began to arrive by both the Nivelles and the Genappe roads. Two brigades of Alten's Third British Division came up from Nivelles; Wellington immediately took the first, Kielmansegge's Hanoverians, to the extreme left and directed it to assist the Rifles in clearing the Bois de Cherris and restoring the position at Thyle.

While Wellington went to the left, Picton was ordered to handle the disposition of Colin Halkett's Brigade which was composed of four British battalions originally from Graham's unsuccessful force. Picton advanced the 2/69th across the Charleroi road a few yards and ordered it to form square so it could support the British squares already strung out more or less in line from this road to the east. The 69th was fresh, had full ammunition pouches and was positioned slightly in front of the west flank of Picton's Division. The fire of this battalion would greatly increase the effectiveness of Wellington's entire centre.

Picton placed the other three battalions of Halkett's Brigade in support of the Brunswickers still holding the northern edge of Bossu wood and some ground to the east between the wood and the Charleroi road. He had Halkett form them individually in square and collectively in echelon, right in front. They extended from the Charleroi road to Bossu wood; all Brunswick infantry appears to have been in the wood itself by this time. Picton's disposition can hardly be faulted; he obtained the maximum tactical support from these reinforcements.

Apparently, the Prince of Orange resented this interference with his authority as second in command over the entire area. The young man, all twenty-three years of him with no line experience, thought he had to make some changes. He ordered the 69th out of their square and into line because of a half-understood principle that lines were better than squares as regards firepower. He then rode across the Charleroi road and again countermanded Picton's orders. Halkett was forced, after vehement protests, to form his other three battalions also in line.

We can follow the Prince's reasoning: Picton's Division needed a maximum of supporting fire. The Brunswickers probably did too. Lines were better for this purpose than squares. Furthermore, they were certainly superior for withstanding artillery fire which was still being delivered by the French batteries around Gemioncourt. Their weakness was, of course, against enemy cavalry.

It would appear probable that the French cavalry concealed in folds of ground near Gemioncourt had scouts posted on vantage points waiting for just such a false movement. The enemy horsemen struck again while these four new battalions were in line. The 69th practically ceased to exist; it lost its colour, many men and all military usefulness for the day at least.[1] Some survivors managed to throw themselves under the bayonets of the 42nd and 44th, now in a single square.

This same French cavalry charge also struck Halkett's other three battalions. Their position was better; they had a little more warning as to what was coming and could have supported each other to some extent. But they were composed of young soldiers whose only active service had been in the unsuccessful campaign of Bergen-op-Zoom. The 33rd and the 2/73rd, the first two battalions in the echelon formation, broke at the sight of the horsemen sweeping down on them, but made their escape into Bossu wood with only a few casualties. The 2/30th seems to have maintained its order and discipline, formed square and beaten off the French cavalry which attacked it. But this unit also retired to the wood a bit later. The survivors of Halkett's Brigade, save for stragglers from the 69th who became part of Pack's battalions, were now in Bossu wood in poor order.

Wellington returned from his left flank; he had restored his line there and ordered a further advance. For the first time in his military career, he found an entire British brigade broken by French cavalry. But there was no time to cry over spilt milk. Besides, he now had the means to remedy the situation. Two more Brunswick battalions and a battery were arriving by the Genappe road. The Duke ordered this infantry to advance in two columns between the Charleroi road and Bossu wood, driving back the French in this area. He then personally rallied and put in order Halkett's Brigade, save for the 69th which was damaged beyond immediate repair. Wellington had commanded the 33rd in the Duke of York's ill-fated Flanders campaign of 1794 and had taken it to India. He was able to restore the morale of these soldiers as no one else could.

Even more important, the all-British Guards Division under Cooke was now arriving from Nivelles. The Prince of Orange sent Maitland's Brigade, which was in the lead, into the west side of Bossu wood in a most disorderly manner. Instead of forming several companies in line and then advancing into the area in formation, individual companies were sent forward as they arrived, some still in column. But the 2/1st Guards threw back the French infantry opposed to them in hand-to-hand

[1] This was the only British colour ever lost in an army commanded by Wellington.

fighting and were soon reinforced by the 3rd battalion of the same regiment. These two units fought a confused action amid trees and undergrowth, but drove the French clear out of the woods. Byng's Guards Brigade appears to have skirted the western edge of Bossu wood; Cooke's whole division arrived south of it in about half an hour.[1]

At about this time, additional supplies of musket and rifle ammunition came up and were issued, particularly to the brigades of Kempt and Pack. The Allied artillery was also greatly augmented. Two batteries appear to have arrived with Alten's Division; one had come with the Brunswickers. Two more were accompanying Cooke's Guards Division. Wellington now had a superiority in every arm but cavalry, and intended to make the most of it. He was informed that the attack he had started on the extreme left flank had been carried through to a successful conclusion. The 95th, the Hanoverians and the Brunswickers had finally taken Piraumont. They had firm possession of the Namur road south and east of Thyle.

Wellington now began an advance in the centre; the 92nd opened this attack.

Two hundred yards south of the hamlet just east of the Charleroi road was a two-storeyed house, and from its rear ran a thick hedge a short way across a field. On the opposite side of the road was a garden surrounded by a thick hedge. Under cover of a cannonade, two columns of French infantry·had advanced, one by the Charleroi road, the other by a hollow in front of the wood of Bossu. The house, hedge, and garden were occupied by these troops. Colonel Cameron's (of the 92nd) fiery temper chafed to be at them, as he paced impatiently up and down, and asked leave to charge. 'Take your time, Cameron, you'll get your fill of it before night,' said the Duke.

Later on when Wellington was ready to deliver his counterattack, he said, 'Now, 92nd, you must charge that infantry!' Instantly the regiment, about 600 in number, leaped over the ditch, headed by Colonel Cameron and General Barnes. The latter called out, 'Come on, my old 92nd!' and though it was not his duty to charge, he could not resist the impulse. The place was carried, although the Gordons suffered severe casualties particularly because 'the enemy pouring a deadly fire on them from the windows and from the hedge'.[2]

Once this improvised fortress had fallen to the 92nd, the brigades of

---

[1] *Becke*, 90, says, 'At last the British Guards drove Jerome out of its friendly shelter.'

[2] These passages are from *Life of a Regiment*, I, 355.

Halkett, Pack and Kempt moved forward on both sides of the Charleroi road accompanied by the Brunswick battalions in this area. These advances occurred about the time Cooke's Guards Division reached the south-eastern extremity of Bossu wood. When, however, the two battalions of the 1st Guards endeavoured to leave the wood in line, French cavalry charged them and drove them back, but with trifling loss. They formed at the edge of the wood, perhaps partly in a ditch, and soon repulsed the French cavalry with fire. The two fresh Brunswick battalions appear to have helped.[1] There is a period of uncertainty here. French infantry, cavalry and artillery seem to have driven back both the Guards and their Allies for a second time, but they soon rallied.

Wellington now completely seized the initiative. Cooke's Division formed a line just south of Bossu wood almost a mile long; the Brunswick infantry in square was in echelon on the left flank. This formation moved forward taking both Pierreponts. The Allied centre drove the French from Gemioncourt and shortly thereafter from Lairalle. Wellington's army recovered every single foot of ground that the Prince of Orange had occupied in the morning. Ney's French forces were pushed back all the way to Frasnes.

The battle of Quatre Bras was the most disorderly in which Wellington ever commanded. The Duke had to fight so as to take pressure off his Prussian Allies, regardless of local terrain and conditions within the Anglo-Dutch Army. The battle, so far as the British units were concerned, began right on the all-important road, so there was no room for manœuvre and no choice of position. The retention of the hamlet of Quatre Bras and the Nivelles–Namur road became a primary consideration. Until the very end, the Duke was seriously outnumbered; he was forced to use every man and gun as soon as they arrived. Tactics of the moment and intuitive decisions, based of course on long years of combat experience, were more important than strategic, or even tactical, planning.

Wellington was unable to join the Prussians at Ligny because he was attacked at Quatre Bras. He retained, however, a French force, at first greatly superior to his own, in action all afternoon and finally conclusively defeated it. Had Ney's army defeated Wellington, driven even a mile north and then swept east on the flank and rear of the

---

[1] Eyewitnesses say they formed a kind of inverted V-formation, or *flèche*, based on the wood.

Prussians, Blücher would have been disastrously defeated at Ligny.[1] Wellington was not cautious at Quatre Bras. He realised the importance of holding the position at Quatre Bras and keeping Ney and his army occupied. He bluffed and gambled and finally won.[2]

Wellington was at his very best at Quatre Bras as a commander of troops in battle. In six hours of combat, he was almost continuously at the right spot at the right time. He flawlessly handled his own troops and those of his Allies right down to battalion level. When necessary, he gave orders directly to the men in the ranks. In a half-dozen critical situations, he managed to stave off defeat; when he finally had the force necessary to win, he took full and efficient advantage of it.

We should perhaps note something else with regard to Wellington's conduct on the field. He had heard rumours in the last fourteen months that he had not over-exposed himself to danger in the Peninsula; he certainly did at Quatre Bras. He remained within range of the French artillery from before 3 until after 9 p.m. During a good portion of this time, he was exposed to the fire of enemy sharpshooters and even of infantry in formation. On several occasions, he was actually threatened with the lances and sabres of French cavalry. He behaved in a manner which left no doubt of his superlative personal courage and set an example to his inexperienced troops.

The performance of the Anglo-Dutch Army was unequal. The Dutch-Belgians did not do well; more than 9,000 of them suffered less than 500 serious casualties. If they had shown a bit more determination, they might have held the French for half an hour which would have allowed Wellington to deploy his force behind garrisoned farms as he did two days later. Van Merlen's cavalry would not charge the French and sustained only scattered casualties, perhaps mostly from the French artillery when it overshot Picton's infantry. Nearly the entire Dutch-Belgian contingent appears to have left the field before the end of the battle.[3]

The Duke of Brunswick's troops seem to have done fairly well. The

[1] This was what Napoleon had in mind when he wrote to Ney, 'You have the Fate of France in your hands.'

[2] *Aubrey-Fletcher*, 368, writes of the first counter-attack, 'Thus in the space of barely half an hour a desperate situation was transformed into one of reasonable security by a piece of sheer bluff on the part of a commander whose reputation among the French was one of excessive caution.'

[3] This conclusion based on many British memoirs is inescapable in spite of what *Boulger, passim,* says and the original and secondary sources he quotes.

Brunswick cavalry could not stand against the French, but did take some part in the fight. The Brunswick infantry was active until the very end. The two late arriving battalions did a particularly good job. The Hanoverian brigades of Best and Kielmansegge were not placed in the forefront of the battle, but performed commendably. One of Best's battalions was caught in line and overrun by French cavalry, but three British battalions suffered the same fate. Halkett's Brigade made as poor a showing at Quatre Bras as any British unit of comparable size did during the entire Napoleonic period.[1] They were, however, to redeem themselves two days later.

We come now to Picton's Division, especially the brigades of Kempt and Pack. Throughout their long ordeal, nearly six hours, these soldiers behaved in a manner which is almost beyond praise. Many of the men and all the battalions were veterans of the Peninsula; their devotion, courage and military efficiency were magnificent. Fortescue said of them:

The battalions of Picton's Division rose to the highest level of excellence attained by British infantry, their constancy under repeated devastation by artillery and incessant attacks of cavalry being superb, but their casualties were heavy. In Pack's Brigade, the Royals had over two hundred killed and wounded, and Forty-second and Ninety-second each over two hundred and eighty, representing in the case of the two last not far from one-half of their numbers. In Kempt's brigade the Thirty-second had very nearly two hundred casualties, and the Seventy-ninth just over three hundred.[2]

The four large Guards battalions also performed well, although for a shorter time. They had marched twenty-six miles, the last four or five allegedly at the 'double', and were badly sent into action, but they quickly cleared Bossu wood of the enemy. The 1st Guards lost over 500 men from their two battalions combined. The entire division took an important part in the last victorious Allied attack.

Wellington's force, although ultimately victorious, may have suffered greater casualties than the enemy for the first time in any of his major battles.[3] The total losses at Quatre Bras were 2,275 British, 819 Brunswick and 369 Hanoverian; the Dutch-Belgians stated they lost in all

---

[1] *Fortescue*, X, 321, says of them, 'It must be frankly confessed that as a body they behaved ill.'

[2] Ibid.

[3] At Toulouse (April 1814) the Duke lost 4,568 casualties to 3,236 for Soult, but this was not a true battle, for it included the storming of the out-works of a fortified town: *Weller*, 359.

1,058 of an Allied total of about 4,521. French casualties appear to have been slighty less; Charras says 4,375.[1] This unusual result was caused by several factors. The foremost of these was that the Dutch-Belgian casualty lists were padded with 'missing' and 'slightly wounded'.[2]

There were other reasons also for the excessive Allied losses. The nature of Wellington's position and his lack of effective cavalry meant that British infantry had to remain exposed not only to the numerous and well-handled French artillery, but often to their tirailleurs also. The 1/95th Rifles were needed on the left flank; the British light companies fought well as skirmishers, but there were too few of them to keep back their more numerous opponents. The Prince of Orange also increased British losses with his inept dispositions. Colin Halkett's Brigade suffered severely when the 69th was overrun by cavalry and the other three battalions driven into Bossu wood. The 1st Guards would have been more efficient if sent into their original combat properly deployed.

The victory was costly: major casualties were sustained where they could be least well afforded, in Picton's British brigades. Wellington, a master of defensive war, had to fight a battle in which, because of conditions beyond his control, he was unable to employ most of his best defensive tactics. But the importance of the modest victory becomes apparent when one considers what a swift defeat might have meant. The Prussians could have been destroyed at Ligny. If Waterloo had not occurred forty-eight hours later, Quatre Bras would be remembered as one of the great days of the British Army. The infantry performed magnificently. Wellington won against almost insurmountable, and for him most unusual, handicaps.

---

[1] French casualties could have been greater: *Robinson*, III, 769, points out that Ney at first reported, 'We have only really lost about 2,000 killed and 4,000 wounded.'

[2] *Gardner*, 88, discusses frankly the Dutch-Belgian casualties.

VI

Retreat to Waterloo and Battle Preparations

Wellington realised by nightfall on the 16th that the Prussians and the French had fought a battle of major proportions around Ligny; the firing was still continuing, but in reduced volume. The battlefields of Quatre Bras and Ligny are only about three miles apart, that is from near edge to near edge. Blücher's battle was more or less visible from positions that Wellington occupied personally during the late afternoon, but what he actually saw is open to question. Topographical research today does little good. Trees have grown up; perhaps there is more industrial haze now. Even with far better glasses than Wellington could have had in 1815, I have been unable to make out anything in the Ligny area from any position around Quatre Bras.

On the other hand, there is evidence that Wellington did see a good deal of the conflict around Ligny.[1] The Duke had spent many years observing battles through his telescope and he received interim reports from Hardinge.[2] He would have been able to gain a great deal from what he could have observed. The sound of artillery and musketry left no doubt that the fight at Ligny was of major proportions. Since the fighting remained static, he knew that neither side had achieved a sweeping victory. As darkness descended, the Duke probably saw that the final Prussian cavalry charge was not successful.

---

[1] The best is his own statement, *Supplementary Dispatches*, X, 526–7, but this was written in September 1842 as a rebuttal to what Clausewitz wrote about the campaign. See also *Robinson*, III, 550–1, who quotes the Duke through *Ellesmere* as saying, 'I positively saw the principal events on the field of Ligny.'

[2] One of these was written after Hardinge was seriously wounded; *Ellesmere's Essays.* 290.

Wellington appears to have left Quatre Bras about 10 p.m. and ridden back to Genappe for food and a little sleep. He was back at his battlefield of the day shortly after sunrise, probably about 4.30 a.m. The Duke did not receive any messages from the Prussians or Hardinge written after 6 p.m. on the 16th. Even though the Nivelles-Namur road was kept open for Allied use throughout the night, it was frequently subjected to small-arms fire. A dispatch, or even a pair of duplicate dispatches carried by different couriers, could have been intercepted.[1] But Wellington was again in the dark as to where the Prussians actually were and their plans for the future. The Duke sent out Colonel Sir Alexander Gordon with a squadron of the 10th British Hussars to reconnoitre the area where the Prussian Army had been. They were back between 7 and 7.30 a.m. with a full account of everything, for Gordon had talked personally to Thielemann, the corps commander in charge of the Prussian rear-guard. Müffling also received news from the Prussian headquarters a little later and described it as follows:

At nine o'clock an officer arrived from Wavre, with verbal messages to me, just as I was sitting with the Duke on the ground. I knew that this officer spoke French and English, and therefore indicated to him by a motion of my hand that he might say to the Duke what he had to report to me. He did so. The Duke put some questions, received sensible and satisfactory replies, and by these was induced to declare to me that 'he would accept a battle in the position of Mont Saint Jean, if the Field-Marshal were inclined to come to his assistance even with one corps only'.[2]

But this intelligence could not have been encouraging. The Prussians had sustained, as Wellington suspected, a severe beating at Ligny on 16 June. Their total loss probably exceeded 20,000 men; some artillery had been taken by the French. Blücher himself had been ridden over by the French cavalry at the end of the battle and was temporarily a casualty. On the other hand, Thielemann was still maintaining a position near the combat area on the morning of the 17th. The French also lost heavily in their battle with the Prussians and had failed to mount any kind of pursuit on the 16th. Gneisenau had taken command of the Prussian Army and was moving the three Prussian corps engaged

---

[1] A Prussian messenger, Major Winterfeldt, did apparently set out for the Duke's headquarters, but was wounded on or near the Namur road and rescued by the Allies. He refused, however, to have his message delivered by someone else: *Chesney*, 151.

[2] *Müffling's Passages*, 241.

at Ligny north towards Wavre.[1] The fresh Prussian Fourth Corps, Bülow's, was moving through Gembloux also in the general direction of Wavre.. (See map 4.)

These Prussian movements definitely constituted a retreat, but in a northerly direction, which would enable them to keep in touch with their allies. The Anglo-Dutch Army obviously also had to retire, preferably in a direction so as to continue the 'in line' front which they had maintained with the Prussians against Napoleon on the 16th. Wellington's immediate problem was that his army was still spread out over a fairly large area including Hal, Nivelles, Quatre Bras and Genappe. The Duke's composite force was now alone in the presence of a magnificent French Army considerably more numerous than his own. He had no Prussian support, for Thielemann's corps was already in motion north. The prudent course was immediately to make a precipitate retreat in a direction parallel to that taken by the Prussians, that is through Genappe towards Brussels.

But the Anglo-Dutch Army concentrated at Quatre Bras had either marched or fought most of the previous day until at least 9 p.m. A scant six hours of darkness left them still in need of rest, food and drink. Provisions were at hand, but was there time to issue and cook them? The Dutch-Belgian forces which had behaved badly on the 16th were now rallying and reassembling behind the Quatre Bras position. Both British and Dutch-Belgian units were arriving at Quatre Bras from Nivelles and would continue to do so for three or four hours. A sudden retreat would disrupt all this and might cause wholesale desertions in the Dutch-Belgian units. They thought Napoleon to be invincible; a sudden move to the rear by their British commander would convince them that he too realised the inevitability of a French success.

Wellington knew a good deal already of the campaign habits of the French and something of those of the Emperor himself. He discussed this matter carefully with Müffling who had served against the Emperor in '13 and '14. The Prussian assured him that the French were now in the habit of remaining quiet for almost the whole morning following a severe battle, even though they won it. Müffling says of this:

[1] This route had been examined and probably mapped for the Prussians by the British Lieutenant Basil Jackson of the Royal Staff Corps: *Cotton*, 20. As *Pratt*, 137, and many others have remarked, Gneisenau retreated by it in order to secure better communications across the Rhine through Maastricht, not necessarily to co-operate with Wellington.

Meanwhile came the question whether the Duke should make his troops, weary with their preceding day's march, break up at once, or first let them rest and cook. He preferred the latter, but was apprehensive that his rear-guard might in consequence be involved in severe fighting. I could not share this apprehension. The enemy had only bivouacked on the 16th (the previous day), in the dusk of the evening; and in such cases it was always Napoleon's custom, in his wars in Germany, to allow his troops first to cook, and to break up at ten the next morning.[1]

In matters such as these, the veteran French professional soldiers were not always a blessing to their commander. They had become in some measure independent of all authority. They felt they had the right to some repose. The French logistics system was seldom adequate for even the simplest sustenance; time was necessary to remedy this deficiency by individual and group marauding.

Wellington made up his mind quickly; he issued instructions for his entire army to cook a meal before they moved. He steadfastly adhered to this procedure, even though skirmishing fire, which might have been a prelude to a French attack in force, was frequent and at one time nearly continuous along the entire Quatre Bras front. The French endeavoured to push in the Allied light troops, but Wellington guessed from long experience that their efforts were calculated to stop just short of a pitched battle. He reinforced his security line as much as was necessary to hold it. An eyewitness, Mercer, of the Royal Horse Artillery, has left us a vivid account of this action.

A smart skirmish was going on amongst the hedges [south of Piraumont]. This was the firing we had heard all the morning. Our infantry were lying about, cleaning their arms, cooking, or amusing themselves, totally regardless of the skirmish. This, however, from our position, was a very interesting sight to me, for the slope of the ground enabled me to see distinctly all the manœuvres of both parties, as on a plan. After much firing from the edge of [Hette] wood, opposite which our riflemen occupied all the hedges, I saw French tirailleurs suddenly make a rush forward in all directions, whilst the fire of our people became thicker and faster than ever. Many of the former scampered across the open fields until they reached the nearest hedges, whilst others ran crouching under cover of those perpendicular to their front, and the whole succeeded in establishing themselves – thus forcing back and gaining ground on our men.[2] The fire then again became sharper than ever, but the French were driven back.[2]

Wellington was issuing orders during this period, however, for a

[1] *Müffling's Passages*, 240.
[2] *Mercer's Journal*, 142.

rearward movement of his entire army. The main part was to move back to Mont Saint Jean by the road through Genappe and by others to either side of it. A minor force was to move on Tubize and Hal to the west. He sent a résumé of his intentions to Blücher and promised, as he had told Müffling, to give battle on the 18th, if he was assured of the support of at least one Prussian corps. Meanwhile, the Duke maintained a firm front at Quatre Bras throughout the entire morning; it extended from Thyle and Piraumont on the east to the two Pierreponts on the west. His masses of infantry, cavalry and artillery appeared to remain constant behind his security lines, as if he were planning to fight again on the same ground. He was actually withdrawing units north as others arrived from the west in such a way that the French saw that his force around Quatre Bras continuously remained about the same size.

By 11 a.m., all the forces due from Nivelles had arrived. Wellington now began to reduce his total concentration at the crossroads, for his entire field army was now in order and under his personal control. Wellington handled the disengaging of his infantry himself and used Cooke's and Alten's Divisions along with the 1/95th from Picton's well-tried soldiers. These chosen brigades and battalions moved alternately to the rear and took up new positions;[1] the light companies of Byng's Guards were the last to break actual contact about 2 p.m.[2] The Duke was finally holding Quatre Bras with British cavalry and horse artillery units only. Save for the skirmishing already described, he was not attacked by Ney's army from Frasnes at all.

Napoleon's army from Ligny moved west along the Nivelles road against Wellington about 2.30 p.m. By this time, the British troops who remained were those best able to make a rapid retreat, if it became necessary, without loss of morale. There was one good metalled road available to Genappe, Mont Saint Jean and Brussels and many secondary ways; all were now free of infantry and baggage. The Duke had refused to be stampeded into anything approaching precipitous movement, but had withdrawn his forces carefully, slowly and in an orderly manner. He could not have escaped from a position of potential danger with greater ease and less damage to the morale of his army.

Napoleon's attack along the Namur road towards Quatre Bras coincided with the breaking of a violent thunderstorm. The British

---

[1] *Siborne*, 265, gives an account of this which sounds like a modern staff manual describing proper procedures for a disengaging operation.

[2] *MacKinnon*, II, 212.

cavalry and horse artillery had no intention of fighting a real battle, but manœuvred skilfully and inflicted casualties as they withdrew through Genappe along the main road and used fords and small bridges to either side of it. Both the British and French horse artillery fired a large number of rounds, but hand-to-hand fighting was limited almost entirely to a cavalry encounter in and near Genappe. This long village was and is built on either side of a relatively narrow street, then the main road from Brussels to Charleroi. For a time, the part of the village north of the Dyle was held by dismounted British light cavalry-men armed with rifled carbines.[1] The artillery of both sides was in noisy action and claimed to be more effective than it probably was. The French forced a passage across the bridge and through the village to its northern outskirts.

So far, no serious fighting had occurred, but now Uxbridge ordered his old regiment, the 7th Hussars, to charge some French lancers that were drawing up on the main road and to either side of it just north of Genappe. The action which followed was not in favour of the 7th Hussars. The enemy received them at a halt in a kind of mounted phalanx with lances extended. The attack was repeated with the same result. The French cavalry then advanced a short distance north, but:

The 1st Life Guards charged the French when they advanced out of the village. They advanced most gallantly, and the enemy ran away before the Life Guards got up to them. They were, from what I could learn, within about 100 yards when the enemy went about, and though the French were awed by their appearance, and ran away before they came near them, yet the charge was entirely attributed to the superior strength of the Life Guards and weight in riding down the enemy. Nothing could be better done than the charge, yet, I much question, had the Life Guards attacked in the situation the 7th attempted, if they would have succeeded. The 7th was Lord Uxbridge's own regiment, and an opportunity desired by him for distinguishing them.[2]

There was no more serious fighting, partly perhaps because of the weather. It rained hard and continuously. There was enough galloping, however, to make lively reading in some cavalry and horse artillery memoirs. Pro-French authors have contended that this retreat was chaotic, if not disastrous. But ascertainable evidence confounds them. A horse pulling a gun in Gardiner's battery of horse artillery cast a shoe. The battery halted while the shoe was replaced. The total casualties

---

[1] *Vivian*, 282. I photographed a 'Baker Cavalry Rifle' with 10th Hussar markings in a small museum at Waterloo in 1953.

[2] *Tomkinson*, 284-5.

suffered by all British cavalry and artillery engaged on the 17th – only British forces were actively engaged on the retreat – were ninety-three killed, wounded and missing. Forty-six of these were in the 7th Hussars and eighteen in the Life Guards. The remaining twenty-nine were spread around in cavalry and artillery units so that they were obviously caused by skirmishing and artillery fire only.[1]

THE WATERLOO POSITION

There can be no doubt that Wellington first evaluated the position at Mont Saint Jean in August 1814; he may have prophesied that he would use it three days before he did.[2] He is said to have had maps made of it, but this is not certain.[3] How good was the position here? Picton who was used to the more mountainous terrain of Portugal, Spain and Southern France thought it poor.[4] Some later critics have considered it ideal. The real answer lies between these two extreme views. Wellington's defensive tactics required a ridge along which he could post his artillery, a slope down which his skirmish line could be pushed towards the enemy, and behind which he could conceal and protect his own infantry. He also needed a system of roads behind the ridge so he could shift his troops as necessary out of sight of the enemy. He liked to have his flanks protected by terrain features.

Often in his career previous to the Waterloo campaign the Duke managed to find nearly perfect positions of this type. If you are familiar with his earlier battlefields, you will be disappointed in some topographical features of the Mont Saint Jean position, later known as the battlefield of Waterloo.[5] On the other hand, there is no question that

---

[1] *Fortescue*, X, 337, quotes these irrefutable statistics and says, 'A pursuit which produced no greater results could not have been very furious.'

[2] At the Duchess of Richmond's ball; see *Guedalla*, 270, substantiated by hearsay only.

[3] *Gardner*, 15–16, says a new map was made the week before the battle. *James*, 188–9, may be referring to the same thing when he says, '. . . the position had been surveyed earlier in the year'. The map made in August 1814 and reproduced in *Yonge*, II, opposite 565, is defective; it can hardly be called a map at all. La Haye Sainte is on the wrong side of the road. The original 'map' was exhibited at Waterloo Barracks, London, in connection with the 150th Anniversary celebration of the battle in 1965 and is like *Yonge's* reproduction.

[4] For a more detailed discussion of this with references see Part Two, Chapter II, 'Wellington's Mistakes'.

[5] The village of Waterloo was Wellington's headquarters before and after the battle; he liked the name better than others of places closer to the fighting, perhaps because it was more easily pronounced by Englishmen. But the village of Waterloo was and is a full three miles north of the northernmost edge of the fighting area.

this position was the best available for the Anglo-Dutch Army to defend Brussels against an enemy moving north from Charleroi through Quatre Bras and Genappe. (See map 5.)

On the credit side, Wellington had a ridge, really a series of them, which was adequate throughout most of his front. Communications were easy north of the position and were fairly well shielded from an enemy deployed to the south. His left flank was protected by the marshy valleys of the Dyle and the Lasne, particularly after many hours of rain. Furthermore, there were three enclosed farms, or groups of buildings, in front of the main line which the Duke planned to occupy. In the centre, just to the west of the Genappe road, there was La Haye Sainte. To the west, there was Hougoumont. To the east, there were the twin farms of Papelotte and La Haye and the hamlet of Smohain, known hereafter as PLHS. All could be occupied by appropriate military force and added considerably to the strength of the position behind them.

There were several defects. First and most important, the ridge occupied by the Anglo-Dutch Army did not run continuously with a single valley to the south, but was cut up with minor indentations, particularly just east of the Genappe road. Second, there were other similar, only slightly lower ridges which an enemy could occupy to the south and use to fire on exposed portions of Wellington's main line. Third, the right flank strategically was 'in the air', although a defile west of the Nivelles road gave some local protection. The country to the west was open and perfectly adapted to the type of manœuvres that the French did so well.

Now for some dimensions. The area actually fought over from PLHS on the east to the Nivelles road next to Hougoumont on the west was about 3,500 yards wide. The Genappe road almost exactly bisected this total front. The PLHS enclave was on the average about 500 yards in front of the eastern flank of the main ridge. La Haye Sainte was some 250 yards forward of the Ohain road which also led to Wavre. Wellington's right flank and its ridge system inclined slightly to the south, but Hougoumont still lay 500 yards down a gentle slope in this area.

By the end of the retreat on the 17th, Wellington had more than 90 per cent of his army in the positions he planned to occupy for battle on the 18th, if Blücher would support him. The Duke planned to take full advantage of the Prussian move west from Wavre and the marshy country to the east of PLHS to protect his eastern flank. He was going to have cavalry only beyond this irregular group of buildings. The château of Frischermont was not to be held at all because it was too far away from easy support.[1]

To the west, as has been said, there were no terrain obstacles and no allied army. The Duke knew well the French powers of manœuvre and Napoleon's remarkable record, particularly early in his military career, of winning quickly by means of flank marches and attack from unexpected directions. Wellington countered this danger, however, by placing an Anglo-Dutch force of about 15,500 men, perhaps nominally under Prince Frederick of Orange, at Tubize and Hal. These two villages were about eight miles west of Hougoumont. This force contained one British infantry brigade, one Hanoverian infantry brigade and two batteries of British artillery under Sir Charles Colville, the commanding general of the Fourth British Division. These troops were destined not to fire a weapon in anger all day; a fuller discussion of their strategic value will be found in Part Two, Chapter II, 'Wellington's Mistakes'.

Closer to where the battle was actually fought, only about 1,200 yards west of Hougoumont, Wellington placed Chassé's entire Dutch-Belgian division in the village of Braine l'Alleud. The road going from this place nearly due west to Tubize passes through Braine le Château which was occupied by Hanoverian and Dutch-Belgian cavalry belonging to Prince Frederick's command. Patrols to the south of this road were to be maintained constantly to detect at the earliest possible moment any French movement to outflank the Duke's army in this direction. The Tubize-Hal force had orders to defend its position to the last extremity in order to allow Wellington time to make appropriate counter-moves, if the French tried to envelop this flank.

As the battle was actually fought, the critical area was from PLHS to the Nivelles road west of Hougoumont. Wellington was quick to appreciate the extreme importance of Hougoumont with its enclosure of buildings, its attached walled garden, orchards and wood. He initially occupied it on the evening of the 17th with the light companies of Cooke's First Guards Division; early on the 18th he sent in a battalion of Saxe-Weimar's Nassauers[2] and two companies of Hanoverian sharp-shooters.

[1] A confusion of names and the actual dispositions of Allied forces in this area will be dealt with in Part One, Chapter XII, 'The Left Flank'.

[2] One wonders why this particular battalion should have been placed so far from the rest of Saxe-Weimar's troops who were in PLHS. Wellington may have had reason to suspect disloyalty and so did not want this unit where it could take other Nassauers over to the enemy.

The Duke placed the rest of Cooke's Division to the immediate rear of Hougoumont and to the east. It was obliged to advance well south of the main ridge at this point in order to be close enough to Hougoumont to support it properly, but the trees to the south and east of the woods gave considerable protection from French artillery fire and observation. Wellington believed and had proved in Spain and Portugal that if a village or large farm was to be defended successfully, supporting troops must be maintained within musket shot of it.

Between Cooke's Division above Hougoumont and Chassé's at Braine l'Alleud, Wellington initially placed Mitchell's Brigade of Colville's Division well to the south almost level with the Hougoumont buildings, but west of the Nivelles road. To the rear and slightly farther to the west, in and around the village of Merbe-Braine, the Duke had the entire Brunswick 'corps' and Clinton's Division which consisted of the Hanoverian Brigade commanded by Col. Hew Halkett, Adam's British Brigade and du Plat's KGL Brigade. These troops were Wellington's tactical reserve; they were stationed more to the west because initially at least he was more concerned about what might happen west of Hougoumont than east of it.

Let us examine the corps affiliations of these troops in and behind Hougoumont and to the west. Prince Frederick of Orange's forces as well as Clinton's and Colville's Divisions were from the Second Corps under Hill, but Chassé's Division of Dutch-Belgians and Cooke's Guards Division were from the First Corps under the Prince of Orange. The Brunswickers were from the Reserve Corps under Wellington's personal command, but the Nassauers in Hougoumont woods were from Perponcher's Division of the Prince of Orange's Corps. Mitchell's Brigade was from Colville's Division, but separated from the rest of it by about eight miles. Wellington had deliberately scrapped his corps organisation, doubtless because of the shortcomings of the Prince of Orange at Quatre Bras. He had separated some of the component parts of two divisions for less obvious reasons. The Duke must have intended to handle as many units personally as he possibly could. He had done this frequently in the Peninsula. To some extent he lost the services of his ablest subordinate, Rowland Hill, but he avoided giving the Prince of Orange exclusive command of a third of the Anglo-Dutch Army. Hill was available for an independent command in the west, were it to become necessary.

We still have to review Wellington's initial postings from Hougoumont to PLHS. Cooke's Guards Division extended a short distance to the east from the rear of Hougoumont and was protected by the main ridge; the lateral road was slightly to the rear of the ridge here. Farther to the east in an area not completely sheltered by the ridge was Alten's Division composed of the brigades of Colin Halkett (British) which had behaved badly at Quatre Bras, Kielmansegge (Hanoverian) which had fought rather well there, and Ompteda (KGL) which had not yet been engaged at all. These three brigades, all in the first line, extended to the Genappe road. Kruse's Nassauers from Wellington's Reserve appear to have been attached to this division throughout the battle and were initially in close support. The farm of La Haye Sainte was occupied by the 2nd Light Battalion, KGL, from Ompteda's Brigade.

On the other side of the Genappe road, Bylandt's Brigade of Perponcher's Dutch-Belgian Division was formed in front of the crest of the ridge. The problem here was that the lateral road and the position which the Anglo-Dutch main line should have taken up were in front of the low crest, not behind it. Picton's Division was slightly behind Bylandt, but contrived to protect itself adequately without moving back too far. Picton formed his brigades in line, west to east, Pack (British), Kempt (British), Best (Hanoverian) and Vincke (Hanoverian). The assigning of Best's Brigade, organised as part of Cole's Division, to Picton had worked well at Quatre Bras and was continued at Waterloo. The sandpit east of the Genappe road and opposite La Haye Sainte was occupied by the 1/95th Rifles from Kempt's Brigade.

As I have briefly mentioned, the PLHS buildings down the slope to the south and slightly to the east of Picton's men were held by Saxe-Weimar's Nassau Brigade of Perponcher's Division, save for the battalion at Hougoumont. Wellington's infantry dispositions ended at this point, but a second line of cavalry composed of Vandeleur's and Vivian's Brigades extended from behind Picton's Hanoverian brigades all the way east to behind PLHS. Patrols from these units were sent out south and even farther east. Infantry skirmishers were advanced well forward of all these main positions, in a line which originally extended from Frischermont to the south edge of the Hougoumont woods.

The bulk of the remaining Anglo-Dutch cavalry was behind Wellington's centre. Three brigades of British-KGL light cavalry (Grant's, Dörnberg's, and Arentschildt's) were in the area behind the Guards Division. The two brigades of British heavy cavalry were on either side of the Genappe road, Ponsonby's Union Brigade to the east and Somerset's Household Brigade to the west. The Dutch-Belgian horsemen were behind the right and centre, although not much could be expected of them after their poor showing at Quatre Bras. A single squadron of the 16th Hussars was behind Mitchell's Brigade between Hougoumont and Braine l'Alleud. The Brunswick troopers were with their infantry near Merbe-Braine. Anglo-Dutch units not moved into their positions on the 17th were settled in them early on the morning of the 18th, save for Lambert's Brigade of Cole's nebulous Division which arrived from Brussels on the morning of the 18th, reaching the junction of the Nivelles and Genappe roads in Mont Saint Jean about noon.

We must now consider Wellington's decision to fight at Waterloo at all. He was willing to do this only if he could be supported by the Prussians. Even though he ordered his troops into position on the 17th, he was not sure at that time that he would fight there. He must have had all kinds of doubts. The Dutch-Belgians had been of little value at Quatre Bras; other Allied units were certainly no better than second-rate. His entire army including all those actually in position or near enough to fight there on the 18th numbered about 68,000 men. He knew that Napoleon still had about 110,000 first-rate veteran troops to use as he saw fit against the Prussians, or against the Anglo-Dutch, or against both. To fight unsupported by the Prussians against the Emperor with most of his army was out of the question, but a retreat without a battle would lose Brussels, Ghent and perhaps the war.

Throughout the 17th, aides-de-camp passed often between the British and the Prussian headquarters. We do not know exactly what was said, nor at what times, because many messages were verbal and others have been lost. Wellington had promised to fight in the Waterloo position, if he was supported by at least one Prussian corps. He received final written assurance from Blücher before 3 a.m. on the 18th that two Prussian corps would move at dawn to support the Anglo-Dutch Army.[1] Wellington immediately and irrevocably decided to fight where he was.

To any other man, the responsibility for making this decision would have seemed extremely heavy, an almost unbearable burden. On the night of the 17th, Wellington knew that a French force, its size as yet undetermined, had been detached to follow the defeated Prussians. Its obvious purpose was to prevent the Prussians coming to the aid of the

[1] *James*, 200, quotes this short dispatch in full.

Duke on the 18th. Conceivably, a relatively small force might accomplish this delaying mission without unduly weakening the main French Army. Wellington did not approve of the Emperor as a man, but appreciated fully his ability as a general, particularly his capacity for using the same troops to defeat different enemy armies in succession.[1] The British commander also realised the probability of Napoleon's using some strategic plan worthy of his previous victories.

Napoleon could have a considerable numerical superiority against Wellington on the 18th as well as all the advantages of a truly professional army from a single nation that had been together for years. It would probably fight superbly because the future of almost every man depended upon a French victory. What might be of more importance, it could manœuvre better than even the British portion of the army commanded by the Duke. Wellington's previous dealings with Allies not under his personal command and speaking different languages had not been encouraging. He must have thought back to Cuesta, the Captain-General of Spain at Talavera, as well as independent Portuguese and Indian Allies of an earlier period. He knew Blücher, however, and was willing to trust him. He committed his army and himself to fight to the death; no secondary plan of any type whatever was formulated from then on.[2]

The weather of the night following the 17th had been atrocious; thunderstorms and drenching rain had made everyone not able to get into the limited number of buildings then standing near the battlefield acutely miserable. But daylight and youth, for most soldiers in all armies are relatively young, restored their spirits. The Anglo-Dutch soldiers, or most of them, prepared on the morning of the 18th to do the best job possible in the battle that was obviously coming. Weapons were cleaned, ammunition was replaced, and men and horses fed. The buildings and garden wall at Hougoumont were to some extent fortified. PLHS buildings probably received the same treatment from Saxe-Weimar and his Nassauers, although La Haye Sainte was only indifferently prepared for defence. There were no field works of any kind outside these positions, however, for Wellington did not believe in sheltering his forces in this way. Trenches immobilised the troops in

---

[1] *Stanhope*, 12.

[2] The absence of anything of this sort is the reason for the uncertainty as to what Wellington might have done if defeated, as is discussed at length in Part Two, Chapter II, 'Wellington's Mistakes'.

them.[1] The Duke was committed to fighting a defensive battle, but the essence of his tactics in such a situation was mobility and the countering of each offensive manœuvre of the enemy with an appropriate move of his own.

On the morning of 18 June 1815, Wellington appears to have considered Hougoumont to have been the centre of his position. If one includes the Tubize-Hal force, half his total strength was initially west of its easternmost corner. As we have seen he had his tactical reserve behind this point. He was a master of defensive war and realised that his army was better constituted for defence than for manœuvring in the open. He undoubtedly hoped that the French would attack Hougoumont and to either side of it, but he can hardly have expected it. He was confident of beating even Napoleon if he would move straight ahead, but he feared the ability of the French Army to act fast, manœuvre and strike at an unexpected place. He knew he could not match this, but hoped that his judicious dispositions, time, the Prussians at Wavre and the Tubize-Hal force would prevent any Jena-like manœuvres.

During the morning hours, Wellington completed his alignment and brought his army into as efficient a condition as possible. Napoleon put on an uncharacteristic review of all his troops and spread them out for his enemies to see. This formal array was something never done before by France during the Republic or the Empire; it was more like Turenne, Condé and Saxe than Napoleon.[2] It was certainly not like the swift, secret movements of the Italian campaign of '96, the flank attack at Marengo and the unorthodox manœuvres at Austerlitz. The Duke realised, however, that it was of a piece with Napoleon's later, more massive, but less inspired battles such as Eylau, Borodino and Leipzig.

The French infantry-cavalry-artillery corps of Reille on the east and d'Erlon on the west formed the first line. Behind these in a kind of second line were reserve cavalry, Lobau's Corps in column, and more

---

[1] Wellington must also have known that the best way to force Napoleon to manœuvre and probably turn the Anglo-Dutch right was to dig field fortifications. *Kennedy*, 75, says that the Emperor actually sent General Haxo, his chief engineer, to make sure that this had not been done before attacking.

[2] Many authors have tried to explain this perfect arraying of the French Army. The most plausible single explanation seems to me to be that the Emperor was trying to make the Belgians desert. He may also have wanted to scare Wellington into retreating and bringing on a running, manœuvring fight.

reserve cavalry. The Imperial Guard, still farther to the rear, was in support of all. Quick calculations by the British staff indicated that Napoleon had a force assembled south of the Mont Saint Jean position which exceeded the entire Anglo-Dutch Army; the Emperor appeared to have between 70,000 and 80,000 men.[1] The numerical odds were stiff enough, but when overall quality was considered they were overwhelming if it had not been for Blücher's solemnly promised support. Fortunately, as early as 10 a.m. Wellington saw in the vicinity of the Paris wood far to the east some Prussian cavalry that could be the advanced guard of assistance from Blücher. The Duke probably refused to reconsider his decision to fight the French with what he had, or to visualise what might happen if the Prussians did not fulfil their promise.

The stage was set. The mighty Emperor with his finest army – the military reputations of both appear still to transcend those of any others the Western world had produced – was at last to meet the British Sepoy general, a man he despised. Napoleon was a master of all that was militarily brilliant and the victor of a hundred actions. Wellington's greatest military virtues were tactical common sense, sound organisation and logistics, and personal efficiency in handling in combat units of all sizes. As the battle came inexorably closer and the circumstances of the coming engagement became clearer, many in the heterogeneous Anglo-Dutch Army lost all hope of victory. The Peninsular veterans and those close to them, however, held a different opinion. Some of them may truly have been the scum of the earth as regards drink, women and honesty. The world was different then. But with 'Old Nosey' to lead them, they could really fight. Their confidence in him and in themselves was based on a more modest, but unbroken series of victories. They and their 'Artie' were not going to be scared by any show, or by reputations alone, no matter how illustrious. Hard fighting lay ahead, perhaps some of the hardest in military history. The battle could go either way depending upon how the armies and their commanders performed.

---

[1] There were three corps plus the Imperial Guard and a Cavalry Reserve, but Reille's Corps was minus a division (Girard's had been left at Ligny and Quatre Bras); Lobau had only two of his usual three divisions (Teste's had gone with Grouchy). These two circumstances would be apparent only under conditions such as this review-like alignment before battle. The French Army at Waterloo, according to *Houssaye*, 185, consisted of 73,835 men and 246 guns.

VII

Hougoumont

The Battle of Waterloo began at Hougoumont; the fighting there throughout the afternoon of 18 June was extremely important in the final outcome. The large farm or château with its walled garden, hedge-enclosed orchard and woods was so located that possession meant a great deal. As we have seen, Wellington may well have considered this rectangle the centre of his position early in the day. It formed a kind of natural strong point which drew enemy units towards it as a magnet does iron filings. The French attacked Hougoumont with ferocity and determination for many hours, but never succeeded in taking it completely. They may have expended more military strength here than was warranted by its value to the Duke, or to them.

What was Hougoumont like in June 1815? To say that it was a typical Belgian farm of the larger sort like Gemioncourt at Quatre Bras is not entirely correct. It was in part a large farm, but it was more than that. It was certainly in part a manor-house, but it was also something of a fortification.[1] The group of buildings which included a private chapel occupied only a small part of the entire Hougoumont enceinte, the north-west corner. (See Map 6 on p. 233 and plates 13–24.) The buildings as a whole were roughly rectangular in shape and about 300 feet long by 100 feet wide. These and their connecting walls formed a complete enclosure pierced, however, at several points by openings with heavy doors. There was a large barn on the west, the château on the east, a farmer's dwelling on the north and various smaller buildings, all joined together by walls. Roofs, floors, ceilings

---

[1] *Cotton*, 28, said in about 1835, 'The buildings are more than 200 years old, and were erected for defence.'

and some interior partitions were combustible, but the buildings themselves and the connecting walls were of brick and stone and proof against the field-artillery of that period.

The greater Hougoumont rectangle was in fact nearly a square of about 600 yards. This was separated from the open fields to the east and partly at least to the south by hedges ditched on one or both sides.[1] The southern two-thirds of this area was woods and a pasture enclosed by hedge and ditch. The woods, because of some tall trees, formed a considerable barrier to observation and artillery fire, particularly to and from Wellington's main ridge position to the north. This southern portion of greater Hougoumont was not of much importance as the battle was actually fought, but the northern third certainly was.

The buildings were at the western border; a formal garden with a brick and stone wall more than six feet high on its southern side came next. This wall joined the farm-house portion of the built-up enclosure and extended east 250 yards to a corner where it turned north and ran along the east side of this garden to a point level with the northernmost end of the group of buildings. The northern end of this wall was connected with the buildings by a stout hedge and ditch only. On a level with the formal garden but to the east, there was an orchard: its southern, eastern and northern boundaries were stout banked up hedges with a ditch on the inside.[2] The orchard rectangle was about 300 yards east to west by some 200 yards north to south. The buildings, walled garden and orchard composed the important third of Hougoumont.

To the north of them lay a kind of sunken road bounded on each side by hedges: this was referred to as the protected or covered way. Behind this, even farther to the north, at the time of the battle there were open fields.[3] To the north the country rose to one branch of the Ohain road and the Anglo-Dutch main position on top of the ridge already described.

The fight for Hougoumont actually began on the evening of 17 June: the light companies of all four Guards battalions advanced from their assigned area on top of the ridge to take possession of the farm. They had to thrust back a small French unit which was apparently

[1] *Clinton*, 399, says that 'a thick hedge and wet ditch ran round the wood and meadow'.

[2] These banked up and ditched hedges were for enclosing cattle in the days before cheap iron wire was available. The ditches were usually on the inside: *Cotton*, 28.

[3] A Belgian manor-house and its grounds now occupy this area which is today thickly wooded. The orchard east of the walled garden has also been removed with only traces of the hedges and ditches remaining.

also bent on the capture of Hougoumont.[1] Some fire was exchanged and the French withdrew. The two light companies of the 1st Guards under Lieutenant-Colonel Lord Saltoun appear to have won this skirmish and were later placed in the orchard and in the eastern sector of the woods south of it. The two light companies of the 2nd Guards Brigade under Lieutenant-Colonel Macdonell occupied the walled garden, the buildings and the western portion of the woods.[2]

Early on the 18th, Wellington to assist these four light companies sent forward two units. These were about 300 Hanoverian riflemen and the often mentioned Nassau battalion from Saxe-Weimar's Brigade. The Nassauers appear to have been deployed in line behind the hedge at the southern end of the pasture;[3] the Hanoverians with some pickets from the Guards held the southern border of the woods. The Duke personally checked the disposition of these troops about 10 a.m. He remained in the area for some time watching the enemy prepare for battle. A French infantry, cavalry and artillery corps (Reille's) was deploying between the Nivelles and the Genappe roads. The three divisions present (Jerome's on the west, Foy's in the centre, and Bachelu's on the east) had all fought well at Quatre Bras. The French were no more than 300 yards away and in heavy strength; the Nassauers appear to have been on the point of panic when Wellington rode up to them and to some extent restored their morale. As he rode away, however, some of them shot at him.[4] The Duke passed off this firing as unintentional, but the history of Europe might have been different if one of these fellows had been a better shot.

The Duke continued his ride back to the ridge behind Hougoumont checking on Macdonell's preparations for the defence in passing. The buildings' enclosure was fairly well fortified. Soldiers were posted to fire through windows and over walls on specially constructed banks and parapets. Both the buildings and walls which connected them, particularly that around the formal garden, already had some loop-

---

[1] *MacKinnon*, II, 213–14.

[2] Rank in the Guards was confusing at this time; many company commanders were lieutenant-colonels.

[3] *Boulger*, 60, disagrees. He says this six company French-type battalion was deployed with three companies in the buildings and three in the woods, an extremely unlikely arrangement.

[4] This incident which has already been mentioned in the last chapter has been described differently by others, particularly as regards time. I have followed *Hooper*, 189, who places it before the beginning of the battle, based on Wellington's own statements.

holes; others were being added.[1] All gates save that to the north had been blocked up; flooring had been removed from above them where possible so that the garrison could fire down on assailants.

As Wellington expected, the battle began with a French attack on Hougoumont. This was accompanied by an artillery bombardment which commenced at 11.50 a.m.[2] Reille's westernmost unit, Jerome's Division, swept forward into the Hougoumont woods. As usual, the tirailleurs came ahead of the main infantry columns. Some eyewitness accounts only mention heavy masses of tirailleurs.[3] The Nassauers appear to have fought better than might have been expected, considering their near panic a short time before. Perhaps small pickets from the Guards helped. The Hanoverian Jaegers, hunters who brought their own private hunting rifles with them to war, inflicted serious casualties with their accurate aimed fire. But the Duke did not reinforce these troops at the southern border of the Hougoumont wood, probably because he had no intention of holding tenaciously so far south.

Jerome's men pushed back their antagonists in confused fighting amid patches of heavy undergrowth. The Allies knew the woods better and managed to retain some order; they kept up a heavy, destructive fire. Finally, they held 'a hedge of large closely-planted trees' which ran across the top of the Hougoumont woods. The French 'cut their way with the axe through this hedge'.[4] Jerome's Division seems to have been committed in its entirety during this advance. As in the Bossu wood fight at Quatre Bras by the same troops, the French appear to have spread out across the entire woods from hedged border to hedged border, but not into the open, because of the Allied artillery now sweeping their flanks. They pushed ahead in spite of losses.

As these Frenchmen pressed forward to and through the tree-hedge, their opponents disappeared from their front. Actually, the Allies were

[1] *Cotton*, 28, and many authorities have pointed out that some of the loopholes were and are carefully faced with stone and obviously not made so recently as the time of the battle. Those which were opened at that time appear to have been filled up shortly afterwards.

[2] *Sidney*, 310, quotes Hill as saying, 'I took two watches into action with me. On consulting my stopwatch after the battle was over, I found that the first gun was fired at ten minutes before twelve.' *Cotton*, 48, says Kennedy and Lord Edward Somerset agreed precisely with Hill.

[3] *Life of a Soldier*, II, 180.

[4] These two short quotations are from *Thiers*, 111. Vestiges of this 'hedge of trees' remain even though the woods are now gone. A few large trees that stand just south of the buildings today have probably grown up since the battle.

withdrawn in accordance with orders into the buildings, over the wall into the formal garden and into the orchard. The French rushed forward and suddenly ran headlong against the southern face of the extremely strong buildings-garden-orchard position now occupied by the Guards, the Hanoverian riflemen and the Nassauers. The assailants emerged from the woods only twenty to thirty yards south of these defences and in unco-ordinated groups. British and Nassau half-company volleys crashed out, aided no doubt by accurate independent fire from the Jaegers. The French fought bravely, in some cases seizing British musket barrels and endeavouring to pull them through loop-holes. Both sides used the bayonet over the top of the garden wall, but the advantage was with the less numerous defenders who were shielded, better organised and better positioned. In spite of cruelly heavy losses, not a Frenchman was left alive in the orchard, garden or buildings at this time. Jerome's Division recoiled back into the woods leaving hundreds of casualties in the strip of open area between the woods and the 'northern third of Hougoumont'.

During this attack, Wellington personally was forward of his main position in the open area north-east of the farm. There was no fighting along the remainder of the Anglo-Dutch line, so he could give his whole attention to this combat. He saw clearly the French units that moved forward into the southern edge of the woods and had a fair view because of the elevation of the position of his firing line. He brought forward Bull's battery of six 5·5-inch howitzers to a position immediately behind Hougoumont and ordered them to open fire on the French in the southern two-thirds of the Hougoumont enclosure over the heads of the defenders with both common shell and shrapnel. This type of shrapnel fire was difficult at that period because of inconsistencies in fuse-burning time, but in this instance it appears to have been unusually effective. It did no damage at all to the allied troops, over whose heads the shells flew, and caused a number of casualties among the French. The Guards, the Hanoverian Jaegers and perhaps the Nassauers dashed forward and recovered a good part of the woods.

The Duke now appears to have withdrawn the Nassauers from the fight, but sent orders to du Plat's KGL Brigade of Clinton's Division to move in behind Hougoumont. He already had the rest of Byng's Guards Brigade stationed in column of companies at quarter distance well down the slope not far from the protected way. Wellington probably guessed that the French were going to continue to press their attack on Hougoumont as had become typical of French tactics in the later·wars of the Empire. Within half an hour Jerome's Division again came forward, this time reinforced with units from Foy's. The French recaptured all the woods, and made dangerous progress both west of the buildings and in the orchard. Lord Saltoun's light companies of the 1st Guards and his detachment of the Hanoverian riflemen were driven back from their hedge to the south of the orchard, through the orchard, and into the protected way. But the French who assailed the south face of the walled garden failed. Those who followed Saltoun's men were badly mauled by a flanking fire from the eastern garden wall to their left. Wellington sent down four line companies of Coldstreamers who helped to recapture the orchard and restored the situation completely on Hougoumont's east flank. Saltoun and his two light companies of the 1st Guards now returned to Maitland's Brigade which was on the crest of the ridge just east of the orchard.

The French attack west of Hougoumont could have been more serious. The enemy surged up to the buildings on the south and on the west, but found all gates blocked and covered with fire from above. They continued round to the north or main gate, however, which they found only closed and barred. The garrison had left it thus to communicate freely with their friends to the north. Ammunition appears to have come in through these doors at intervals.[1]

A giant French lieutenant[2] seized an axe from one of his pioneers and weakened the bar where it was exposed between the doors. He then led a charge which crushed the doors inward breaking the bar. In an instant, many French rushed into the courtyard. But Macdonell himself and several officers and men including Sergeant Graham[3] closed the gates by main strength, replaced the bar and killed or incapacitated every enemy soldier inside, probably helped by musket fire from the surrounding buildings.

Wellington now sent down four more companies of Coldstreamers to restore the situation north and west of the buildings. These were to be added to Macdonell's garrison. Before they arrived, however, the French again forced the north gate and rushed in only to be cut off by

---

[1] *MacKinnon*, II, 216–17, says that 'a cart of ammunition came in about 1 p.m.'. Colonel Sir H. Seymour, *Siborne's Letters*, 19–20, mentions the arrival of an ammunition tumbril 'late in the day'. Both references are vivid, interesting and from eyewitnesses.

[2] Sous-Lieutenant Legros of the 1st Légère, nicknamed 'L'Enfonceur'.

[3] Sergeant James Graham received in 1817 a small annuity as being 'the bravest man' at Waterloo: *Creasy*, 410.

these reinforcements and killed, wounded or captured inside. Macdonell now had a sizeable force in hand to hold the buildings and garden, probably more than 600 men.

But the French continued to attack: they retook the orchard by sending a mass of tirailleurs down outside the eastern hedge and firing at the British and Hanoverian defenders from flank and rear. Again the Guards retreated through the orchard, but the French who followed them from the south were themselves taken by a flanking fire from the eastern wall of the garden. Wellington sent down two companies of the 3rd Guards to intercept and defeat the tirailleurs moving along the east hedge; once the French skirmishers were driven back, the orchard was recaptured and the east as well as the south hedge manned.

The Hougoumont garrison was reorganised about this time, but probably not all at once. Macdonell received all nine available companies of the Coldstreamers for the buildings and walled garden; the tenth was with the colours still kept to the north on the main ridge.[1] The 3rd Guards, probably six companies of them at first, were moved into the orchard. Wellington had now used up almost all his immediate supports by adding them to the garrison; all Byng's Guards Brigade were eventually inside 'the northern third of Hougoumont', save for the company of the Coldstreamers with their colours and a similar company from the 3rd Guards. At this time, or a little later, the 2nd Line Battalion, KGL, and the other light companies of du Plat's Brigade were also added. The advance Guard Battalion of Brunswickers also finally became a part of the garrison.[2]

The Duke must have been pleased with the fight so far. The French attacks on Hougoumont were neither successful nor well co-ordinated. Neither lines nor columns could move through the wooded area to the south of the main Allied defences. British and KGL artillery swept the flanks. Jerome's and Foy's Divisions had already suffered heavy piecemeal casualties. Wellington solved the immediate support problem by bringing forward part of Hew Halkett's Hanoverian Brigade, also from Clinton's Division, from the other side of the Nivelles road and stationing it with du Plat's just north of the protected way. Part of

---

[1] The chief command probably passed to a more senior officer, but memoirs continue to name Macdonell.

[2] Conflicts in original references make it impossible to determine exactly when and what reinforcements were sent into Hougoumont. Because of his long association with the battlefield and the various units and their movements on it, I have trusted *Cotton*, 101.

Mitchell's Brigade which had been west of the Nivelles road was brought east and posted along the lane leading from Hougoumont to the Nivelles road. The 1/23rd from this fine formation was placed directly north of Hougoumont, probably at the Duke's specific orders.

The Hougoumont fight began approximately an hour and a half before there was any other serious fighting along the entire battlefront; it did not stop, however, when fighting started elsewhere. Jerome's and Foy's Division, finally supported by some battalions from Bachelu's Division, continued the see-saw fight. The orchard was taken and re-taken, but the buildings and the walled garden were never lost. When the French surged north through the orchard, they suffered from the flanking fire of the 3rd Guards who lined the eastern garden wall. The buildings were set on fire directly or indirectly by French howitzer shells,[1] but resistance continued unabated, since a large part of the actual fortified area was in the open behind bare walls. Although now pre-occupied with fighting elsewhere, Wellington sent a note pencilled on 'ass's skin' (probably goatskin) to Lieutenant-Colonel James Macdonell which read:

I see that the fire has communicated from the hay stack to the Roof of the Château. You must however still keep your Men in those parts to which the fire does not reach. Take care that no Men are lost by the falling in of the Roof or floors. After they will have fallen in occupy the Ruined Walls inside of the Garden, particularly if it should be possible for the Enemy to pass through the Embers to the Inside of the House.[2]

The only serious loss due to this fire was the tragic burning to death of British, French and Hanoverian wounded.

During the period of the French cavalry attacks to be described later, Hougoumont was isolated, but Wellington personally brought up to its support Adam's veteran British Brigade, the last formation of Clinton's Division to be brought into action. Grant's light cavalry was also present to give assistance as required. Much later in the afternoon, all three divisions of Reille's Corps, artillery and cavalry made a con-certed attack across the whole breadth of the Hougoumont enclosure and to some extent on either flank of it. By this time, however, the individual efforts of the French soldiers from these units had declined appreciably. Byng's Guards, du Plat's KGL Brigade, part of Mitchell's

[1] *Maxwell*, II, 73, says a haystack next to the barn started the buildings burning. *Siborne*, 437, says that a battery of French howitzers specially assembled on Napoleon's orders caused the fire directly.

[2] *Brett-James*, 112.

fine infantry and some other units threw back this heaviest of the French attacks.

The Hougoumont fight was, of course, only a part of the battle of Waterloo; victory or defeat was not finally determined within this enclosure. But its effect on the final outcome can hardly be over-estimated. As the day wore on, the defenders gained strength, efficiency, and confidence as they learned how to make the most of their unique position. Wellington used only about 3,500 men all told inside the area and a lesser number as direct support. They kept about 14,000 veteran French infantry busy throughout the day and finally defeated them.

As many as 10,000 men from both armies are said to have fallen in and around Hougoumont.[1] At least three-quarters of these casualties must have been French, mostly in Reille's fine divisions. But their direct losses were probably not so valuable to Wellington as the strategic advantages which accrued to him from holding the place. Allied possession of the Hougoumont position throughout the day seriously cramped the French attacks to the east. Those made west of the Genappe road, both by cavalry and infantry, just did not have enough room to operate efficiently and were often taken in the flank by British infantry firing from the orchard and by Allied artillery from a little farther north. Hougoumont may have been merely a thorn in Bonaparte's side early in the battle, but it became a thrusting spear towards the end.

[1] *Robinson*, III, 599, says, 'Within half an hour 1,000 men fell in the orchard of Hougoumont; and throughout the day, including both armies, some 10,000 men.'

VIII

D'Erlon and Uxbridge

During the Hougoumont fight, Wellington from his position on the right had seen movements within the French Army suggesting an impending attack on his left. Napoleon in his morning grand review had displayed two corps in his first line. Reille's was west of the Genappe road and used mainly in the Hougoumont fight just described, but d'Erlon's was deployed east of that road and extended to a point south of the PLHS enclave.

As the battle progressed around Hougoumont, Wellington kept an eye on the French preparations to the east. Napoleon appeared to be preparing one of his characteristic artillery-infantry power attacks. D'Erlon's Corps had not fired a shot so far in the campaign;[1] it was obviously going to be used now after a preliminary artillery bombardment. These units would probably attack with all the fire and efficiency that had gained them their illustrious reputations. A grand battery of approximately 80 guns, including many 12-pounders, had been formed on an intermediate ridge east of the Genappe road.[2] Wellington could see that the principal usefulness of this battery was to fire on the portion of his first line from La Haye Sainte to PLHS and that the range would be as short as 500 yards.

The second phase of the battle of Waterloo, that involving d'Erlon's

---

[1] *Cotton*, 37, rightly observes that Durutte's infantry division and Jacquinot's cavalry did do a little fighting at Ligny – very little, actually – but the rest of the corps was, on 16 June, marching back and forth between battlefields, equally useless at either place.

[2] *Kennedy*, 107, says 74; *Siborne*, 384, also says 74; *Ropes*, 302, says 78; *Oman* in *Cambridge Modern History*, IX, 634, says 80; and *Becke*, II, 54, says 84. All base their calculations on full batteries less reported losses in action on 16 June.

Corps, began about 1.30 p.m.; the French artillery opened on the Anglo-Dutch left. By this time, Wellington was on his way east from above Hougoumont. The fire of this grand battery was at first concentrated on the unfortunate brigade of Dutch-Belgian infantry under Bylandt which had formed in front of the crest of the ridge.[1] Picton appears to have been in overall command in this area and had his two brigades of British infantry, already reduced at Quatre Bras, somewhat sheltered.[2] Kempt's was next to the Genappe road and Pack's just beyond Bylandt's. Considerably farther to the west, Picton's Hanoverian brigades (Best's and Vincke's) extended his line east to support Saxe-Weimar in and behind PLHS.

The real problem for historians to understand is not how and when Bylandt moved, but the topography of the area. The greatest defect of Wellington's crest or ridge position was here; the Ohain road is in front of, rather than behind, the line of greatest elevation. If the Anglo-Dutch Army had been arrayed behind the crest, a re-entrant angle would have been formed behind[3] La Haye Sainte, a situation which would have been tactically undesirable. Picton's own men were to some extent exposed, but lay down behind convenient hedges; some of these soldiers appear to have been fully protected by the south side of the slightly sunken Ohain road.

Wellington ordered Bylandt to realign with Kempt and Pack either before he took his position beside his elm[4] or immediately he arrived there. Bylandt's troops were probably in line with Picton's veterans during all the French artillery fire, but the Dutch-Belgians could not be trusted to lie down. They were about ten times as likely to be hit standing as lying in the open. An insignificant ditch or bank would protect them still more. But this brigade was already shaken by its

[1] Authorities do not agree as to when and how Bylandt moved back. *Boulger*, 22, claims it was before the opening of the 'action'; the movement certainly came before d'Erlon's infantry began to advance, probably before the French grand battery opened.

[2] Picton was senior here and had his four brigades immediately in hand, but the general mixing of units had disarranged the command structure. Perponcher's Division (Bylandt's and Saxe-Weimar's Brigades) was split between this area, PLHS and Hougoumont. Picton probably did not have Bylandt's men under his direct control.

[3] As mentioned previously, the Waterloo position was not perfect. The crest is behind the three post-Waterloo buildings west of the Genappe road and runs in an inverted 'V' first north-east and then south-east behind Picton's position.

[4] At the time of the battle, a large elm stood in the south-west corner of the intersection of the Ohain and Genappe roads. A new, much smaller sycamore is now growing up on this spot.

none too distinguished fighting at Quatre Bras; it just did not contain the type of troops to stand a concentrated artillery fire. They were obviously not steady.

La Haye Sainte played a considerable part in the fighting in this area which was now about to start. This farm was located just to the west of the Genappe road and approximately 250 yards south from Wellington's main line and the Ohain road. It was similar in many respects to Hougoumont, but smaller and not so well suited to defence. It consisted of a compound of masonry and brick buildings with the necessary connecting walls, a long, relatively narrow rectangle of pasture and orchard inside a stout hedge to the south, and a much smaller hedge-enclosed kitchen garden to the north. (See Map 7.) Relatively little had been done to fortify this position beyond a few loopholes and some scaffolding; one of the main gates had been destroyed the evening before to provide fuel for a bivouac fire. But the troops assigned as a garrison were of excellent quality; they were initially Major Baring's 2nd Light Battalion, KGL. These men were veterans armed with British Baker rifles and held not only the buildings, but also the pasture and orchard to the south and the kitchen garden to the north.

In accordance with Wellington's orders, the Anglo-Dutch artillery did not reply to the French grand battery. These heavy pieces fired on the Anglo-Dutch army for about twenty minutes without any return. Finally, about 1.45 p.m., the French tirailleurs from d'Erlon's Corps and also from Bachelu's Division of Reille's Corps moved forward against Wellington's skirmishers. The quality of the French light troops was uniformly good, but this was not so in the Anglo-Dutch Army. The riflemen of the 1/95th and the light companies from veteran British and KGL battalions were at least able to hold their own in spite of heavy odds. But the Hanoverians and companies from some British non-veteran battalions were not efficient at this work; the Dutch-Belgian skirmishers from Bylandt's Brigade were useless. The French drove back Wellington's security line. There was soon spirited fire between the tirailleurs and the German riflemen in La Haye Sainte, supported by the 1/95th to the east in the sandpit and on the knoll behind it.

There was more to come, much more. Wellington saw that the main columns of d'Erlon's Corps were beginning to move forward in echelon, left in front. D'Erlon's infantry stretched from slightly west of the Genappe road east as far as PLHS, a distance of perhaps 1,200 yards. It was supported on the west by Reille's Corps and additional

French cavalry. Jerome was again attacking Hougoumont; Bachelu was moving north in support of d'Erlon's westernmost division. Foy was keeping these two connected.[1]

Mindful of his Peninsular defeats by British infantry in line, d'Erlon appears to have adopted a relatively new formation used with minor variations by three of his four divisions. Each was composed of two brigades of four or five battalions. Instead of having the individual battalions in columns one or two companies wide, that is with a front of about 30 to 60 files and a depth of 18 or 9 ranks,[2] d'Erlon deployed each battalion in line three ranks deep and about 180 files wide. Columns were formed by placing these in-line battalions one behind the other at five- or six-pace intervals. The westernmost French division, which we will call Quiot's[3], advanced first with one brigade on each side of the Genappe road. The two French divisions farther east had their brigades one behind the other. A French brigade mass probably had a width of about 150 yards and a depth of about 35 yards including the spaces between the battalions. This arrangement for forming a column, or really a succession of lines, had a good deal to recommend it, at least in theory. D'Erlon's Corps had probably practised the manœuvre often in the immediate past.[4]

D'Erlon was using at Waterloo a line formation similar to that often employed successfully by Wellington, except that there were three ranks rather than two and the individual battalions advanced one behind the other. In the lead battalion, at least, every single musket could be used.[5] D'Erlon was trying to avoid the firepower disadvantage that French infantry in column usually had when meeting British lines. In order to give mass to his formation, always important in

[1] Too often Ney has been criticized for delivering unsupported attacks; this was just not so. See Part Two, Chapter III, 'French Mistakes'.

[2] The exact mechanics of these manœuvres are complicated by variations in the total strength of each battalion and the number of men detached as tirailleurs.

[3] I have followed *Fortescue* here; the same French division had two commanders in this short campaign, Allix and Quiot. There are authorities (see *Robinson* III, 595), who believe Donzelot rather than Quiot was on the west. From the British point of view, it makes little difference.

[4] Some writers in condemning this formation appear to have overlooked the fact that Napoleon's generals were professional soldiers and battle tacticians of a high order with a lot of skill and combat experience. The formation was certainly not invented on the field of battle and tried there for the first time.

[5] The third rank may have occasionally singed the hair of those in the first, but Continental infantry regularly fired in three rank lines.

French tactics, he supported his first battalion by others deployed directly to the rear in an identical order. The following battalions could march easily and simply to either flank alternately, face to the front, advance to the level of the lead battalion, and increase the firepower of the brigade or division as required.

The first battle test of this alignment was favourable. Quiot's left brigade under Bourgeois advanced against Baring's Germans in the La Haye Sainte orchard. The first battalion halted and opened fire. The second and third moved out to either flank, advanced so as to embrace the enclosed area, and began firing. In a few moments, the French infantry drove the Germans back with their much heavier firepower. Baring's men retired all the way back to, but not into, the buildings. They appear to have formed a line with their left flank terminating at or near the open barn passage into the courtyard of La Haye Sainte.

Quiot's right brigade was advancing against the 95th in the sandpit and on the knoll behind it. Two more French divisions with their brigades one behind the other were beginning to ascend the slope to the right of Quiot. Far to the east, Wellington could see d'Erlon's fourth and final division under Durutte beginning to move forward against PLHS with a mass of French cavalry on his outer flank. There were even French light artillery batteries moving forward with this infantry. The French were mounting an attack by 18,000 fresh veterans supported by a considerable force of cavalry on their right flank, and infantry and cavalry on their left. Their grand battery would continue to fire when not masked by their own troops.

Wellington appreciated immediately that this was to be a full-scale test of infantry power in the open and checked quickly to make sure that Picton had his partially sheltered brigades ready. The attack would fall mainly on them. The Allied artillery finally opened against the enemy infantry, at first at fairly long range save above La Haye Sainte. The Duke ordered the 1st Light Battalion from Ompteda's Brigade, German riflemen, to move across the Genappe road to support the 95th in the sandpit and on the knoll behind it. He appears to have gone with them personally, for two or three minutes later he was well to the east. Even though he must have seen the precarious situation at La Haye Sainte he did nothing about it at this time, perhaps because he realised the danger of sending down reinforcements.

The young Prince of Orange who was nominally in command of Alten's Division had no such misgivings. When Wellington rode east, he sent forward the Lüneburg battalion from Kielmansegge's Hanoverian Brigade to support Baring in the open west of the La Haye Sainte gateways. Baring extended his riflemen and these reinforcements in line and began a counter-attack against Bourgeois's French Brigade which had been unable to take the buildings and was suffering severely from the accurate rifle fire of the garrison, the 95th, and perhaps of the new reinforcements that the Duke had taken across the Genappe road. Baring had his left flank protected by the buildings.

Quiot's other brigade had been forced to the east by the 95th and their newly arrived reinforcements. Quiot's men in their wide, shallow column were moving straight north towards Picton's veterans. Bylandt's Belgians now took themselves out of the fight, perhaps in accordance with orders from their officers,[1] but this can hardly have come as a surprise to the Duke. At least, they had not deserted. A quick realignment might have been needed, but appears to have been unnecessary. The French 'columns' were advancing in the area, but Kempt's Brigade less the 1/95th was already in line almost directly in front of Quiot's left brigade. Pack's was across the path of Donzelot's French Division. Neither British brigade had as yet stood up.

Now let us return to what was happening just west of La Haye Sainte. It will be remembered that d'Erlon's left flank was protected by a mass of French cavalry headed by cuirassiers. These moved forward on Bourgeois's left, but considerably to the rear of the infantry. They were in the covered ground and not seen from the crest above or from west of La Haye Sainte until they emerged opposite the western end of Baring's new line. The French cavalry immediately charged the luckless Hanoverians of the Lüneburg battalion who were on the right and had no real chance to form square. The cuirassiers broke them completely and inflicted terrible casualties; Baring's own men also suffered, but were closer to the buildings and took refuge under the walls. The French cavalry continued their charge to the crest of Wellington's position.

Meanwhile, things were happening all along the eastern front more or less concurrently. The first French infantry columns which advanced past La Haye Sainte on the east were badly mauled by Allied artillery. The British and KGL batteries had not been allowed to fire at the French guns and were fresh. They went into action against the

---

[1] Siborne, 395–6. Some of these troops rallied and took a position farther back, but no single soldier from this unit appears to have been within musket range of French infantry all day. See particularly Tomkinson, 295, who was an eyewitness.

French 'columns' with canister as well as solid shot. According to the Duke's orders, the pieces were to remain in action where they were until overrun. They did great damage with their last rounds delivered against the 'columns' at ranges below fifty yards. But the gunners were shaken by the French attack; some of them did not understand their orders and lost their heads.[1] Artillerymen streamed to the rear; one gun was actually spiked by the British sergeant in command of it.[2]

Both brigades of Quiot's Division saw victory within their grasp; that on the east was now well past La Haye Sainte. Although the building still held out here, the Rifles and their reinforcements had been forced to retreat from the sandpit and knoll to the Ohain road. The right French brigade appears to have thought Bylandt's Belgians to be their only antagonists until they were suddenly confronted by Kempt's men in line. In spite of an unusually wide French formation, the three British infantry battalions overlapped both flanks by a considerable extent. The first British volley, delivered by every musket in the brigade, was followed by regular half-company volleys. The Frenchmen were stopped in their tracks, momentarily paralysed.

Donzelot's whole Division in its single column of battalions, one brigade behind the other, was coming along within supporting distance of Quiot, perhaps 400 yards farther east and 200 yards to the rear. Marcognet's Division was similarly arrayed and positioned farther to the east and south. Pack moved to oppose Donzelot and opened fire in the same manner as Kempt, probably with four battalions in line. Best and Vincke were moving to meet Marcognet, but appear not to have actually made contact.

We must now return to the area just to the west of the Genappe road which was overrun by French cuirassiers. A crisis more serious than any at Hougoumont was at hand, but so also was Wellington. The French horsemen had just destroyed one battalion of Hanoverians. Quiot's infantry was not yet brought to a stand. The French were close to achieving an outstanding success. The Duke was ready, however, to meet each offensive manœuvre with an appropriate countermeasure. He knew that Picton's men would do their duty; he had left them only moments before.

---

[1] The misbehaviour of even the British artillery was temporary and amply made up for later, but was the basis of Wellington's long secret letter to the Earl of Mulgrave dated 21 December 1815 and quoted by *Duncan, History of the Royal Regiment of Artillery*, II, 447–8, as well as by others.

[2] *Anglesey*, 138, and other sources.

Wellington threw the remaining infantry battalions of Kielman-segge's and Ompteda's Brigades into square to avoid damage by the cuirassiers. He then ordered Uxbridge to form Somerset's Household Brigade of British heavy cavalry in line and attack the French horsemen who were just reaching the crest of the Anglo-Dutch position.[1] The French cavalry were taken by surprise, outnumbered and out-weighed; the British horses were stronger and less tired.[2] The cuirassiers were swept back and, to some extent, to the east into a cutting in the Ohain and/or Genappe roads, losing heavily.[3] In a moment, the French infantry in this area was also ridden down. The Rifles returned quickly, collecting prisoners; La Haye Sainte was again firmly held.

While this action on and near the roads was taking place Kempt's Brigade had riddled with fire the French pseudo-column arrayed against it. As in Spain, the initial single tremendous volley followed by regular platoon firing halted the French advance and caused heavy casualties at the head of the formation. But d'Erlon's 'column' had been invented to deal with such a situation. French columns in Spain had been unable to deploy because of the complicated movements necessary to go from a close column into line.[4] The French could now easily triple or quintuple their front and their fire as already described. They appear to have been in the process of doing this when Uxbridge led Somerset's heavy cavalry into them.

Ponsonby's Union Brigade of British heavy cavalry to the east of the Genappe road had received orders, apparently from Uxbridge, to be ready to support Somerset's horsemen. They appear to have crossed the crest of Wellington's position less than 100 yards behind the Household Brigade. The Union Brigade struck both Donzelot's and Marcognet's Divisions at about the same time as Somerset's Brigade

---

[1] Some authorities have given Uxbridge credit for originating this movement. He certainly led it, but is unlikely to have ordered it without permission, considering what we know of Wellington's long record in combat. *Clinton*, 142, says, '. . . Wellington sent forward the Household Brigade . . .' Neither Uxbridge nor Wellington said anything one way or the other for many years.

[2] *Fortescue*, X, 338, was convinced by the research of *Houssaye*, 274, that many of the French cavalry spent the night of the 17th sleeping in their saddles. This treatment of horses is not only despicable, but would also have handicapped them the next day.

[3] These cuttings were greatly reduced in depth when the mound for the Lion monument was constructed after the battle. This action probably gave rise to the sunken road incident in Victor Hugo's *Les Misérables*.

[4] There is some evidence that French columns of companies were supposed to advance at 'full or half distance' which would have allowed easy deploying, but in an attack they soon became 'close' with only a pace separating the ranks.

crashed into Quiot's men. D'Erlon's formation of in-line battalions one behind the other may have had considerable merit for meeting infantry in line, but no conceivable formation could be so unsuitable to receive a charge by British heavy cavalry. Every British trooper was superbly mounted, knew how to ride, and was strong enough and skilful enough to make lethal use of his long straight sabre. They caught most of the ill-fated French battalions already demoralised by fire and disordered by their flank marching. The infantry was either in line without space to form square, or in what amounted to an extremely narrow column which was attacked on its northern flank.

Ponsonby's Union Brigade was composed of the 1st Dragoons (Royals), the 2nd Dragoons (Scots Greys) and the 6th Dragoons (Inniskillings); the mingling of British, Scottish and Irish units led to its name. These men not only completely broke Donzelot's Division, but also smashed Marcognet's; the same squadrons were perhaps not involved with both divisions. The Royals on the right certainly struck Donzelot, while the Greys on the left charged Marcognet.[1] In both cases, the carnage was awful; many horsemen killed or wounded several French. Two eagles were taken[2] and upwards of 3,000 prisoners actually secured; many others surrendered and then escaped because there were insufficient men left to guard them.

Save for Durutte's French Division in front of PLHS which did not come into contact with the British heavy cavalry at all, d'Erlon's Corps was temporarily destroyed. Their entire original attack was utterly defeated. Two batteries of French light artillery which were advancing to support the infantry at close range were completely wrecked. So far the British heavy horsemen had achieved a magnificent success, perhaps the finest in the history of the British mounted arm.

Unfortunately, they now yielded individually and collectively, officers and men alike, to their greatest weakness. They became intoxicated with what they had already done, and endeavoured to accomplish the impossible. Superbly mounted young officers were determined to demonstrate their personal gallantry and forgot that they were supposed to be professional soldiers. Older officers who should have

---

[1] *Gardner*, 250, and others. The eagles mentioned in the next note certainly came from different divisions.

[2] Sergeant Ewart of the Scots Greys took the eagle of the 45th French regiment. The eagle of the 105th was taken by Captain A. K. Clark of the Royals. *Cotton*, 60–61.

known better joined them with no more appreciation of the proper employing of cavalry on a battlefield than a novice in a nunnery. Nearly 2,000 heavy horsemen, who had suffered trifling loss until this time, crashed through the French grand battery, inflicting casualties and putting some guns out of action. They were now completely out of hand; all order and formation were lost. They dashed forward, however, individually and in small groups, on blown horses, in muddy fields, against 30,000 formed French infantry, cavalry and artillery including the entire Imperial Guard. Uxbridge himself, as gallant and dashing a man as ever lived, led the Household Brigade, but lost all control of it.[1] Ponsonby led his own with equal bravery and even less knowledge of his job.

Napoleon immediately appreciated his rare opportunity and took full advantage of it. The British horsemen were stopped by infantry and artillery fire as well as cavalry in formation. They were taken in the flank by other French cavalry units under specific orders from the Emperor. Jacquinot's Lancers from the extreme eastern flank were particularly effective in overthrowing disorganised men on tired horses, either singly or in small groups.

The British light cavalry brigades of Vandeleur and Vivian moved forward on the eastern flank and prevented their heavier companions from being exterminated; one regiment of Vandeleur's Brigade, the 12th Light Dragoons under another Ponsonby,[2] achieved a considerable success and then also to some extent went out of control. It did not suffer such severe casualties as the two heavy brigades, but neither did it accomplish so much. The brigades of Somerset and Ponsonby were magnificent at first, but then sacrificed themselves against senseless odds. Total casualties appear to have been only about 50 per cent, but those who survived were so disorganised that the brigades lost far more than half their efficiency.[3]

Wellington never criticised Uxbridge personally for this rather astonishing misadventure; it may not have been the Chief-of-Cavalry's

---

[1] Uxbridge quoted in *Siborne's Letters*, 9–10, frankly admits his mistake. *Cotton*, 69–71, is more diplomatic and mysterious, but sides against his old chief.

[2] Sir Frederick Ponsonby commanded the 12th Light Dragoons and was severely wounded, surviving all night on the ground. Sir William Ponsonby commanded the Union Brigade and was killed after being captured.

[3] *Fortescue*, X, 366, says, 'Of two thousand troopers and horses that had charged, over one thousand horses and from seven to eight hundred men were killed, wounded and missing.'

fault.[1] British horsemen had often done the same thing on a small scale in the Peninsula. There was no appreciation of the professional duty of an officer in cavalry regiments; they insisted on thinking of combat as a kind of glorious foxhunt. The be-all and end-all of their existence was to be in the forefront of a magnificent spectacle and to demonstrate their personal intrepidity at the expense of the real interests of their units and their army. Their men were not slow to follow their example.

The final defeat of the heavy cavalry does not entirely alter the importance of their early success. The situation before their charge had been critical. Even though they finally destroyed themselves, they inflicted further casualties on the enemy, temporarily broke three divisions of French infantry and completely drove back Napoleon's second main attack. 'It was a harrowing sight to see the English cavalry breaking through and slaughtering these fine divisions as if they were flocks of sheep. Intoxicated with slaughter, inciting each other to kill, they pierced and cut down the miserable mass with glee. The columns were shattered, divided, scattered, and hurled down to the slopes by the swords of the dragoons.'[2] The final broken retreat of the British heavy cavalry was covered in part by rockets discharged by Whinyates's Battery, R.H.A.[3]

[1] One wonders, however, at the difference between the discipline in the infantry and cavalry. *Cope*, 202–3, in speaking of the 1/95th says, 'Leach's two companies and Johnston's company running out to and beyond their former positions in the sandpit and at the hedge, slew many men, and made many prisoners. But the Duke's orders were peremptory that the troops were not to quit their positions, and the Riflemen, having disposed of their prisoners, returned to theirs.'

[2] *Houssaye*, 198.

[3] Wellington thought less than nothing of rockets because of their extreme inaccuracy and, according to *Mercer*, 91–92, ordered Whinyates to place his in store and draw guns. But this battery definitely used both at Waterloo. *Duncan*, 438, says that it fired 52 rockets on the 18th, all probably at this time.

IX

The French Cavalry Attacks

Wellington began reorganising his forces even before the British heavy cavalry had come to grief. Picton had been killed, but Kempt took over that victorious division; the position remained secure. La Haye Sainte was a more difficult problem: Baring and his men through no fault of theirs had lost the hedged orchard and pasture south of the buildings and had come close to losing the buildings themselves. The Duke sent Baring part of the battalion of Nassauers previously employed in the Hougoumont woods,[1] and appears to have told the KGL major to give up trying to defend the enclosure to the south and to concentrate on holding the farm proper. He was to block up the open passage through the barn from the west with farm implements.

Wellington personally inspected the 1/95th which was again firmly re-established in the sandpit and on the knoll behind it. Bylandt's Brigade was not up to fighting in the first line, but might be of some use in support. It was confirmed in its position some 400 yards to the rear of the Ohain road. Its absence from the front line meant that the three eastern brigades of Kempt's Division must move to the west, but they had already made this adjustment. The two Hanoverian brigades had suffered little so far and were capable of efficiently handling their new responsibilities on the east flank. Lambert's British Brigade which had been stationed in Mont Saint Jean just in front of where the Nivelles and the Genappe roads divide was brought forward to a position behind and slightly to the west of PLHS. These three fine

[1] Perhaps only the flank companies went into La Haye Sainte, but three are also mentioned. All six could have gone in, but this seems unlikely. La Haye Sainte is also said by some authorities to have contained some non-KGL Hanoverian riflemen.

strong Peninsular battalions were temporarily in the second line, but could be used to reinforce any part of Wellington's left flank.

The Duke was now reasonably sure that Napoleon was not contemplating a direct attack on the Anglo-Dutch Army along any route much farther west than Hougoumont.[1] The Duke's forces originally deployed beyond the Nivelles road were now probably disposable for use to the east. He had already, as we have seen, moved the brigades of du Plat and Mitchell to reinforce the area north and immediately west of Hougoumont. He now ordered forward both Hew Halkett's Hanoverians and the Brunswick infantry from the vicinity of Merbe-Braine.×All Halkett's battalions were placed behind Hougoumont; the Brunswickers were divided into two parts.[2] Two battalions were placed above and to the east of Hougoumont to take the place of Byng's Guards, now all employed in garrisoning that place. Mercer's battery of horse artillery was eventually placed between these two Brunswick battalions, while the 1/23rd was also moved into the same area to steady them. The remainder of the Brunswick infantry was placed as a ready reserve some 400 yards behind Maitland's Guards. Following his usual custom, the Duke was providing for a continuous supply of reinforcements to feed into any sections of his main line which might need them.

Even though this chapter is devoted mainly to the French cavalry attacks, an infantry action of considerable importance preceded them. The French launched another attack against La Haye Sainte with troops from Donzelot's, Quiot's, Bachelu's and probably Foy's Divisions. Some French cavalry and light artillery also participated. A heavy mass of tirailleurs, probably regular battalions advancing in open order, pressed forward on a front extending about 500 yards both east and west of the Genappe road. The Allied skirmishers were quickly driven in, but Kempt's Brigades east of the Genappe road restored the situation in their area by advancing in line and repelling the tirailleurs. The French west of the road were prevented from exerting any appreciable pressure on the Allied main line because of accurate enfilade artillery fire from the batteries immediately behind Hougoumont. The attack on La Haye Sainte itself, however, was again made in

---

[1] Wellington was still convinced that a semi-independent French force might turn his flank by the Mons-Brussels road and did not want his Tubize-Hal command moved, although about this time, or slightly before, he received from Colville a request for orders.

[2] As has already been mentioned, the advance Guard Battalion may have been added to the Hougoumont garrison.

strength and pressed with determination. But Baring's reinforced garrison was now too strong and too well settled into their makeshift fortress.

For some minutes fighting was hand-to-hand, particularly near the only imperfectly blocked passage through the barn into the courtyard. The assailants could not enter the place, but managed to set it on fire. The newly arrived Nassauers, however, were equipped with light sheet-metal cooking pots which served admirably as buckets for a bucket brigade from the pond; the fire was soon put out. The French were repulsed fairly easily after this; they were still suffering from their earlier defeats by Picton's infantry and the British heavy cavalry. Baring's men were victorious, although rifle ammunition was running low.[1]

While the action at La Haye Sainte was still going on, the French grand battery was realigned; some pieces were moved across the Genappe road. Other batteries were added. Napoleon's artillery was now capable of firing on the entire Allied line, although the enemy artillery units west of the Genappe road never seem to have been as effective as the guns on the east. As all the French pieces opened fire, Wellington saw a mass of French cavalry begin to advance in strength towards the gap between Hougoumont and La Haye Sainte. He could scarce believe his eyes. His troops here were certainly not all of uniform high quality, but most of the men were fresh. In many battalions, only the light companies had fired a shot. The French artillery was too far away to do them serious damage quickly. Was the great Napoleon going to try to break fresh infantry in good positions, with ample artillery and cavalry support, by cavalry and long-range artillery alone?

The Duke must again have checked what he had ready to receive this onset. La Haye Sainte and Hougoumont were surely proof against horsemen and left an opening no more than 1,000 yards wide between them. His main line consisted of at least seven batteries supported by infantry just to their rear, but in many cases over the crest of the ridge and safe from the French artillery. He had immediately available infantry and artillery reserves; his own cavalry was behind his artillery-infantry line. Allied brigade and battalion commanders could be counted upon to arrange their forces properly to receive cavalry.

[1] Baring's own men were certainly armed with Baker rifles; their shortage of ammunition, when the various units of the 95th armed with the same weapons appear to have had enough, has never been satisfactorily explained.

Wellington had already given his artillery careful instructions for their procedure in an attack of this type; they had even had some practice in carrying these out.

The French cavalry came forward in all its magnificence. Men, horses, uniforms and weapons were remarkable.

The First Line of Cuirassiers shone in burnished steel, relieved by black horse-hair crested helmets. Next came the Red Lancers of the Guard in their gaudy uniform and mounted on richly caparisoned steeds, their fluttering lance flags heightening the brilliancy of their display. The Third Line comprising the Chasseurs of the Guard in their rich costume of green and gold, with fur-trimmed pelisses *à la hussard,* and black bearskin shakos completed the gorgeous, yet harmonious, colouring of this military spectacle.[1]

These were the French veterans who had been so often victorious under Murat. Marshal Ney, the bravest of the brave, now led them. Hearts quailed in the Allied army; more than one young soldier has set down in his memoirs that he could not see how anything could withstand the mighty host of mounted Frenchmen.[2] Only the Penin-sular veterans realised how little they had to fear cavalry so long as they kept their formation and fire discipline.

Ney's task was beyond human capability. Even though the first charge was made by perhaps 5,000 horsemen, they had scarcely 700 yards of front, the distance between the limits of effective musketry from La Haye Sainte and the Hougoumont orchard. A proper forma-tion would have been a line two files deep, an interval of at least 100 yards, and another similar line.[3] If two lines each two ranks deep could not accomplish the task, adding more horsemen in depth was not going to help. But France and Napoleon had often used mass far beyond the requirements of military efficiency and won because of its psychological effect.

The French actually attacked by squadrons and regiments in echelon, right in front. The individual units were in perfect order, but they appear to have been crowded together; far less than 100 yards separated the lines from each other. To some professional soldiers in the Duke's army the formation looked more like cavalry in column than in a series

---

[1] *Siborne,* 443.

[2] *Morris,* 219, says, 'Their appearance was of such a formidable nature, that I thought we could not have the slightest chance with them.'

[3] A cavalryman occupied 36 inches of front; 624 files of them, roughly 12 squadrons placed end to end with narrow intervals between each squadron, could have been in such a line. A total of 2,500 troopers would have been needed for the whole formation.

of lines. The first charge was delivered, however, with courage and discipline. The slope up which the French came was sufficiently gentle not greatly to impede their speed. The rye fields were still heavy with rain, but the footing on the slope was not yet bad.[1] The fire of the Allied artillery was galling everywhere and particularly effective when a battery could catch a squadron or two in enfilade as often happened in the area north-east of Hougoumont.

The French cavalry must have been astonished to receive a final round from all the exposed British and KGL guns and then apparently to capture these pieces as the gunners ran to the rear. French horsemen who had served in the Peninsula were elated, for never before had they captured and retained a single cannon belonging to the Duke. They did not know it yet, but they were not about to improve their record. The surviving cavalry pressed on through the abandoned batteries, but suddenly came to the squares and oblongs.[2]

If the French cavalry, the very first squadrons of it, could have maintained their speed and formation they would have won. A cuirassier and his horse probably weighed about 2,000 pounds. Half a dozen acting together with kamikaze courage in man and beast could have broken any battalion. This never happened for a variety of reasons. The firepower of the squares was probably most important, but the horses themselves often refused, perhaps with some help from their riders. The lines of bayonets and the regular volleys from such compact small human fortresses were too much for the Frenchmen and their horses. The squadrons tended to funnel between the squares rather than careering into them. An average battalion square was only of about 60 feet on a side; there was a much wider open space between two squares. A maximum swerve of about 35 feet would take horse and rider around the formation and clear of its bayonets.[3] Even the oblongs were usually less than 100 feet wide.

Most British infantry battalions received the cavalry with a volley from the third and fourth ranks of each square, but retained the muskets

[1] I have walked about this battlefield during periods of rain lasting several days – they are not uncommon – and have been astonished at the variation in footing. Mud of unusual tenacity will form quickly in spots used by medium-sized farm animals, but other areas remain firm even where heavy Belgian horses tread frequently in the same place.

[2] Oblongs could always be formed easily in manœuvres and were particularly effective at Waterloo because they had more frontal firepower: *Kennedy*, 115. The sides of an oblong generally consisted of a single company. This formation required better than average discipline, however, because of the relatively long line exposed to shock attacks.

[3] More details of this in Part Two, Chapter V, 'Cavalry Against Infantry Squares'.

of first and second lines loaded until the third and fourth were able to reload. After all had discharged their weapons once, the squares sometimes began their rolling fire by half companies. This was particularly important because of the presence of the apparently abandoned British and KGL guns. Wellington had ordered the pieces left where they were. The gun crews had taken with them only the implements necessary for operation. But the French cavalry who tried to seize the pieces and either damage them or pull them away were shot by the squares.[1]

The mass of French horse continued to pour forward; some squares received three, four and even five charges, always with the same result. The leading units penetrated to the north of Wellington's first line and received in turn a charge from Allied squadrons placed in support here for just this purpose. Wellington still had more mounted soldiers in this area than Ney used in his first cavalry attack, but the brigades of Ponsonby and Somerset were sorely missed. No one could get the Dutch-Belgians to charge at all. The Duke of Cumberland's regiment of Hanoverians abandoned the field entirely and rode off to Brussels with the news that Wellington and his army were defeated.[2]

Even though the Allied counter-charges were delivered by British and KGL cavalry only, they were effective. The enemy was in disorder as well as a poor state of morale because of their experiences with the Allied artillery and infantry. They were driven back towards the squares and through them, receiving further fire from the rear and side faces. As they finally retreated back the way they came, the gunners ran out to their pieces and opened fire again. One sizeable group of French cavalry tried to get away down the Nivelles road, but came to grief opposite the Hougoumont lane where an obstruction had been placed across the road and the hedges on either side lined with Allied infantrymen.

Wellington could hardly have been more pleased with the results of the first French cavalry attack. In spite of the bravery of individual Frenchmen and small groups, they had accomplished nothing and suffered heavy casualties. But there was more to come; it was not yet 4 p.m. So far, at least, the French had been using the straight-ahead,

---

[1] Uxbridge wrote, *Siborne's Letters*, 9–10, 'Some cuirassiers were in possession of several of our guns and remained there to be picked off.'

[2] This unit was composed of young Hanoverians of wealth and social position. They furnished their own horses and were almost a part of the British Army, but behaved worse than any other Allied unit. They were the only Hanoverian cavalry regiment at Waterloo.

pounding type of attack which had been characteristic of Napoleon's battles since 1809. Manœuvres stressing surprise, speed and precision, which had done so well earlier in his career, apparently were not now to be revived. The Duke made a decision based on this assumption. He would maintain Hougoumont and the area close to it just across the Nivelles road to the west. But he ordered Chassé's Dutch-Belgian Division to move from Braine l'Alleud as unobtrusively as possible through Merbe-Braine to a position on the Nivelles road behind the main line. This manœuvre involved considerable marching and was to be covered by the extremely skilful 2nd Hussars, KGL. It would not yield actual new reserves in less than an hour, but they were soon on their way.

Meanwhile, the French cavalry came on again in even greater strength. We have now reached another period of uncertainty; the original records do not help. The battle, and particularly these French cavalry charges, looked different from points as close to each other as 400 yards. The French cavalry attacked again and again until nearly 6 p.m. Units were added so that finally at least 10,000 French sabres were in action at once. Some eyewitnesses claim that Ney brought forward cavalry in as many as twenty-three different attacks. This was hardly impossible: there was not sufficient time nor could any horse have lived through such an ordeal. An individual square of British infantry may well have been charged by twenty-three, or even more French squadrons in the course of the several cavalry attacks, but there were probably not more than six or eight of these general attacks.[1]

The French horsemen accomplished nothing of importance, even though their force was increased. They and their horses became tired and discouraged; parts of the battle area became knee-deep in tenacious mud. The British artillery learned through practice how to get the most from each round and how best to carry out Wellington's instructions for taking cover and returning to their pieces as soon as possible. But the personnel of one battery at least, Mercer's, never left their guns at all.

The Brunswickers were falling fast; French shot were every moment making great gaps in their squares. The officers and sergeants were actively employed

---

[1] *Thiers*, XII, 125, says 'eleven', but this seems too many if an entire forward movement by all or most of the French cavalry in this area is considered to be just one attack. On the other hand, *Wood*, 170, who studied the battle carefully from a cavalry point of view, says, 'Ney led or sent forward the cavalry twelve times.'

in filling up the spaces by pushing their men together. Sometimes they had to thump them ere they could make them move. These were the very boys whom I had but two days before seen throwing away their arms, and fleeing, panic-stricken, from the very sound of our horses' feet. Today they fled not bodily, but I feared they would if our men ran from their guns.[1]

The Allied infantry also gained in confidence and in efficiency; they had plenty of ammunition.[2] Their most severe trials were when the enemy horsemen retired and the French artillery reopened fire on them while still in square and somewhat exposed. But the artillery casualties inflicted by the French at relatively long range were only a small fraction of those which their cavalry suffered at the very muzzles of the Duke's guns. Mercer

allowed them to advance unmolested until the head of the column might have been about fifty or sixty yards from us, and then gave the word, 'Fire!' The effect of the case was terrible; nearly the whole leading rank fell at once. The round-shot penetrated the column and carried confusion throughout its extent. The ground, already encumbered with victims of the first struggle, became now almost impassable. Still, however, these devoted warriors struggled on, intent only on reaching us. The thing was impossible. Our guns were served with astonishing activity, whilst the running fire of the two squares was maintained with spirit. Those who pushed forward over the heaps of carcasses of men and horses gained but a few paces in advance, there to fall in their turn and add to the difficulties of those succeeding them. The discharge of every gun was followed by a fall of men and horses like that of grass before the mower's scythe. When the horse alone was killed, we could see the cuirassiers divesting themselves of the encumbrance and making their escape on foot.[3]

Throughout the French cavalry attacks, Wellington was riding from place to place. He sometimes entered a square, but more often relied on his own dexterity as a horseman and the speed of his horse. About 4.30 he heard a cannonade to the south-east indicating that the Prussians were finally taking some part in the battle, but not actually supporting him. Their active intervention in the fight between Hougoumont and PLHS was still some time away.

The Duke now brought forward Adam's superb Brigade of British infantry which contained Colonel Colborne's famous 1/52nd, a light infantry battalion of more than 1,000 bayonets, the 1/71st with 810

[1] *Mercer*, 170.

[2] Wellington had made arrangements early in the morning for carts and wagons to deliver casks of cartridges to all units in his main line as required.

[3] *Mercer*, 175.

rank and file and eight companies of the 2nd and 3rd battalions of the 95th.[1] It advanced across the Nivelles road and occupied a position in echelon north and east of the north-east corner of the Hougoumont orchard. Some artillery along the road above them could continue to fire over their heads. At least one battery also occupied their position. This new brigade of veteran light infantry would be acting on the flank of the advancing French horsemen, and could do severe damage with accurate aimed fire, particularly from the riflemen of the 95th. This was the strongest British brigade in the entire army; all units had served in the Peninsula. Wellington had delayed bringing it into action, perhaps because of its strength and efficiency. He now placed it where it could do the most good, but where it was not dangerously exposed to fire from the French artillery.[2]

The final French cavalry attack appears to have come about 5.30 p.m., or slightly later. The assailants were more numerous than ever, but many horses were so weary that they could not even trot. The field was so cluttered with horses and men killed and wounded in former charges and the ground in places so churned to mud that no squadron could keep its alignment. Few even of the leading squadrons could reach the guns. The Allied artillery continued to fire; as ranges closed the infantry squares and oblongs opened fire with little regard for the old rule of keeping at least 50 per cent of muskets loaded at all times. No one, not even the French, believed that cavalry could now do harm to this battle-hardened, confident infantry. The slaughter was extreme; the rampart of dead horses and men was built up so high in some places as almost to create a field fortification. The French horsemen finally broke, not to return in strength again.

There was one more attack in this area before the crisis of the battle. Before 6 p.m., Ney launched a combined force of cavalry, infantry and artillery behind a heavy mass of tirailleurs. They put extreme pressure on du Plat's KGL Brigade and three battalions of Hew Halkett's Hanoverians behind the Hougoumont enclosure, where French field-guns went into action against these infantry squares at relatively short range. The swarm of skirmishers continued up the slope to the east.

---

[1] The battalions of the 95th were ordinarily at this time composed of six large companies each, total battalion strength near 600 rank and file. The 2/95th with six companies acted as an independent battalion; the two companies of the 3/95th appear to have been combined with the 1/71st.

[2] The Hougoumont woods shielded them from some frontal fire; the French grand battery, still largely on the other side of the Nivelles road, had other, closer targets at which to shoot.

French cavalry was in close support of both the skirmishers and the artillery; several French columns were also coming north. The French attack, however, was directed against an area that was now full of British and KGL infantry battalions and artillery batteries; it was also directed at a point where Wellington commanded in person.

The British and German squares suffered casualties from artillery and tirailleur fire, but British and KGL batteries were soon sweeping the southern slopes. Maitland's Guards advanced in line to defeat the tirailleurs. Adam's Brigade came in on the flank of the French columns as they advanced past the Hougoumont enclosure and defeated them utterly. Several of the artillery pieces brought forward by the French were left where they had briefly gone into action. This combined arms attack seems to have been doomed to failure before it started by the exhausted condition of the forces which made it. But it refutes the many criticisms of Ney for not combining his three arms in a single attack. There just was not sufficient space to do this effectively in the narrow area between Hougoumont and La Haye Sainte, or anywhere else on the Waterloo battlefield for that matter. Napoleon's massive tactics were in part defeating themselves.

X

The Loss of La Haye Sainte

The fourth phase of the battle of Waterloo concerns the enclosed farm
of La Haye Sainte and the tirailleur fighting which went on north of
it on both sides of the Genappe road. We have already discussed what
happened here before 6 p.m. Major Baring and his 2nd Light Battalion,
KGL, were originally entrusted with the defence of this post. This
battalion had a total strength of 376 men divided into six companies all
armed with Baker rifles.[1] As we have seen, Baring defended at first the
hedge-enclosed orchard in front of the buildings, the buildings enclosure itself and the garden to the rear, probably with three, two and
one of his companies respectively.

La Haye Sainte was a·typical Belgian enclosed farm and not a
semi-fortified château like Hougoumont. Map 7 shows the plan;
modern aerial photographs give a good idea of what it was like
in 1815. (See plates 27–33.) Some loopholes were opened, particularly
through roofs; a firing step or platform was erected against the inside
of the south and east walls. But, as has been pointed out, the passageway through the barn into the courtyard could not be closed
satisfactorily.

After the repulse of d'Erlon's attack, Wellington sent in two companies from the 1st Light Battalion, KGL, and part at least of the
Hougoumont Nassau battalion. The Duke gave Baring orders to allow
the orchard to be taken, but to hold the buildings at all costs. As we
have seen, Baring defeated a determined attack by French infantry,

[1] *Beamish*, I, 352 and *passim*, is the best and most complete authority for the force inside
La Haye Sainte. *Blackmore*, 118, says that the 1st and 2nd Light Battalions, KGL, received
Baker rifles in 1806.

cavalry and artillery which was delivered between d'Erlon's infantry advance and Ney's cavalry assaults. The buildings were held, but there was a serious shortage of rifle ammunition. Baring received another company of KGL riflemen, the light company of the 5th Line Battalion,[1] and maintained his post stoutly throughout the period of the French cavalry attacks.

Soon after the French cavalry attacks had finally ceased, or perhaps while they were still continuing, the French brought literally thousands of men to bear against the farm. This operation probably started when the French also attacked east of Hougoumont with infantry, cavalry and artillery.[2] Once again, masses of infantry were thrown forward as skirmishers isolated La Haye Sainte on both west and east. French cavalry used the blind area under the Anglo-Dutch main position to give support from the west. D'Erlon's many battalions, now partially restored to effectiveness, were so threatening that Wellington moved Lambert's Brigade from behind PLHS to beside the Genappe road, to the right rear of Kempt.[3] The French made no headway against the main line, but they made their strongest attack on La Haye Sainte.

French infantry in overwhelming strength supported by some artillery[4] forced themselves right up to the building enclosure, fired through the loopholes and windows, and tried to wrest away the weapons of the defenders. They stubbornly assaulted the blocked-up barn passage facing to the west. Siborne tells us that seventeen Frenchmen were killed here in hand-to-hand fighting, their bodies being used by the defenders to reinforce their barricade.[5]

Baring's men were falling fast. Worse still, his rifle ammunition was running out. Only the Nassauers had muskets which could use standard ammunition; cartridges for the rifles had been called for at least three

---

[1] *Kennedy*, 122, who would have the Nassauers go in at the the same time as this company. But they were certainly there in time for their camp kettles to be used as buckets before the French attack just referred to.

[2] Napoleon ordered Ney to take La Haye Sainte at all costs.

[3] *Harry Smith*, I, 370, says, 'We were ordered to the very spot where the Duke, early in the morning, had expected we should be required.'

[4] *Siborne*, 475. He lived for several months at La Haye Sainte while gathering data for his map; the artillery damage which was still obvious to him probably occurred at about this time. But field-guns, even the heavy French 12-pounders, were comparatively useless against good masonry buildings.

[5] ibid., 440.

times, but none had arrived.[1] Baring and his Germans refused to surrender, even after they fired their last rounds, but the French soon realised their advantage and began climbing over roofs and walls, knowing that the Germans could not shoot them. Frenchmen took deliberate aim and killed man after man of Baring's force like sitting ducks. The end was near, for the odds were at least four to one in favour of the French. A door next to the open passage through the barn was broken down, but the Germans held the passage beyond with bayonets and musket butts only.

About this time, the Prince of Orange observed that La Haye Sainte was surrounded. He ordered Ompteda to use what was left of his brigade to attack the tirailleurs covering the principal French forces attacking the place. The gallant German, a professional soldier of many years' experience and a Peninsular veteran, told the Prince of the French cavalry concealed in the blind area to the west of the farm. But the Prince would not listen; at the age of twenty-three, he knew all the answers and retorted with words implying doubt of Ompteda's personal courage.

The KGL brigade commander formed his two remaining battalions, the 5th and 8th Line, and advanced.[2] They drove back the tirailleurs and may have reached the north-west corner of the garden. They were not far from clearing the approaches to the open barn gate and passageway facing west when a strong force of French cavalry burst from the hollow south-west of the farm, swept up the slope and caught them in line. Ompteda was killed and the 8th Line practically destroyed;[3] the 5th Line to the east was more fortunate, managed to form square and retreated under cover of a partial charge of what remained of the Household Brigade which stopped and drove back the cuirassiers. But La Haye Sainte was not relieved.

The end came for Baring and his men a few minutes later, shortly

---

[1] This shortage of ammunition is difficult to explain and has been the subject of considerable controversy. The Duke is said by *Chad*, 3, and others to have blamed Baring for not cutting an opening in the rear wall of the dwelling, but *Kennedy*, 96, points out that there was a doorway. *Cotton*, 32, says that there were four windows also. Rifle cartridges were in use by the 1/95th and other units nearby. *Beamish*, II, 363, was probably right when he says, 'The cart which should have brought it was upset in the general confusion that existed on the Brussels road', but why was none borrowed from another brigade?

[2] The companies of the 1st Light not in La Haye Sainte were probably skirmishing.

[3] *Cotton*, 89–90: 'The 8th was dropped upon quite unawares, and nearly all destroyed. Colonel Schroder was wounded mortally; ensign Moreau, who carried the King's colour, was severely wounded, and the colour carried off by the enemy.'

after 6 p.m.[1] They were driven through the courtyard and into the farmhouse; they did not have a single round of ammunition, but held the doorway for several minutes with bayonets only. The French could take almost any liberties with the riflemen now; they climbed on a cart and fired at a range of under ten yards. The fight was hopeless; Baring tried to retreat through the small doorway on the northern side of the dwelling. Only a few made it, for the French took the house by storm. A pitiful remnant, Baring and forty-two men, managed to get through the garden.[2] Once in the open, they were comparatively safe, for the 1/95th still held the sandpit and the knoll to the rear of it. The British riflemen shot any French who pursued.

The capture of La Haye Sainte was the first tangible success achiéved by the French all day, but it dangerously weakened the centre of Wellington's position. The French had a strong base for further operations in this immediate vicinity. They reinforced their troops in the garden north of the buildings and in the buildings themselves and forced the 1/95th to retire from both the sandpit and the knoll. At such close range, French muskets were almost as effective as the British rifles and could be loaded and fired more rapidly. The 95th fell back to the hedge in front of the Ohain road.

The French tirailleurs now extended irregularly, but in dense firing lines, both east and west of the newly won farm and sandpit. They advanced under the crest to positions from which they could fire on the Allies while at least partly protected themselves. They even brought forward some light field-pieces and placed them in the garden north of La Haye Sainte. The guns opened on Kempt's, Lambert's and Alten's squares at ranges of below 300 yards, but they could not be kept in action because of the accurate fire of individual riflemen of the 95th. Other pieces, however, were brought up in this area and to the west of it which could and did maintain their fire.

The French grand battery was still able to fire on some of the Allied troops over the heads of the tirailleurs; French infantry and some

[1] The exact time has been widely debated, but *Robinson*, III, 601, says, 'Charras, Hooper, and Ropes make the farmhouse itself fall also before 4 p.m., but the evidence now is that it did not fall till 6.30 p.m. See Schwartfeger's *Geschichte der Koniglich Deutschen Legion, 1803–1816* (1907); also Oman, in *Cambridge Modern History*, vol. ix., p. 638. Probably the smoke and flames of the farmhouse, and the capture of the garden and orchard, led to the contradictory opinions formed.' *Pratt*, 176, *Wood*, 153, *Creasy*, 390, and *Wolseley*, 178, also agree roughly on 6 p.m., give or take a few minutes.

[2] *Saunders*, 235.

6-pounders moved up to ranges of less than 100 yards all along the line. In favourable places where the tirailleurs could take advantage of undulations in the ground, they were less than 50 yards from their targets. Wellington's light troops could no longer hope to cope with the tirailleurs, for entire French brigades were now operating as irregular infantrymen, each man pressing forward to do as much damage as possible. The French artillery at close range plus the 'tirailleurade' had temporarily silenced most of the Allied guns in the area behind La Haye Sainte almost as far west at Hougoumont. These were the tactics of the early French Republican Armies, but had not been used much during the Empire.

Wellington reacted to this new system with characteristic efficiency. He was above Hougoumont when La Haye Sainte fell and faced with the same sort of problem. An eyewitness tells how he solved it. 'The exposed situation of the 3/1st Guards, the fire from which in square was necessarily so vastly disproportioned to that by which it was assailed, caught the eye of the Duke who immediately rode up to the battalion, and ordered it to form line' in a special way four deep by wheeling a side and half the rear face around each end of the front of the square as a pivot. The battalion drove off the tirailleurs with volleys and a controlled charge. 'A body of French cavalry was now seen approaching, but the battalion reformed square with great rapidity and regularity. The cavalry refused the square, but receiving its fire, and then dashing along the front of the 52nd regiment, it exposed itself to another vigorous fire by which it was nearly destroyed. The 3rd battalion of the 1st Guards retired in perfect order to its original position.'[1]

Wellington then sent the 1/52nd and perhaps other units of Adam's Brigade against the tirailleurs, probably in the same four-rank lines, with similar success.[2] The other Allied units in this area appear to have done more or less the same thing. Actually, the French formation was too compact for its own safety and vulnerable to fire. The French cavalry behind these tirailleurs should have been reliable, but did not protect them. Most of the horsemen remembered their unsuccessful attacks earlier in the afternoon and did not want to charge British and KGL infantry again regardless of its formation.

We should remark that this tirailleur type of attack would have been suicide if Wellington's best battle cavalry had not destroyed itself

[1] *Leeke*, I, 89.
[2] *Gardner*, 321.

earlier. Even the light brigades of British and KGL horsemen behind the centre had been used up against the French cavalry attacks. The Dutch-Belgian horse was still in this area, but these units would not charge at all.

Once the French began to retire in the angle above Hougoumont, they retreated all the way almost in panic. The Allied ascendancy was completely restored. Farther east, however, things were going badly. For once, Wellington was not personally at the point of greatest stress. Alten's Division, together with the Nassau contingent under Kruse which acted with it all day, was now in serious trouble. The brigades of Kempt, Pack and Lambert to the east were also subjected to a lethal combination of artillery and tirailleur fire. The 1/27th of Lambert's Brigade in square next to the Genappe road received a heavier fire than any endured by a force that Wellington commanded in the Penin-sula.[1] If casualties continued long at their present rate, the battalion would literally be killed where it stood. The eastern square of Halkett's Brigade, the 2/30th and the 2/73rd together in a single formation, suffered severely from heavy artillery fire from the grand battery, fire from lighter guns at close ranges, and finally from the intense 'tirail-leurade'. Their ammunition was temporarily so low that they were unable to return an adequate volume of fire in their own defence. The other square formed by the 33rd and 2/69th had suffered almost as much; both were in poor shape. Colin Halkett had 'asked that his brigade, which had lost two-thirds, should be relieved for a short time; but there was no reserve to take its place; and Wellington replied, "Tell him, what he asks is impossible: he and I, and every Englishman on the field, must die on the spot which we now occupy."'[2]

The rest of Alten's Division had also been sorely tried. Alten himself had been wounded and carried from the field. Ompteda was dead and his brigade sacrificed partly owing to the folly of the Prince of Orange. Kielmansegge now commanded the division, but his own four re-maining Hanoverian battalions were in two squares and receiving an extremely heavy fire. Kruse's Nassauers were not much better off, although they had been a trifle more protected by terrain.

The gap which was opening in Wellington's line from Lambert west almost to the Guards was extremely serious. The Duke had just driven back the tirailleurs with the 1/3rd Guards, the 1/52nd and some

---

[1] *Life of a Soldier*, II, 189, says, 'The 27th had not been long in their new position before they lost 400 men, without firing a shot . . .' See also *Leach*, 391.

[2] *Clinton*, 421.

other units above Hougoumont when Shaw Kennedy, Alten's chief executive officer, brought him the bad news.

This very startling information he received with a degree of coolness, and replied to in an instant with such precision and energy, as to prove the most complete self-possession. He left the impressions that he was perfectly calm during every phase, however serious, of the action. He felt confident of his own powers of being able to guide the storm which raged around him; and from the determined manner in which he then spoke, it was evident that he had resolved to defend to the last extremity every inch of the position which he then held. His Grace's answer to my representation was, 'I shall order the Brunswick troops in reserve behind Maitland to the spot, and other troops besides [Vincke's Hanoverians and Vivian's light cavalry from the east]. Go you and get all the German troops of the division to the spot that you can, and all guns that you can find.'[1]

The importance of Wellington's system of reserves now appears with startling clarity. He ordered forward the fresh battalions from the Brunswick contingent which he had saved for just such an emergency. He may have led these personally east, turned them north after a march of about 300 yards, and brought them forward to the crest. He ordered Vincke's Hanoverians to the same general area from behind PLHS and sent Freemantle to the east to hurry up the Prussians.[2]

Wellington also decided to bring Vivian's Brigade of light cavalry from the extreme left flank to the centre; the Duke sent Seymour with this order who delivered it apparently just as Vivian was making up his mind to do the same thing.[3] Years later Vivian wrote:

About six o'clock [more likely 6.45 p.m.] I learnt that the cavalry in the centre had suffered terribly, and the Prussians having by that time formed to my left, I took upon myself to move off from our left, and moved directly to the centre of our line, where I arrived most opportunely, at the instant that Buonaparte was making his last and most desperate effort; and never did I witness anything so terrific; the ground actually covered with dead and dying, cannon shots and shells flying thicker than I ever heard even musketry before, and our troops – some of them – giving way.[4]

We return now to Alten's Division. Vivian arrived and deployed in line behind it just as the Brunswick battalions moved up between

---

[1] *Kennedy*, 128.
[2] *Siborne's Letters*, 21, quoting Freemantle.
[3] ibid., 20, quoting Seymour. See also *Müffling's Passages*, 245-7.
[4] *Vivian*, 303.

Lambert and Maitland against the near-victorious tirailleurs and French light artillery. The young Brunswick soldiers, thrown suddenly into an extremely dangerous situation, recoiled and broke, but were stopped by Vivian's line. Wellington himself managed to rally these troops and brought them forward again so that they formed a base of fire just out of musket range of La Haye Sainte. What was left of Ompteda's and Kielmansegge's Brigades rallied on the east; Kruse's Nassauers and Halkett's Brigade did the same to the west.[1] British and German infantry in formed lines exchanged fire at close range with the French tirailleurs. For several minutes the issue hung in the balance; then Wellington's new deployments suddenly won. The tirailleurs broke and retreated, so British and KGL artillerymen could re-man some of their pieces and go into action against the French infantry and light artillery. The situation now changed abruptly; the French melted away again, leaving some of their cannon. The Duke's main line was restored from Hougoumont to PLHS, save that La Haye Sainte still remained in French hands.

The Prince of Orange played his final part in the battle of Waterloo during this period. At about the time that Wellington was rallying the Brunswickers, the young Prince, who certainly did not lack physical courage, did the same with Kruse's Nassau infantry and led them forward in the area just to the east of Halkett against French infantry and artillery which was apparently supported by cavalry under the slope to the south. But the Nassauers did not stay together long enough to suffer the disaster that usually followed the Prince's orders. At the first discharge from the tirailleurs, they broke and fled, but were stopped again by the Allied cavalry lines. One musket ball hit the Prince in the left shoulder and knocked him off his horse; he was carried from the field.[2] The Nassauers were rallied again and brought forward into place as French pressure was reduced.

The respite which followed the tirailleur fight was welcomed; the Duke reorganised his batteries and supplied them all with ammunition. Cartridges were served out to all Allied infantry battalions. The 1/95th cleaned their rifles and again took over the handling of the French sharpshooters in La Haye Sainte. Wellington also brought up units

[1] The Nassauers had been caught by Vivian's British-KGL cavalry in line behind the Allied centre. According to Morris (of the 73rd), *passim*, Halkett's Brigade also retired a short distance without orders during this ordeal. Morris seems to remember the battle through a kind of alcoholic haze.

[2] The wound was not mortal; he attended a ball not long afterwards.

not yet seriously engaged. Detmer's Brigade of Chassé's Division was placed in the first line between Colin Halkett's well-tried men and Kruse's Nassauers. D'Aubreme's Brigade from the same division was placed in support where the four battalions of Brunswickers had been until they were required.

About this time, Wellington received positive assurance that at least some Prussian troops were finally moving to support him. A part of Thielemann's Corps was advancing on PLHS by the lower Ohain road. Vandeleur's light cavalry Brigade was brought over from the left and aligned with Vivian's, extending this reasonably fresh line of effective cavalry almost to a level with Hougoumont.

XI

The Prussians on 18 June 1815

We should learn something of the movements of the Prussian Army on the 18th in order to understand the last two phases of the battle of Waterloo. These were dependent upon what had occurred before, during and after the battle of Ligny. Ziethen's Prussian Corps had been in action on 15 June as we have seen; Ziethen's, Pirch's and Thielemann's Corps had fought at Ligny on the 16th. They initially had a combined strength over 88,000, but with battle casualties and later desertions had lost more than 25,000 of these.[1] The three corps had a total strength of slightly more than 60,000 men when they finally arrived at Wavre in the late afternoon of the 17th. Bülow's Corps, so far unengaged and numbering more than 28,000, did not arrive in the area until after nightfall.

Wellington knew before midnight that Blücher had his entire force concentrated in the vicinity of Wavre. The most distant corps (Bülow's) was less than fourteen miles from PLHS. About 2 a.m. on the 18th the Duke received Blücher's assurance that the Prussians were marching 'at dawn' to support the Anglo-Dutch Army. In this latitude the sun rose on the 18th of June about 3.50 a.m., so that a literal interpretation of 'dawn' would mean a start at about 3.30 a.m.

Wellington always made allowance for human weakness. Armies that march and fight in the long days of June in northern Europe must have more hours for rest and food than those of darkness only. Perhaps the most common failing of historians who have written about this campaign is to forget this completely. A dawn start just was not possible under the logistical conditions of that era when men had been fighting

[1] *Ropes*, 159, citing particularly Charras and Gneisenau.

and/or marching for the previous three days. The Duke realised that a 3.30 start was impossible, but undoubtedly expected one between 6 and 8 a.m.

Wellington knew also that the Prussian Army relied to a considerable extent on its artillery and that the Prussian field-guns were considerably heavier and clumsier than his own. In the Prussian Army 100 per cent of the artillery was assigned to corps; each would undoubtedly bring all its pieces. The Duke also appreciated the rain-sodden and generally poor condition of the lateral roads by which Blücher's forces would have to move.[1] On the other hand, armies of all ages have had to march and fight in mud; the Prussian equipment and march procedures had been evolved in part to contend with just such conditions.

The distance from the centre of Wavre to the midpoint of PLHS was 13,730 yards or 7·8 miles.[2] The distance by roads as they then existed cannot be precisely determined because of changes in the road system, but it probably was not more than about 10 miles.[3] An 8 a.m. start should have meant an arrival on the battlefield between 12 noon and 2 p.m. in spite of all road troubles. Wellington certainly did not expect to have to fight a battle against the entire French Army without any active help from the Prussians until between 4.30 and 5 p.m. and no direct support until after 7 p.m.

The final tremendous victory which Wellington and·Blücher jointly gained and Wellington's own inflexible resolve not to blame subordinates or Allies has badly beclouded this entire feature of the campaign. The gallant efforts which Blücher himself made to fulfil his promises and the ultimate successful arrival of the Prussians on the scene has further thrown into the background the fundamental question of why they did not come at a reasonable time to support Wellington's army in its fight against the French.

Why did the Prussians take so long to move ten miles when the fate of Europe might have depended upon their speed? One factor which

---

[1] *Bain*, 131, quotes Wellington as saying, 'The roads are heavy. They cannot be here before two or three o'clock.'

[2] This was computed from modern 1: 50,000 Ordnance maps supplied through the courtesy of the Belgian Army and Lieutenant-Colonel Stan Leon McClellan, U.S. Army, who was a member of the U.S. Military Assistance and Advisory Group in Brussels in 1960.

[3] Topographical research in this area is difficult because of changes in place names and the location of roads. Even Commandant Emile Dehond of the Belgian Staff College, a true expert in this field, cannot follow the old roads everywhere. Some have degenerated into farm tracks, and some have been lost entirely in ploughed fields and pasture.

contributed to their late arrival was the poor and waterlogged roads already mentioned. Another was the strange set-up at Prussian head-quarters.

It was no secret to Europe that old Prince Blücher, who had passed his 70th year, understood nothing whatever of the conduct of a war; so little, indeed, that when a plan was submitted to him for approval, even relating to some unimportant operation, he could not form any clear idea of it, or judge whether it were good or bad. This circumstance made it necessary that some one should be placed at his side, in whom he had confidence, and who possessed inclination and skill to employ it for the general weal. Gneisenau had proved himself to be such a man during two campaigns; and since it was by these very campaigns that Blücher had gained his European renown, there was no reason for not entrusting him with the command of the Prussian Army precisely as in the two past years.[1]

Gneisenau practically ran the Prussian Army; as we have seen, he was senior to three of the four Prussian corps commanders. Müffling and Grolman were also on this staff and both Lieutenant-Generals. As we know, Müffling had been assigned to Wellington's headquarters as liaison officer. His British counterpart with Blücher was Lieutenant-Colonel Sir Henry Hardinge, aged thirty. The Prussian staff was even at this time more powerful than in most other armies and Gneisenau was Chief of Staff.

There was a distinct personality clash between Gneisenau and Wellington; the Duke can hardly have been ignorant of this. Although never explained, this state of affairs is easy to prove. 'General von Gneisenau warned Müffling to be much on his guard with the Duke of Wellington, for that by his relations with India, and his transactions with the deceitful Nabobs, this distinguished general had so accustomed himself to duplicity, that he had at last become such a master in the art as even to outwit the Nabobs themselves.'[2]

Gneisenau not only disliked Wellington, an attitude of mind that is not at all unusual either during the Duke's life or later, but also appears to have doubted his integrity, honesty and sense of duty to

---

[1] *Müffling's Passages*, 225. *Stanhope Conversations*, 119, says, 'I asked the Duke whether General Gneisenau had not been an excellent tactician? "Not exactly a tactician, but he was very deep in strategy. By strategy, I mean a previous plan of the campaign; by tactics, the movements on the field of battle. In tactics Gneisenau was not so much skilled. But Blücher was just the reverse – he knew nothing of plans of campaign, but well understood a field of battle."'

[2] *Müffling's Passages*, 212.

his country and to his Allies. Even Wellington's worst enemies have rarely accused him of anything of this nature. The Duke's rectitude was beyond question.

Gneisenau was temporarily in command of the Prussian Army after Blücher was unhorsed and injured at Ligny; Bülow and his Corps had not yet come up. Even though the new commander ordered the move in the direction of Wavre, he endeavoured on the night following 16 June to have the Prussian Army move in such a way that they would leave an even wider gap between themselves and Anglo-Dutch Army. Blücher and Grolman finally persuaded him to continue the retreat north instead of turning east towards Liège.[1] Even though Gneisenau had been persuaded to support the Duke, he conjured up phantoms in his own mind of a possible predicament into which the Prussians might get if they moved promptly west from Wavre on the morning of the 18th. For unknown reasons, he suspected Wellington of some sort of plan to fight a rear-guard action only and then retreat in order to leave Blücher's army to be destroyed.

On the night of 17 June three of the four Prussian corps were bivouacked around Wavre on both sides of the Dyle. Bülow's Corps, the one not engaged at Ligny, was at Dion-le-Mont some three to four miles farther east. Even though this corps was the most distant from Wellington's army, it was ordered to lead the Prussian advance towards Waterloo and given a specific route which led across a small bridge and through the town of Wavre. Pirch's Corps was ordered 'to follow behind Bülow's', even though it was initially four miles closer to the battlefield, and did not have to cross the Dyle or march through the narrow streets of a small Belgian town. Finally, Ziethen's Corps was ordered to move by a route more to the north, but to wait for both Bülow's and Pirch's Corps to pass across its line of march before starting. This kind of thing was certainly poor staff work, unless the staff had an object other than military efficiency. The movement was not even scheduled to start 'at dawn' in the orders issued, even though the promise to Wellington was made in these words.

We cannot blame Gneisenau for the condition of the roads or for a fire that broke out in Wavre and caused Bülow's Corps an additional

---

[1] *Fuller's Decisive Battles*, II, 217, says, 'Gneisenau, who did not trust Wellington and considered him to be a knave, urged that the army should fall back on Liège, but Blücher, still full of fire and supported by Grolman, disagreed, and it was decided to maintain contact with the English.' *Fuller* cites *Stanhope's Conversations*, 108–10.

delay, but we can for his extreme restrictions on the free movement of his corps, which must have been intentional. An objective researcher many years later concluded that 'The Prussians were late, very late, partly because of muddy roads and a fire in Wavre, but chiefly because Gneisenau intentionally delayed the troops, owing to his mistrust of Wellington.'[1]

In spite of everything, the head of Bülow's infantry and artillery column was at Saint Lambert before noon; this little village is no more than two miles from Ohain and four and a half miles from Plancenoit. Saint Lambert was situated on an eminence to the east of the so-called Lasne river.[2] The road west descended the hill, crossed the stream by a small bridge and went up the other side. It was so waterlogged that it presented extreme problems for the heavy Prussian artillery; Grolman called this stretch a defile.

The Prussian Army halted at Saint Lambert for two reasons. First, the fire in Wavre had caused a gap in the column which would take an hour to close. Second, Gneisenau thought of the Lasne as a kind of Rubicon which once crossed would leave the Prussians irrevocably committed to fight the French to a finish regardless of what happened to Wellington. Blücher and Grolman had to argue for some time to persuade the Chief of Staff to advance beyond this point. No subordinate could ever have caused ten seconds of irresolution in Wellington's mind, but Gneisenau appears to have dominated Blücher completely, save when the old gentleman was actually commanding troops in battle. This Saint Lambert-Lasne delay probably lasted for about two and a half hours, although the break in Bülow's column because of the Wavre fire would have cost one of these anyway.

Bülow's Corps started down the hill, across the stream and up the other side about 2 p.m. The going was bad, but Blücher exerted himself personally to the very limit to get his army forward over those last two and a half miles. 'Forward, boys!' he cried. 'Some I hear say it can not be done, but it must be done! I have given my word to Wellington and you will surely not make me break it.

---

[1] *Aldington*, 239. *Fortescue*, X, 342, is less charitable and says, 'No intellectual eminence can exalt a nature so essentially low as this, a nature which, from sheer terror of that which is high, abases all others to its own vile and despicable level. It was not the fault of Gneisenau that the campaign of Waterloo did not end disastrously for the Allies.'

[2] This stream is insignificant now, no more than a moderate brook which a middle-aged historian can jump without difficulty. It appears likely, however, that it was larger 150 years ago and did not have such strong banks. It may have presented on 18 June 1815 a much greater military obstacle than we can now visualise.

Only exert yourselves a little longer, children, and certain victory is ours.'[1]

Blücher could not have been more steadfast and loyal to his ally and friend. On the other hand, the Prussians were not really moving in support of Wellington, but to take the French Army in the flank while it was attacking the Anglo-Dutch. This was undoubtedly a fine military decision and led ultimately to the completeness of victory, but it was not the quickest way to bring the support originally promised to Wellington's army much earlier. Gneisenau was moving as he had not wished Wellington to do on the 16th from Quatre Bras because of the additional time involved.[2]

Even though the Prussian infantry and artillery were not in sufficient strength to go into action south-west of Paris wood until 4.30 p.m., they had relieved Wellington indirectly of some possible French pressure well before that time. About noon of the 18th Napoleon and his staff had observed a concentration of unidentified troops east of the Emperor's headquarters at La Belle Alliance.[3] These were 'the advanced guard of General Bülow', according to a dispatch carrier from Bülow to Wellington who was captured and gave information willingly.[4] He said further that the whole Prussian Army 'passed last night at Wavre'. The Emperor ordered two divisions of cavalry to move east about 3,500 yards towards these Prussians and supported them with Lobau's two infantry divisions. This French force made no effort to advance further; throughout the mid-afternoon the only fighting in the area was cavalry skirmishing. But if these troops and guns had not moved east to face the Prussians, they would have been available for assaulting Wellington's position. They appear to have numbered about '8,000 infantry, 3,000 cavalry, and 32 guns'.[5]

Between 4.30 and 5 p.m., Bülow's Corps was sufficiently closed up to begin a combat advance. The Prussians attacked towards Plancenoit from west of Paris wood by deploying infantry and artillery behind a cavalry screen. A Prussian infantry brigade, equal in size to a division in other armies, advanced in line of battalion columns on each side of

---

[1] *Henderson's Blücher*, 301; *Siborne*, 491.

[2] See Chapter IV, p. 51, above.

[3] The Emperor spent most of the battle seated on a chair with a small table and charts in front of him on an eminence behind this small inn. His method of command was so very different from that of the Duke who personally looked to everything possible.

[4] *Houssaye*, 190, who believes that this took place a bit before 1 p.m.

[5] *Fortescue*, X, 359.

a straight road leading towards Plancenoit.[1] Initially the Prussian advance appears to have been quickly checked, but Blücher brought up reinforcements and pushed Lobau back into and through Plancenoit with heavy fighting.[2] Napoleon threw in the 'Young Guard', expelled the Prussians from all parts of the village, and drove Bülow's Corps back apparently for more than a mile. Pirch's Corps was now up, however, and the two together pushed back both Lobau and the 'Young Guard', regaining possession of this vital village. Prussian field artillery was sending round shot across the Genappe road in the vicinity of La Belle Alliance at about 7 p.m., perhaps while Wellington was undergoing north of La Haye Sainte the most serious trial of his military career.

Napoleon now reinforced his eastern flank in two ways. First, he confirmed by orders the existing arrangements south of PLHS. Durutte's Division, the most easterly of d'Erlon's Corps, was now facing to the east rather than the north; Lobau continued this line south to the 'Young Guard' opposite Plancenoit. Second, the Emperor reinforced these troops with two battalions of the Imperial Guard, the 1/2nd Grenadiers and the 1/2nd Chasseurs. Seldom have 1,000 bayonets accomplished so much: 'With their drums beating, these old veterans charged forward in close columns of platoons [a column with a front of about 30 files and a depth of 36 ranks]. They outdistanced the Young Guard, which Duhesme was striving to rally, assaulted Plancenoit at two different points, forced their way in, without deigning to fire a shot, overthrew, trampled down, and drove out the mass of the Prussians. The attack was so impetuous, that in twenty minutes the whole village was swept.'[3]

The French eastern flank was restored, but at last Wellington and Blücher had achieved a concentration on the field of battle. Part of Ziethen's small Prussian Corps was finally in actual support of the Anglo-Dutch Army. We will discuss what was done in this area

[1] This road is no longer passable throughout the year by motor vehicles, but is still easily recognisable. Commandant Dehond pointed it out to me as the 'axial road down which the Prussians came'. We traced it from Plancenoit back through the area formerly called Paris wood to the village called Lasne in 1815, opposite the old Saint Lambert on the hill towards Wavre.

[2] The smoke from the artillery engaged in the action was seen by Wellington from behind Hougoumont towards the end of the French cavalry attacks on his right centre. One can see the spire of the Plancenoit church from several points in the Anglo-Dutch position, but no roofs of ordinary houses or anything lower.

[3] *Houssaye*, 218.

in the next chapter which is devoted to the left flank of the Duke's army.

We must now survey briefly the portion of the French Army which had been sent after the Prussians from the battlefield of Ligny. This force under Marshal Grouchy began its movement early in the afternoon of 17 June fettered by all sorts of specific directives.[1] It would appear that if this most unfortunate and most junior marshal had carried out his instructions, he could not possibly have been at Waterloo.[2] He did, however, attack the Prussians he was told to follow on the afternoon of the 18th both at Wavre and farther west along the Dyle at Limale. Grouchy had about 33,000 men including ample cavalry and artillery.

Blücher was informed of Grouchy's attack, which soon developed into a battle. Thielemann's Corps was alone and considerably outnumbered; Bülow's, Pirch's and Ziethen's were either already engaged at Waterloo, or on their way there. Blücher realised that the fate of Europe rested on what happened against Napoleon – the Grouchy-Thielemann fight was really unimportant – and he only sent Thielemann instructions to do as well as possible with the force he already had. There would be no reinforcements.[3]

---

[1] The attempts to make Grouchy responsible for Napoleon's defeat at Waterloo are discussed in detail in Part Two, Chapter III, 'French Mistakes'.

[2] *Gardner*, 153, claims that 'a strong Prussian detachment of all arms was at Mont Saint Guibert to prevent an unopposed union of Bonaparte and Grouchy'.

[3] *Henderson's Blücher*, 300.

XII

The Left Flank

We should take a brief look at what happened on the left flank, an area hardly mentioned so far. The fighting in and around PLHS is the least known of any that occurred at Waterloo because of several factors. No British or KGL infantry units were involved; Wellington personally did not figure in this combat. He was certainly east of the Genappe road, but did not go as far as Papelotte after the Hougoumont fight started. The British cavalry brigades of Vivian and Vandeleur which were stationed more or less behind PLHS were not called upon actively to support the Netherlands infantry in the area, so no memoirs and little in the way of original records of this fighting survive in English. Further, the Netherlands infantry brigade most involved were Saxe-Weimar's Nassau troops serving in the Netherlands Army. The papers of their officers seem to have disappeared.[1]

Most studies in both French and English have, at least by omission, tended to conclude that the fighting on Wellington's left flank was unimportant. Relatively speaking, this is probably correct because the French in this area were never close to gaining anything of real value. We should not lose sight, however, of the contribution to the final victory made by these Nassauers, nor the peculiar conditions under which they fought.

Combat in the PLHS area was quite different from that farther west because of terrain and buildings. (See Map 8 which is based on Craan's

[1] I acknowledge with gratitude and pride the great assistance that Commandant Dehond has been to me in this area also. He has passed on to me not only some of his own great knowledge, but also several books about which I would not have heard without his aid. But there is still far less known of this part of the battlefield, and even more contradictions.

map and my own actual tramping about in the area.) The most important feature here is the defile directly south of the two farms, Papelotte and La Haye.[1] The hamlet of Smohain is situated in this deep small valley astride a stream of the same name which originates a short distance to the west.[2] A branch of the Ohain road runs south-east past Papelotte and follows this stream east to Ohain and Wavre; other less important roads, all uncobbled at the time of the battle, connect Smohain with Plancenoit and Papelotte with La Belle Alliance. Another road runs south-east from Smohain past Frischermont,[3] a château similar to Hougoumont. All these roads cut so deeply into the sandy clay hillsides as to present extreme problems for cavalry or infantry in formation trying to cross them.[4] The small stream running through marshland, the sunken roads and the defile itself were considerable military obstacles, particularly in view of the wet condition of the countryside on 18 June 1815.

The farms of La Haye and Papelotte were both enclosed structures, but had detached dependent buildings south of them. Further, there were two isolated dwellings in the defile south-west of Papelotte.[5] Smohain, situated on both sides of the brook, contained about twelve separate major buildings. The centre of this hamlet was about 630 yards from La Haye, 900 yards from Papelotte, and 540 from Frischermont.[6] The last is a full 1,170 yards from Papelotte and high up the southern side of the valley.[7]

The low hill used by the French grand battery in preparing the way for d'Erlon's attack and in the later fighting comes to an end about

[1] Papelotte was rebuilt and enlarged during the nineteenth century, but La Haye remains much as it was in 1815.

[2] Names have been confused in this area also. Smohain is also known as La Marache. The Nassauers in their official report almost certainly confused Papelotte with Frischermont.

[3] Occupied by Marlborough as his headquarters in 1705.

[4] These roads show clearly on Craan's map (made in 1816) and are still in use. The roadbeds are now partially cobbled, but in some places 15 feet below the surface of the fields. Banked hedges bordered most of these roads on both sides in 1815.

[5] Craan's map. They seem still to be in use in 1965. But a row of newer attached houses in this area makes positive identification difficult.

[6] I have used a 1:20,000 Ordnance map made in 1865 and last revised in 1906 for these estimates. Commandant Dehond gave me this map which shows clearly all places mentioned. I have used the Smohain crossroads and the centres of the three buildings enclosures for my measurements.

[7] Only the foundations and part of the outer walls of Frischermont remain, but the place was never fought over by infantry in spite of what *Boulger, passim,* says.

800 yards south and 200 yards west of Papelotte. A rather steep small valley enters the main mass of rolling upland south of this French artillery position. North of Papelotte and La Haye, where Vivian and Vandeleur spent most of the day, the land was again high and open, but no one any distance south or north of the two farms can see into the area around them because of the covered nature of the PLHS defile which begins west of Papelotte and extends east all the way to the village of Ohain, two miles away.

On the morning of the 18th, Wellington placed Saxe-Weimar's Brigade of Perponcher's Dutch-Belgian Division in the area between Smohain and the isolated dwellings west of Papelotte. This force of about 3,300 men consisted of both battalions of the Orange Nassau regiment and two of the three battalions of the 2nd Nassau Infantry, the 2nd and 3rd. The first battalion of the 2nd Nassau had been used, as we have seen, by Wellington in front of Hougoumont.[1] Saxe-Weimar sent out as skirmishers his four light companies which advanced well up the hill to the south. One battalion became the garrison for Smohain, La Haye and Papelotte. The other three were held in formation behind these buildings about half-way from the bottom of the defile to the crest of the ridge to the north, that is in front of Vivian's and Vandeleur's light cavalry brigades.[2] Saxe-Weimar had a battery of field-artillery at Quatre Bras, but was down to two guns and a howitzer at Waterloo which he placed on an eminence behind Smohain on his left.[3] He derived considerable benefit from Rettberg's KGL battery on his right and Picton's left. The Nassauers occupied a position about 1,000 yards long with many defensible structures on either side of the east-west defile and small stream.

The first serious fighting on the 18th probably occurred in the PLHS area. A French force of cavalry, artillery and some infantry penetrated as far as Frischermont well before the fighting at Hougoumont started. The French reconnaissance in force discovered nothing helpful. The defile was too serious an obstacle to be crossed easily; the country farther east appeared even worse. Although artillery fire was exchanged, the French retired after pushing the Nassau skirmishers back as far as the buildings. Saxe-Weimar did not attempt to hold Frischermont, probably because of specific orders from Wellington.

---

[1] Part of this battalion was later used in La Haye Sainte and part assigned to Cooke's Guards Division. See *Beamish*, II, 363 and *passim*, and *Harry Smith*, I, 268–9.

[2] *Aerts*, 225.

[3] *Boulger*, 22.

As we have seen, the Duke would only fight for a large farm or village if he could maintain supporting troops within musket shot of it as at Hougoumont. There was no chance of doing this at Frischermont because it was definitely too far up the southern face of the defile.

A great deal has been written about the infantry attack made by d'Erlon's four fine divisions. Most authorities, however, really discuss in detail only what the divisions of Quiot, Donzelot and Marcognet did. These were ranged in that order from west to east; the fourth under Durutte was in front of PLHS and is usually either ignored, or only given a few perfunctory words. The fate of the three western divisions has already been described in detail. Durutte on the east was probably ordered to advance in the same manner as the others, in a column formed of battalions in line, and presumably in echelon with the other three divisions. After careful study of this part of the battle-field as well as of the Waterloo literature, I believe not only that Durutte did not come forward with his division in close column of battalions in line, but that he could not have done this even if he wanted to. If he had headed for either Papelotte or La Haye, or any point between them, he would have had to negotiate the hedge-bordered sunken roads already described and then the defile. A talented professional soldier just would not have attempted the movement. He actually left two of his eight battalions as a kind of flank guard for Napoleon's grand battery and took forward only six, probably all in individual battalion columns at half or quarter distance, on a front of one or two companies. These smaller formations were better able to negotiate the difficult terrain of this area. Four probably attacked Smohain, La Haye and Papelotte, while the other two extended to the west to support Marcognet.[1]

Durutte's battalion columns were preceded by the usual tirailleurs and accompanied by light artillery. The Nassau skirmishers were quickly pushed back down the hill and through the defile.[2] Smohain fell quickly, probably to tirailleurs alone, but Durutte's columns met stiffer resistance as they tried to advance up the south face of the defile. They may have deployed into line so as to increase their firepower. The Nassauers fought stubbornly in favourable positions, however, while Saxe-Weimar fed in reinforcements from his battalions above. Ultimately he held both La Haye and Papelotte, but the French took isolated dwellings in the defile and some small outbuildings south of

---

[1] *Wood*, 143.
[2] *Life of a Soldier*, II, 182.

the two major farms, and temporarily may have penetrated into one of these built-up enclosures.[1] There were fairly heavy casualties on both sides.

The total defeat already narrated of d'Erlon's other three divisions placed Durutte in a dangerous position. Since he was the last to move forward in this echelon attack, he may not have had time fully to engage all his forces. A further advance up the hill would not only be difficult because of the determined resistance of the Nassauers, but extremely dangerous because both his flanks were 'in the air'. Vivian and Vandeleur had moved their light cavalry brigades forward into the area just west of Papelotte. If Durutte's infantry did gain ground and appear in the open, it might be exposed to a charge from flank and rear by British cavalry. Even more important, the temporary collapse of the entire French right must have caused Durutte to assume a kind of defensive holding position running from the high ground south of the two farms to the eastern end of the French grand battery. His troops were the only unbroken French infantry within a mile. He may have left small garrisons in some of the buildings that he had taken in the defile, but Saxe-Weimar's counter-attack certainly pushed the French back into the defile and may have forced them up the other side.

The next severe fighting in the PLHS area came about 6 p.m. following the French cavalry attacks on the right. In co-operation with the French tirailleur attacks all long the line east from Hougoumont, Durutte sent forward several battalions, not in column now, but as heavy masses of light infantry. The Nassauers were again forced back to the north side of the defile, probably again lost several isolated buildings, but continued to offer an efficient and successful resistance. The fighting continued for the better part of an hour; the French may have forced their way into one or both farms, but they could not hold them. Saxe-Weimar used his reserves wisely, adding companies to his garrisons as required.

Durutte seems to have made a final determined attack at the very end of this period of tirailleur fighting, say about 6.45 p.m. He wished apparently to seize the strong position held by Saxe-Weimar in order

---

[1] Several authorities including *Thiers*, 137, and *Saunders*, 240, believe that Durutte took the farms and held them for hours; *Clinton*, 409, says Papelotte was lost and then recovered by the Nassauers. It would appear that this irreconcilable confusion comes from mistakes in regard to names; Frischermont and perhaps Smohain, or part of it, did fall and may have remained in French hands for a long time, but I believe that the two main farms did not.

to offer more effective resistance to the Prussians who were now obviously approaching from the east along several different roads. This advance made some headway, but the farms did not fall. Durutte's Division had now, to some extent at least, become separated from d'Erlon's Corps and was starting to function as part of Lobau's. It was beginning to face east rather than north.

Saxe-Weimar's position was naturally strong; the Nassauers appear to have had both time and tools to strengthen it with barricades, loophole walls and buildings, and to post artillery so as to be partially protected, but able to support the infantry. Saxe-Weimar was a first-rate leader and a better than average tactical commander. He held La Haye and Papelotte securely during a period that was perilous for the Duke's first line farther to the west.

Saxe-Weimar and his Nassau Brigade must have felt isolated and alone, something almost unique for a brigade in a battle army commanded by Wellington. Why did this occur? Essentially, because the Nassauers did their job so well they did not need help. The Duke, after assigning them their defensive position, supported them with the two fine British cavalry brigades, those of Vivian and Vandeleur, and placed at least one battery, Rettberg's, so as to aid them with fire.[1] The two brigades of Hanoverian infantry assigned to Picton's Division were more or less connected with the Nassauers.

When the Duke realised that d'Erlon's whole corps was about to attack, he dispatched Lambert's Brigade, recently arrived on the field from Brussels,[2] to occupy a station behind and slightly to the west of the Nassauers. Saxe-Weimar probably never knew he had this support because of the configuration of the ground. When it turned out that the Nassauers did not need it, Wellington used Lambert's battalions – there were three only for the 2/81st had been left in Brussels – near the Genappe road to prevent any breakthrough there, as has already been related.

Wellington may have given unofficial command of the Allied forces on his left to the Prussian General Müffling, an able commander and a man of considerable professional ability and diplomacy. There were no British troops here after Vivian and Vandeleur left. Müffling had kept in constant communication throughout the day with the Prussian

---

[1] *Aerts*, 225, says that Vivian had a battery of British Horse Artillery which may have been in direct support of PLHS.

[2] They had arrived in Belgium from America only days before and had just reported to Wellington: *Harry Smith*, I, 268–9.

forces coming towards Waterloo from the east. He undertook no actual direction of combat forces, but was certainly instrumental in bringing the Prussians more quickly into the battle than would otherwise have been possible. Another source says of this:

The stability of Wellington's left virtually depended upon his connection with the Prussian Army; and the Duke recognised that on this flank General von Müffling could be most effectively employed. The Prussian Attaché, if placed on this flank, could direct the Prussian troops to their stations on the battlefield as they came up; for Blücher's Army were unacquainted with the topography of the field. Also it was essential that the Anglo-Dutch left, and the supporting Prussian troops, should act in complete accord, union and cohesion. To ensure this end would require the immediate presence of a superior officer, well known to both armies, and one who was capable of taking upon himself considerable responsibility. The Duke's selection of General von Müffling, to carry out these most important duties, was extremely wise; and with these ends in view he [the Duke] referred the Generals of the Anglo-Dutch left to General von Müffling.[1]

Because of the unusual marching arrangements and other troubles already discussed, Ziethen's infantry and artillery did not begin to reach the Smohain area until about 7 p.m. A real misunderstanding of serious proportions was narrowly avoided.

General Zieten's advanced guard, which I was expecting with the utmost impatience, suddenly turned round, and disappeared from the height. I hastened after this advanced guard and saw them in full retreat. General von Zieten, whom fortunately I soon overtook, had received instructions from the Field-Marshal, to close up to him, and wished very properly to effect this by going by Papelotte; but he changed his intention, when one of his officers, whom he had sent forward to ascertain how the battle was going, returned with intelligence that the right wing of the English was in full retreat. This inexperienced young man had mistaken the great number of wounded going or being taken to the rear to be dressed, for fugitives, and accordingly made a false report. On my assuring General von Zieten of the contrary, he instantly turned about and followed me.[2]

Müffling directed Ziethen's Corps to attack the hinge of the French line where it turned at a right angle from the forces engaged with Wellington to those facing Blücher. The Prussians arrived from Ohain, probably by a road beside the small stream in the defile, and saw the farms of Papelotte and La Haye still in possession of troops who

[1] *Becke*, II, 71.
[2] *Müffling's Passages*, 248–9.

appeared to be French because of their uniforms. They attacked immediately with artillery and fresh infantry. Saxe-Weimar and his men were taken by surprise, but assumed that they were being assaulted by Grouchy's French command which was known to be in the area to the east. They offered considerable resistance and caused fairly heavy casualties among the Prussians, but the Nassauers were tired from a whole day of working and fighting. Their barricades were not properly placed to resist an attack from the north-east. They were forced back up the steep hill to the north-west for a distance of several hundred yards.[1] The mistake was discovered, and the Nassauers rallied and brought back to the positions they had held for so long. They were not able, however, to take a prominent part in later fighting.

Ziethen's Corps turned south-west against Durutte's Division.[2] They were temporarily held up by the gallant Frenchmen in heavy fighting.[3] Blücher's whole force was making little progress, although it was engaged from the defile of Papelotte all the way south to Plancenoit. The situation remained essentially unchanged while Napoleon prepared and delivered his famous attack by the Imperial Guard on Wellington between Hougoumont and La Haye Sainte, known as the Crisis of the battle of Waterloo and to be described in the next chapter.

Saxe-Weimar and his Nassauers appear to have fought longer and better than any other part of the Dutch-Belgian Army. They held their assigned position against veteran French professional soldiers, even though initially outnumbered in men and guns. They were the only Netherlands brigade, with the exception of Detmer's of Chassé's Division, that Wellington did not have to rescue almost as soon as he sent it into combat. The Nassauers held for ten hours; if they had not been attacked from flank and rear by their allies, the Prussians, they might have taken an effective part in Wellington's final victorious counterstroke.

---

[1] There is evidence that the Nassauers discovered the identity of the Prussians before the Prussians realised that they were fighting friends. One wonders what Müffling was doing at this time and if he actually was in any sort of overall command.

[2] Ziethen's Corps numbered no more than 17,000 men because of casualties and desertions suffered 15-17 June. It was the only Prussian Corps to fight on the 15th and lost heavily at Ligny on the 16th also. It is probable that no more than 5,000 men of this unit were actually engaged at Waterloo. Their artillery fire seems to have done more harm to the Anglo-Dutch Army than the French.

[3] *Aerts*, 258, and some other authorities believe that the Prussians had to take Smohain from the French.

13. Hougoumont and the area south east, taken from above 13 in map 6. A was once covered by an extensive copse which somewhat shielded the building from French observation and fire. B was the garden and orchard area surrounded on three sides by walls and buildings and never taken. C changed hands several times. D was the 'protected' way which was held throughout. X is the Lion monument; Y the farm of Mont St Jean; Z the position of the Wellington elm.

14. Another aerial view of Hougoumont, taken from above 14 in map 6.

15. Hougoumont, showing entrance lane and 'protected' way.

Stone Garden Wall

Covered Way

Entrance Lane

16. Hougoumont. The ruins of the chapel are in the courtyard; the south garden wall centre left.

17. The buildings and garden wall of Hougoumont seen from the south, the way the French approached.

18. Hougoumont from the south, taken from 18 in map 6. The trees in the foreground remain from the once extensive copse.

19. The Hougoumont courtyard showing the chapel ruins, farm house and barns. The manor house once stood in the left foreground.

20. A closer view of the south entrance to Hougoumont, taken from 20 in map 6. Note bullet holes and commemorative plaques.

21. The middle of the 'protected' way, taken from 21 in map 6. The end of the east wall on the left, with the farm house seen beyond.

22. The 'protected' way north of Hougoumont.

23. Hougoumont, the south garden wall and what remains of copses and hedgerow, taken from the top of the east garden wall 23, in map 6. Area A was open but the French had to make their way through the copse to get to it. B is the farm house; C the chapel with the large barn behind. X is the old garden; the orchard lies behind the camera.

24. Hougoumont, corner of south and east garden wall. The bricked-up loopholes show clearly in the right foreground section. Farther to the left are some stone-lined loopholes, still open, made when the wall was built.

25. The intersection of the Genappe and Ohain roads. On the former (left) the farm of La Haye Sainte. The positions of the Lion monument and Hougoumont can be quickly determined.

Ohain Road

26. A general view of the centre and western sections of Wellington's position. Left to right foreground: La Haye Sainte, monuments, Ohain road.

27. La Haye Sainte with its orchard extending along the Genappe road. Below left, the KGL or Hanoverian monument; below right, the Gordon monument. La Belle Alliance, Napoleon's command post, was at A. The sandpit was at B.

28. La Haye Sainte from the west. This photograph and numbers 29–33 should be viewed in conjunction with map 7.

29. La Haye Sainte from the air.

30. The old main gate at La Haye Sainte with the dove- or pigeon-cote above. The entrance to the right, through which the Genappe road can be seen, was opened in the wall long after the battle.

31. The second door broken open by the French at La Haye Sainte. This east–west passage was held for several minutes by KGL riflemen, who were out of ammunition, with bayonets and rifle butts only.

32. The entrances to La Haye Sainte from the west (the small door, right, is post-Waterloo). The door of A was burnt on the night of 17 June, so the passage was barricaded with farm machinery and French dead. B was broken into, but held by KGL riflemen (see number 31).

33. North side of La Haye Sainte farm house showing the small projecting 'wing', formerly an enclosed well, mentioned in several battle accounts. French field pieces were placed there but their crews were shot by the 1/95th Rifles from south of the Ohain road.

34. The farms of Papelotte (left) and La Haye (bottom left).

35. Papelotte (centre) with La Haye on its right. On the far right is the hamlet of Smohain. Some of the outbuildings and detached houses were there in 1815.

36. Junction of the sunken roads south of Papelotte (left). La Haye appears right. Craan's map shows these roads as bordered by hedges at field level in 1815.

37. In the foreground, a La Haye outbuilding; in the background Papelotte, somewhat changed since the battle.

38. Smohain, left, and the site of the Château of Frischermont, centre. The Smohain brook shows clearly above the hamlet.

39. La Belle Alliance and the Genappe road running north to La Haye Sainte and the junction with the Ohain road.

40. The French Waterloo staging area.

Genappe Road

De Costa's House

Hugo Monument

La Belle Alliance

Plancenoit

41. Plancenoit. The church and churchyard changed hands many times during the afternoon of 18 June.

42. Plancenoit, seen from the direction in which the Prussians moved. The farm track in the foreground was once the best road there from Lasne–Chapelle St Lambert and was the axial road down which Bülow's Corps attacked.

43. The old bridge over the Lasne river near Chapelle St Lambert. The modern road is behind the camera.

44. The farm of Mont St Jean from across the Brussels–Charleroi (Genappe) road. This large block of buildings, like most of the other large farms, remains essentially unchanged. It was used as a hospital after the battle, but no French came near it on 18 June save as prisoners.

45. The forest of Soignes today, probably much as it was in 1815. An army, including artillery, could have passed through easily, either between the trees or along roads similar to that in the foreground.

46. The exterior hornwork and main gates of Péronne, fortified by Vauban. The Guards Light Companies blew in the doors to the hornwork and took this whole rather minor portion of the defences on 26 June. The city then surrendered in a couple of hours.

47. An example of the glorification of Bonaparte and the French Grande Armée. This was once the house and Museum of Sergeant-Major Cotton of the 7th Hussars. His relics are now gone and have been replaced by a 'Naporama'.

48. French 12-pounder of the Waterloo type. Les Invalides, Paris.

49. British Waterloo 9-pounder. Tower of London.

50. British Waterloo 6-pounder. The carriage is a replica. R.M.A., Sandhurst.

51. French Waterloo 6-pounder. R.M.A., Sandhurst.

52. French 6-inch (actual bore diameter 6.5 inches) field howitzer of the Waterloo type. A heavy, powerful weapon which fired both common shell and canister. Les Invalides, Paris.

53. British 5.5-inch howitzer and carriage of the Waterloo type. Rotunda Museum, Woolwich.

54. French small arms ammunition wagon of the Waterloo type. Les Invalides, Paris.

55. A Belgian innkeeper, now dead, and two of his many fine Waterloo relics: a British Baker carbine marked as having belonged to the 10th Hussars and a French heavy cavalry sword.

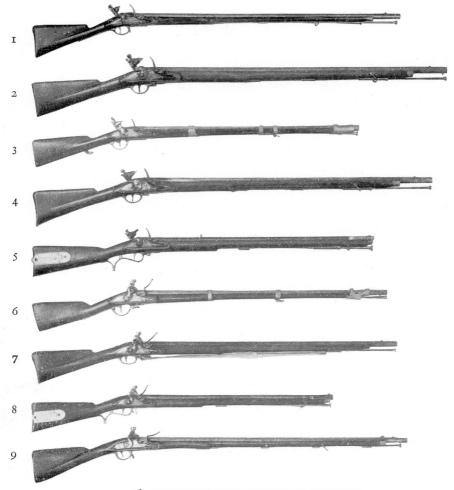

56. WATERLOO-TYPE SHOULDER FIREARMS

1. British Brown Bess musket, model II, with 42-inch barrel, four rammer pipes and fluted stock.

2. British Brown Bess musket, East India type, stamped 'Dublin Castle' with three rammer pipes and 39-inch barrel. Note, however, the goose-neck cock.

3. French musketoon, model 1777, which was standard throughout the Napoleonic period.

4. British Brown Bess musket, model III, with 39-inch barrel, three rammer pipes and fluted stock. Note the reinforced cock.

5. British Baker rifle, standard issue in the 60th, 95th and KGL light companies and battalions.

6. French infantry musket, model 1776, made throughout Napoleonic period.

7. British Brown Bess musket, East India model.

8. British Baker rifle.

9. Prussian Potsdam musket.

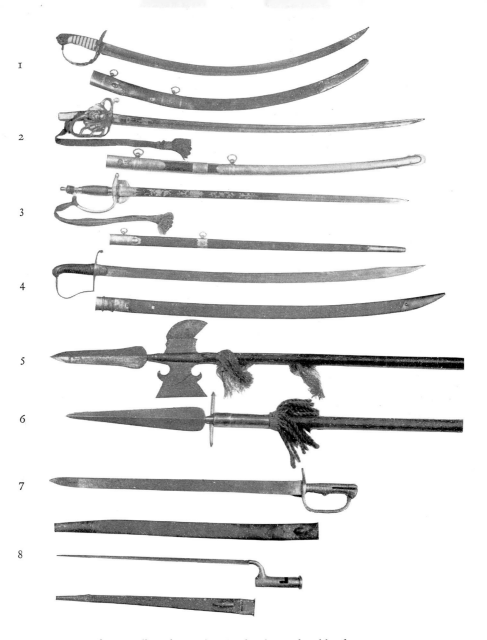

57. 1. British general's and Guards officer's sabre and scabbard.
2. French Imperial Guard sword and scabbard.
3. British infantry officer's sword and scabbard.
4. British Militia sabre and scabbard.
5. British Government issue infantry halberd.
6. British Government issue infantry spontoon.
7. Baker rifle 'sword', actually a bayonet, and scabbard.
8. Brown Bess musket bayonet and scabbard.

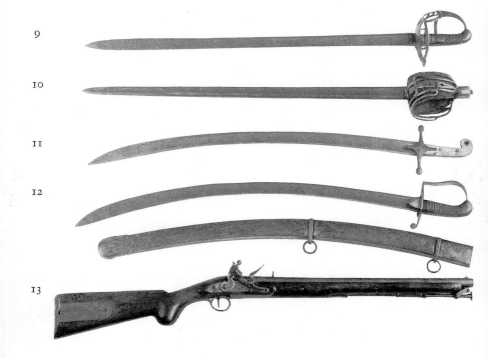

58. MISCELLANEOUS WATERLOO-TYPE WEAPONS

   9. British heavy cavalry sword.
10. Military claymore (broadsword).
11. Oriental-type sabre actually carried by British officer at Waterloo.
12. Standard light cavalry sabre and scabbard.
13. Baker rifle carbine.

XIII

The Crisis

We return to Wellington and the troops under his personal command. As we have seen, he had weathered the tirailleur attack and then restored his position, save for La Haye Sainte. The Duke's army was now compressed into a strong front extending from Hougoumont well to the east of the Genappe road. A pause of about half an hour followed the defeating of the tirailleurs. Only the French grand battery was firing and it slowly. Skirmishing died down to the lowest ebb of the day. The tirailleurs could now be held in check by the Duke's skirmishers, even though in some instances it was necessary to add line companies to the light companies in order to build up sufficient firepower in the security line.[1]

Wellington used this time to reorganise his artillery and repair pieces where possible. Many guns and howitzers had been out of action because of lack of gunners, damage to the pieces by enemy action, enlarged touch holes due to excessive firing and drooping barrels. Guns beyond repair were cannibalised for parts which could be used to get others back in action; crews were more evenly distributed along the front, even though to some extent pieces and men were interchanged between batteries. Infantry ammunition was served out, flints replaced, and the muskets and rifles cleaned where necessary.

Wellington's position was now as secure as it could possibly be from a direct attack, even though his army had probably shrunk to less than 35,000 men.[2] Many Dutch-Belgians had left the fight without excuse;

[1] *Morris*, 198–9, mentions that his line company as well as the light company of the 73rd was sent forward as skirmishers.

[2] *Müffling*, 31, says, 'Wellington's whole disposable force could not be more than 30,000 to 35,000 men.'

some unwounded men from other units had made their way to the rear 'to assist wounded comrades'. The foremost historian of the British Army says of these, 'Hundreds of the Netherlandish soldiers were hidden away in the forest of Soignes, where they lay at their ease with piled arms, cooking their soup and smoking until the time should come for them to advance in safety or to disperse to their homes, as the fortune of the day might dictate.'[1]

Chassé's newly arrived Division was fresh; at least a part of it was to play an honourable and important part in what lay ahead. As mentioned, Detmer's Brigade with Chassé personally in command was in the front line.[2] Vincke's Hanoverian Brigade was also reasonably fresh and now posted in reserve on both sides of the Genappe road. The Duke's flanks were secure. Hougoumont had become practically impregnable, due mainly to the skill, know-how and soaring morale of its defenders. The Prussians were finally arriving in strength beside PLHS. Farther west, where d'Erlon had attacked six hours before, all was well. The brigades of Best, Pack, Kempt and Lambert were depleted, but again efficient and confident.

We should review, however, Wellington's dispositions from the Genappe road west to Hougoumont, the area where the final French attack struck hardest. These units were, east to west, the remnant of Ompteda's KGL Brigade next to the road, Kielmansegge's Hanoverian Brigade, Kruse's Nassauers, the four Brunswick battalions brought up during the tirailleur fight, Detmer's recently added Dutch-Belgians,[3] and Colin Halkett's sadly reduced British Brigade, which in spite of two days of dreadful mauling, bungled commands and internal troubles was still in the first line. These units were all in the area occupied in the morning by Alten's Division; six brigades now held a front where three stood earlier. Two original batteries had been increased to at least five. In spite of casualties, there were now more Allied muskets and guns on this front than ever before during the day.

Farther west, there were Maitland's Guards, Adam's Brigade of still almost fresh light infantry, two battalions of Brunswickers held to-

---

[1] *Fortescue*, X, 367-8.

[2] Chassé did well in the French Army at Talavera and at Maya, and fifteen years after Waterloo was able to hold Antwerp with a garrison of 6,000 Netherlanders against a French force more than ten times as large.

[3] The position and accomplishments of Detmer's Brigade in defeating the final French attack are controversial. I have not followed my usual authorities in this connection and have placed particular reliance on *Houssaye* who was thorough, to some extent unprejudiced and acquainted with all the Dutch-Belgian writings.

gether by Mercer's Battery, R.H.A., and the 23rd. These troops were not quite so thick when their whole line was considered, but they were formed around an eighty-degree angle with Hougoumont at its apex and were protected by that bastion. The artillery here, what remained of five to seven batteries, was posted in part to fire on an enemy force advancing past Hougoumont from the flank, the most efficient angle for artillery before the advent of high-explosive bursting charges.

The brigades now in Alten's old area were to some extent fought out, or of questionable quality, but Wellington reinforced his position here by keeping Vivian's and now Vandeleur's cavalry in line close up behind the crest. In the earlier tirailleur fight, this type of line held both the Nassauers and Brunswickers close to their positions. It could do the same for Detmer's Brigade of Dutch-Belgians if necessary. The other brigade of Chassé's Division, D'Aubreme's, was placed in the second line behind Maitland's Guards.

Wellington realised that Napoleon had not used against the Anglo-Dutch Army any considerable portion of the Imperial Guard.[1] He sensed also that the recent slow-up in the battle so far as his troops were concerned was only a lull before a storm. In his battles since 1809, the Emperor had frequently softened up an area of the enemy's front before finally sending forward the Guard to clinch the victory. A French cavalry officer appears to have deserted at this time and confirmed the conclusion which Wellington had reached already. The Frenchman said, 'Get ready. That scoundrel Napoleon will be upon you with his Guard in less than half an hour.'[2]

We must digress for a moment to look at the formation of the infantry within the Imperial Guard as it fought at Waterloo. Their organisation was known to Wellington and other Allied commanders. There were three Guards infantry divisions, each composed of four regiments. One of these was the 'Young Guard', exhausted by the Prussians; these units do not concern us. There remained, however, two divisions of four regiments each, save for two or three battalions also now at Plancenoit. Four regiments were Chasseurs, numbered 1 to 4; four regiments were Grenadiers, also numbered 1 to 4. All authorities agree so far. But was there really a 'Middle Guard' division

---

[1] Cavalry and artillery from the Guard had been engaged, but no infantry.

[2] *Houssaye*, 224. The advice was of doubtful value, for what else would a commander and an army in this position be likely to be doing?

at Waterloo? If there was, it probably comprised the 3rd and 4th Grenadiers and the 3rd and 4th Chasseurs.[1] Each regiment was composed of two battalions, save for the 4th Grenadiers which had but one; the 4th Chasseurs may also have had only one.

From 7.30 p.m. on, the Emperor probably had eleven fresh battalions of Imperial Guard infantry. These, or some of them, were to spearhead the final French attack on the Duke's army; this attack would also include many other French units. Wellington, from his vantage point above Hougoumont, saw the Old and Middle Guard battalions start to move north from behind La Belle Alliance; French artillery was increasing its fire and probably planning to concentrate on the point or points to be attacked. Reille's three divisions were getting ready to attack Hougoumont again; three of d'Erlon's were forming as if to come forward alongside La Haye Sainte and to the east of the Genappe road. The battle would be decided, however, by what happened at the point where the Imperial Guard struck the Allied line, not by any additional fighting to be done by Reille and d'Erlon; they were already beaten. The Duke, partly perhaps by intuition, foresaw where the Guard would strike and rode east from Hougoumont calmly issuing orders.

The coming French attack would be delivered mostly by infantry, but all that remained of their exhausted cavalry would undoubtedly also come forward, perhaps by paths that would allow them to arrive unexpectedly close to Wellington's own foot battalions. He ordered the Brunswickers above Hougoumont, Adam's Brigade and Maitland's Guards to form in line, but four ranks deep. Good troops not overtired by combat were nearly as strong against cavalry like this as in square, and not so exposed to casualties from artillery.[2] A battalion in this formation could deliver almost as much fire on enemy infantry as if in a normal two-rank line.

The Duke continued on his way to give the same orders to the brigades in Alten's old area as far as, or even past, the Genappe road. He then rode back to the west, to a spot on the crest of the hill just above where Maitland's Guards joined Adam's light infantry. The French attack was taking definite shape; the Imperial Guard

---

[1] *Anatomy of Glory*, 469 and *passim*, does not agree. See also ibid, 506–7.

[2] The weakness of this line was not in its thickness, which was the same as each face of a British, KGL or Hanoverian square, but in its length which was four times as long as the face of a square. This could lead to unsteadiness. It was also vulnerable from the flanks and rear.

infantry was not definitely heading so as to advance between Hougoumont and La Haye Sainte. Wellington rode forward and cautioned
Bolton's Battery and probably other Allied artillery units in this area
to keep a sharp lookout to their front and open fire as soon as they had
a target; he wanted just as much damage done as possible to these
élite units before they came into contact with his infantry. There was
so much smoke that a column might slip past undetected. The great
virtue of his refusal to let his gunners engage in counter-battery fire
was that his pieces were still reasonably effective even after hours of
combat[1] for a crisis like the coming one.

The French artillery had again picked up its speed of firing; heavy
lines of tirailleurs were once more pushing back Wellington's skirmishers. The lower portions of the battlefield were still thick with
smoke, and becoming thicker, but the crests were reasonably free of it.
The Duke from his position above Hougoumont saw through his
telescope a single column of seven battalions of the Old and Middle
Guard advancing one behind the other, each in a short column with
a front of two companies.[2] A six-company battalion so formed would
have been about 60 files broad by nine ranks deep. Closed up tight –
the expression then was 'close column' – each battalion would have
been only eight yards deep. But the battalions undoubtedly had their
companies separated from each other by about either 24 or 12 yards,
at 'half' or 'quarter distance' as it was then called. So deployed, each
battalion would have occupied 56 or 32 yards of depth; seven battalions
would have theoretically extended in such a formation to a total depth
of 536 yards or 396 yards including 'half' or 'quarter distance' intervals
between battalions.

This column was advancing north on a course roughly parallel to
the Genappe road, but 200 yards farther west. As the Guard moved
past the bottom of the Hougoumont enclosure, Wellington saw it
assume an echelon formation of battalion columns. The individual
battalions, starting with the second, inclined successively farther to their
left which meant that they were separating from each other both

---

[1] *Duncan*, II, 438, says that the 11 British batteries present fired 10,400 rounds, an average
expenditure per piece of slightly over 140 rounds. The Duke did all in his power to prevent
his gunners firing at French artillery. This was not always successful: *Mercer's Journal*,
164–5.

[2] Authorities do not agree as to the number and identity of these battalions, nor do they
see eye-to-eye on formations or the places struck. I have followed a consensus of opinion
as to major details and my own conjectures in small matters.

laterally and vertically. If this manœuvre had been carried out perfectly, they would have struck the Duke's line at seven different points. The tirailleurs were ahead of the Guard; all French artillery which was in position and could still fire was doing so. The light artillery of the Guard was coming forward beside it. Reille's and d'Erlon's infantry was now coming forward too, but in support, rather than ahead of the Guard.

There must have been several minutes of waiting while the French veterans ascended the gentle slopes and went through smoke-filled minor valleys. The Guard battalions were mostly lost from sight now in dead ground and smoke. The Duke could not see them, but knew they were coming. He had heard much of the Imperial Guard infantry, but had never met it in battle before. This picked French force kept from harm by the Emperor[1] for just such a critical situation had often turned a close-fought day into a resounding French victory. Had Wellington done enough? Would his disposition and troops hold up against the most dangerous offensive commander of history using his favourite soldiers in a characteristic attack? Unknown to the Duke, two battalions of the Guard had, only a few minutes before, led a victorious French advance which tumbled 25,000 Prussians almost in panic from Plancenoit.

The answer was close at hand. In passing through the smoke and low ground, the seven French Guards battalions had lost their echelon formation and appear to have reunited into two columns. One of these, the most powerful, was heading for where Wellington was sitting his horse, but was still some 400 yards away. Suddenly, the ranks within this column were cut by furrows; muskets and shakos were hurled high into the air. These Frenchmen were now visible to the British and KGL gunners. Every piece that would bear was being fired individually and carefully with double charges; ranges differed, but all were short.[2] The gallant Frenchmen – they were the pick of twenty-three years of combat – came on in spite of terrible casualties. Wellington moved in behind Maitland's line of British Guards who were still prone. As the French came over the low crest scarce forty yards away a strong, confident voice rang out.

---

[1] The soldiers of the Guard were called by the French Line 'The Immortals' because they were shielded from day-to-day combat casualties by the Emperor.

[2] Double charges at that time meant one charge of powder behind either a round shot and a canister, or two canisters. The piece and its carriage were overstrained, but each discharge was more lethal at close range.

'Now, Maitland! Now is your time!' A pause, and then the same voice roared, 'Up Guards! Make ready! Fire!'[1]

Maitland's Guards were soon firing their half-company volleys under their company officers and sergeants.[2] They still had a front of near 400 men and were all firing on a column only about 60 files wide. Since the British line overlapped on either side of the French column, the Guards (British) were raking the head of the French column with a crossfire. Even worse for the French, adjacent British units were also taking a part in this musketry duel. On the east, two now weak British battalions of Colin Halkett's Brigade, the 33rd and the 2/69th in a single four-deep line, advanced and opened fire on the French right flank, in accordance either with the Duke's orders or Halkett's Peninsular training.

To the west where the Hougoumont salient reached far to the south, Colonel Colborne in anticipation of the Duke's orders brought forward the 1/52nd in the same four-deep line against the left flank of the Imperial Guard. This famous light infantry battalion, because of its large size, had a front of over 200 yards even though arrayed in double depth. The 52nd appears to have enveloped the entire rear portion of a column of Imperial Guards in fire; the light infantrymen closed towards the enemy as they fired until the range was under forty yards.[3] Musketry by these Peninsular veterans was terribly destructive; a young officer recently joined was to maintain years later that the 52nd alone beat the French Guard.[4] But the crossfire of five British battalions against five similar French units who could make only an inadequate reply was extremely effective. Frenchmen were falling fast and accomplishing nothing. Gallant officers tried to deploy their columns into lines under fire so as to meet firepower with firepower. The Imperial Guard was meeting Wellington's veterans for the first time. Its commanders had not taken seriously what French officers who had fought in the Peninsula had said of British infantry and their firepower. For a considerable interval, British volleys from three sides poured into those

---

[1] Both sets of words have come down to us from too many sources to be in error. A simple explanation of their apparent inconsistency is that at first Wellington intended to let Maitland fight his brigade, but could not resist the temptation to take command personally, as he so often did in battle.

[2] There is some evidence that the 1st and 2nd ranks were firing and the 3rd and 4th loading.

[3] The French columns always became shorter under fire.

[4] *Leeke, passim,* maintains that Maitland's Brigade only met skirmishers from the Imperial Guard, a story which is impossible on several counts.

five battalions of the Imperial Guard. Ranges on the north and west shortened to thirty yards.

Veterans from both nations were locked in mortal combat, but the British commander had protected his men by terrain and formation, formed them so as to take maximum advantage of their more efficient fire discipline and created severe artillery casualties among their assailants just before the moment of contact. In addition, 'Nosey' was but a horse's length behind them, more exposed than any man on foot, and in complete personal command. They had seen him among them time after time all day long, directing coolly and effectively. The great Emperor had at last risen from his chair, but was safely behind La Haye Sainte while his men met death to secure his throne.[1]

Columns never beat lines in the Peninsula, and they did no better at Waterloo. The individual companies of the Imperial Guard crowded too much together; there was no room to deploy. Men who attempted to leave the mass and re-form in the open were exposed to the withering fire of Maitland's Guards, Colborne's 52nd and even Colin Halkett's right-hand battalions. The Frenchmen who still survived broke completely and melted to the rear. Maitland led his men in a short pursuit, but Colborne restrained his; French cavalry was on his flank near Hougoumont.

The force defeated as just described probably consisted of the 1/3rd Chasseurs, 2/3rd Chasseurs, the 4th Chasseurs (one or perhaps two battalions) and the 2/3rd Grenadiers. There may have been a break in this column, for some men remembered it as not one column, but two.[2] The important point is not how precisely it was constituted, nor even by what units it was defeated, but that it was, and how it was defeated. It dispersed completely routed with a loss of near half its total strength because of the valour of the all-British units which met it, the tactics they employed and the personal direction they received from the Duke.

During the time the Guards of the two nations were exchanging fire, or perhaps a minute or two before, a smaller force of the French Imperial Guard came up the slope of the Anglo-Dutch position farther to the east. It struck the Allied line, apparently in two battalion

---

[1] Jerome Bonaparte was particularly critical of his brother for not leading his Guard in person.

[2] The British 1st Guards became the Grenadier Guards because they were at first thought to have defeated the French Grenadiers of the Guard. *Houssaye*, 225, is perhaps the best single authority for the French arrangement. *Gardner*, 368, says that there were two French Guard columns in this fight. See also *Fuller's Decisive Battles*, II, 534–5; *Fortescue*, X, 386; and *Thiers*, XII, 132–5.

columns, right in front, about fifty yards apart laterally. These two received the same kind of concentrated Allied artillery fire as directed on the more powerful French column farther west. Even though this French Guard attack was delivered by two battalions only, probably the 1/3rd Grenadiers and the 4th Grenadiers, it was more closely supported by the line infantry of d'Erlon's Corps than the other attack had been by Reille's Divisions.

Colin Halkett's left-hand formation, the 2/30th and the 2/73rd together in a four-deep line, fought hard, but finally retreated a short distance. The Brunswickers and Nassauers here were driven back precipitately, but were stopped by Vivian's cavalry. Wellington somehow sensed this new crisis, rode over from behind Maitland's Guards, and again rallied the Brunswickers. Colin Halkett was also able to rally his two skeleton British battalions, but was badly wounded in the process. Detmer's Brigade of Chassé's Dutch-Belgian Division probably did a good job.[1] As has been pointed out, this is the most confused portion of a battle which abounds in confusions. Chassé personally was certainly present and ordered a battery of Dutch-Belgian horse artillery with fresh guns to open fire with canister on the French Guard and their supports at a range of less than 100 yards.[2] Once Allied confidence was restored in this area by the Duke person-ally, the two battalions of the Imperial Guard, which numbered no more than 1,000 men together, were so outnumbered that they were quickly smothered with fire. The survivors were pushed back down into the valley beside La Haye Sainte, but more than half were left on the bloody crest. It is interesting to note, however, that here at least the French columns won a momentary ascendancy over Allied lines by psychological shock. A four-deep formation 'of Brunswickers fled from a column of the enemy. The Duke rallied the Brunswickers, returned to the charge, and beat back the assailants.'[3]

Wellington sensed a sudden and drastic change in French morale. He could hear incredulous cries of '*La Garde recule!*' These units full of honours and past victories had at last met complete and humiliating

---

[1] Some British writers have supposed that Detmer's Brigade was incapable of doing well because D'Aubreme's men from the same division, but in the second line, were shattered by noise only from the other side of the crest. The Duke, according to *Siborne*, 537, said of D'Aubreme's panic-ridden men, 'That's right, tell them the French are retiring.'

[2] This battery is said by *Houssaye*, 226, and others to have been van der Smissen's, but he was Chassé's Chief of Artillery; the battery commander was Krahmer.

[3] *Alexander*, II, 386.

defeat. If the Guard had been beaten, what chance had ordinary French soldiers against this Sepoy general and his steadily changing, but continuously effective combinations?

The Duke paused to order Vivian forward by a route east of Hougoumont. He rode to his position of vantage on the ridge he and his army had defended so long, and took a careful look at the French. What he saw confirmed what he heard; the portion of the French Army fighting the Prussians was still holding out. The units fighting the Allies were beaten, but they needed to be driven from the field. It was 8.10 p.m. when after an overcast day a shaft of evening sunlight revealed him to his army.[1] The Duke took off his hat and decisively motioned with it several times. The entire Allied army was to move south towards the French.

Wellington galloped forward to where Colborne and the 52nd had advanced in a south-easterly direction after contributing so much to the defeat of the more numerous of the two Guard columns. The 52nd was still in a four-deep line, since French cavalry might be encountered. In front of them, there were several French Guard battalions which had rallied after their recent defeat. One may have been as yet unengaged. They were formed on a height east of the Genappe road near where the French grand battery still stood, but now was abandoned. Colborne was uncertain as to whether to attack or not; he was probably outnumbered. The Duke rode up and surveyed the situation for a few seconds only.

'Go on, Colborne! Go on!' he said. 'They won't stand. Don't give them a chance to rally.'[2]

The 52nd did go ahead until they were no more than fifty paces away from the Frenchmen, halted and opened fire. After a few volleys at ever decreasing range, the French Guards broke and melted into the stream of fugitives that was now flowing fast towards the rear.

Vivian meanwhile was delivering controlled charge after controlled charge with his three light cavalry regiments in the area between Hougoumont and La Belle Alliance. Vandeleur soon came up and joined Vivian on his left with three additional light cavalry regiments. In spite of the exhaustion of the Allied army, Wellington managed to get enough of it forward in fighting formation to break every semblance of formal resistance the French could organise almost as soon as it came into being. He appreciated the great resiliency of French

[1] *Cotton*, 124.
[2] *Clinton*, 430.

soldiers and did not want to give them one extra minute to reorganise and restore their morale.

Soon the Prussians swept around Plancenoit, both north and south of it, and emerged on the Genappe road. A British cavalry unit actually briefly fought Prussians; Ziethen's artillery did more damage to the Allies than the French. But these mistakes were soon rectified. As the two armies mingled, a Prussian band struck up 'God Save the King'. Blücher and Wellington met and embraced while still on horseback.[1] Through the many trials of a long, long day these two leaders had remained staunch and true to each other, their armies and their countries. They had won according to their original plans, beating the greatest of military commanders with his finest army. There was honour and glory enough for all, for Napoleon had sustained his greatest and his final defeat.[2]

---

[1] The meeting place is traditionally La Belle Alliance, but was probably a mile or more closer to Genappe. *Robinson*, III, 615, says, 'after 10 p.m. *at* Genappe'. *Hooper*, 237–8, says, 'Somewhere between La Maison du Roi and Rossome.'

[2] Wellington wrote in his famous Waterloo dispatch, *Dispatches*, XII, 484, 'I should not do justice to my own feelings, or to Marshal Blücher and the Prussian Army, if I did not attribute the successful result of this arduous day to the cordial and timely assistance I received from them.'

XIV

The Pursuit and the End of the War

For Wellington and his troops the battle of Waterloo ended between 9.30 and 10 p.m. with the breaking or driving to the rear of some fresh battalions of the Old Guard near Decosta's house behind La Belle Alliance. There may have been as many as four, but two or three seems more probable. We know that both battalions of the 1st Grenadiers, the *élite* of the *élite*, had been left in this vicinity for just such an emergency. Napoleon tried to use these fine units to stem the tide of the Duke's final attack so he could rally his army behind them. It was useless; Allied and perhaps Prussian infantry, cavalry and artillery broke these veteran battalions comparatively easily. Through all this Wellington remained in the thick of the fight, often in as much danger from friends as from foes, for many units were confused in the smoke and gathering darkness. When some remonstrated, he replied, 'Never mind, let them fire away. The battle's gained; my life's of no consequence now.'[1]

Wellington and Blücher made several rapid decisions at their meeting somewhere south of La Belle Alliance. The defeated French Army had to be pursued relentlessly and with a maximum of military strength. It was obvious, however, that a joint pursuit would not be advisable; Britons and Prussians had already exchanged fire and sabre cuts, each mistaking the other for the enemy. If units from the two forces mingled in the wake of the enemy, more clashes were likely. This probability was increased by the fact that most communications between English and Prussian troops were carried on in the French language. So addressed, each nationality could easily mistake the other

[1] *Life of a Regiment*, I, 375.

for the enemy. Besides, save for Vivian's and Vandeleur's cavalry, Wellington's army was practically exhausted by more than ten hours of fighting. The Prussians agreed to take over the pursuit and keep pressure on the French for as long as possible. The only organisation from the Anglo-Dutch Army that had a part in this rapid advance was the Brunswick cavalry which was allowed to join the Prussians.[1] They were apparently more useful in pursuing a defeated French force than in standing against a fresh one in the open field.

The French were now completely broken and retreated mainly by the Genappe road. They were badly hampered in passing through the village by the long narrow main street and the small bridge.[2] Here they suffered additional severe casualties in killed, wounded and prisoners and lost practically all of their wheeled transport. The Prussian cavalry even took the Emperor's coach a few seconds after he had jumped out of it and on to a horse.

Gneisenau was in charge of the Prussian pursuit and conducted it in a manner to disrupt enemy units rather than to take prisoners; the Prussians did not really have sufficient men to guard them. The tired French Army was driven out of position after position that they took in order to bivouac for the night. The Prussian Chief of Staff had mounted a Prussian drummer on one of Napoleon's carriage horses and took him along with the cavalry. When French infantry were found encamped, or at least halted, the drummer would beat the charge indicating that Prussian infantry was up; the Prussian cavalry would move as if supported by foot soldiers and artillery. The French would then continue their retreat. They are supposed to have been driven out of no less than seven bivouac positions.[3]

In the process of this harassment, French units broke up completely and became disorganised mobs moving across country. Even veterans were seized by panic and threw away not only their weapons, but all other equipment also. French officers with experience from Russia in 1812 and Germany in 1813 had never seen anything like it. *Élite* units under commanders of resolution and efficiency were so infected with the spirit of stampede that they lost their sense of duty and disappeared into the general mass.

Gneisenau finally called off his pursuit near Frasnes not far from the

[1] Vivian wanted to join the pursuit, but Wellington saw the dangers involved and would not hear of it.

[2] Already described in Chapter VI of this work in connection with the cavalry action there on 17 June when Wellington retreated through the place.

[3] *Fortescue*, X, 393, says 'nine'.

Sambre, but many Frenchmen, even some on foot, crossed the stream before sunrise on the 19th. The Emperor, accompanied only by a handful of soldiers on horseback, escaped into France and in the morning arrived at Philippeville. In the battle and pursuit the French Army which fought at Waterloo lost 30,000 men killed and wounded and some 6,000 to 7,000 prisoners together with all their artillery, about 250 pieces.[1] The soldiers of the Emperor's army who were not casualties were completely disorganised and most of them beyond recall. There was a rumour that Napoleon had set out for Paris, perhaps leaving Soult in charge of the wreck of his army.

To return to Wellington at the conclusion of his part in the battle, he rode back in moonlight from his meeting with Blücher to the little inn at Waterloo which had been his headquarters the night before. He arrived about 11 p.m., tired physically and mentally past the capacities of most men. He still had to face the details of the most staggering casualty list of his career. His personal staff, or military family, numbering more than thirty officers, appears to have been particularly hard hit. Sir Alexander Gordon, wounded while aiding the Duke to rally the Brunswickers during the tirailleur fight, died that night in Wellington's bed while the Duke used a pallet on the floor. He was still there when the chief medical officer gave him the preliminary casualty list.

As I entered, he sat up, his face covered with the dust and sweat of the previous day, and extended his hand to me, which I took and held in mine, whilst I told him of Gordon's death, and of such of the casualties as had come to my knowledge. He was much affected. I felt the tears dropping fast upon my hand, and looking towards him, saw them chasing one another in furrows over his dusty cheeks. He brushed them suddenly away with his left hand, and said to me in a voice tremulous with emotion, 'Well, thank God, I don't know what it is to lose a battle; but certainly nothing can be more painful than to gain one with the loss of so many of one's friends.'[2]

The British Army including the KGL and the Hanoverians had suffered more than 10,000 casualties; Wellington's Brunswickers and Nassauers had 1,300 more.[3] Several British and KGL units had lost in

[1] Oman in *Cambridge Modern History* (1st edition), IX, 641.

[2] Dr John Hume, as quoted by *Brett-James*, 182.

[3] *Gardner*, 406, gives these precisely and also questions those reported by the Dutch-Belgians which were probably too high. The 4,200 reported by the Prince of Orange appear to have contained 1,600 missing, mostly deserters who got clean away. *Fortescue*, X. 397.

killed and wounded more than a third of their strength at the beginning of the battle. The loss in officers was disproportionately large; 680 including many of high rank had fallen. Picton was killed; so were William Ponsonby, du Plat and Ompteda. Uxbridge, Alten, Cooke, Kempt, Pack, Adam and Colin Halkett were all wounded. Barnes and Fitzroy Somerset of the staff were wounded; De Lancey and Canning were killed. There were many, many more. The battlefield itself was a shambles. About 44,000 men lay dead and wounded within an area of about three square miles centring at La Belle Alliance. Many wounded were untended for as much as three days. In spite of large graves, containing in some instances scores of bodies, burials were too long delayed.

Wellington did what he could for his own wounded, but had to leave general medical care mostly to civilians; there were not nearly enough military surgeons. The Anglo-Dutch Army spent the 19th on or near the battlefield not only in caring for the wounded, but also in restoring order among the survivors. Equipment had to be replaced, but there was a plentiful supply in the fields near by. Orders were issued for a forward movement towards France on the morning of the 20th. If maximum profit was to be reaped from the recent victory, it had to be followed up.

We should now look briefly at what had happened to the Prussians under Thielemann who fought the French under Grouchy at Wavre. When last seen, these two armies of about 33,000 Frenchmen and 18,000 Prussians were locked in battle along the Dyle on the evening of the 18th. The Prussians were finally pushed back towards Louvain, but early on the morning of the 19th the troops of both sides received details of the battle at Waterloo. Blücher sent Pirch's Corps to trap Grouchy, but the latter avoided being surrounded, managed to retreat through Namur on the 19th and 20th, and was safe back in France on the 21st with nearly 30,000 organised French soldiers together with their artillery.

Long before Grouchy had made good his escape, Wellington and Blücher had decided upon their next move. They could only surmise that Napoleon would reorganise and re-equip the wreck of his Waterloo army and combine it with other French forces north of Paris. Even though all the French artillery used at Waterloo had been captured, many of the gunners and horses escaped.[1] There were spare

[1] *Napoleon*, 138-9.

guns in the French arsenals nearby.[1] After the Russian disaster of 1812 and the French defeat at Leipzig in 1813, matériel had been replaced, and patriotism revived, to an astonishing degree.[2]

Wellington and Blücher realised that the way to prevent such a revival was to take full advantage of their victory and move rapidly on Paris. They decided to put into operation their original plans for moving into France, whether or not the Austrian and Russian Armies were ready. Their two armies would advance south-west by routes parallel with those of the Prussians to the east. Wellington and his army, now mostly British and Hanoverian, moved to Nivelles on the 20th and the next day in two columns crossed the border into France by way of Bavay and Mons.

These operations were complicated, however, by the triple line of French fortified towns extending from the channel to the Ardennes. The two Allied armies could easily march between these, but communications had to be kept open after they had passed. Each army had to detach some strength to protect its lines of supply. Young Prince Frederick of the Netherlands with a considerable force was to operate in the area between the Sambre and the Scheldt taking as many towns as he could, but preventing any restoration of French general control of the area. Blücher left a similar force operating between the Sambre and the Meuse, nominally under Prince Augustus of Prussia, which included the corps of Pirch and the newly arrived forces under Kleist.

Wellington blockaded and by-passed the French first line fortress of Valenciennes. He established his headquarters on the 21st at Malplaquet where Marlborough had fought his last great battle in 1709. The second line fortress of Cambrai was taken by the veteran British battalions of Colville's Division on the 24th. A professional soldier who witnessed this attack says, 'In few words, the Duke designated which troops should make fascines in a thicket, and which should bind the ladders. He designated the point of attack, and all the rest went on of itself. The battalions in two contiguous columns, behind a swarm

[1] Douai and other fortress towns in the area had been cannon foundries for centuries.

[2] *Marbot*, 287, casts doubt on this possibility in 1815, however, when he says, 'The men are deserting, and no one stops them. Whatever people may say, there are 50,000 men in this neighbourhood who might be got together; but to do it we should have to make it a capital offence to quit your post, or to give leave of absence. Everybody gives leave, and the coaches are full of officers departing.'

of skirmishers, carried the fascines as a protecting wall and the ladders on their shoulders. All went off just as if they had been on the practising-ground.'[1]

The city-fortress in the third belt below Valenciennes and Cambrai was Péronne, a strong place with massive walls of fine Vauban design. The garrison was more than adequate in numbers, but had heard all about Waterloo. The light companies of the Guards took a hornwork outside one entrance on the 26th by blowing in its gates. The Duke was still far from capturing the town, but the place surrendered. On the same day, Valenciennes asked for an armistice. Wellington had cleared a wide path for his own army through all three lines of the fortresses. Blücher and the Prussians also managed to penetrate these three lines of fortress-towns, partly because of British siege artillery units loaned to them. Once in the open, however, they encountered stiffer resistance, in part because they were ahead. The Prussians requisitioned all they wanted from the towns and villages and treated civilians so viciously that they dared not refuse anything. Wellington had to follow a different pattern because he was incapable of cruelly forcing delivery of supplies or billeting his soldiers in the homes of French civilians. He said so to Müffling, 'Do not press me on this point, for I tell you, it won't do. If you were better acquainted with the English Army, its composition and habits, you would say the same. I cannot separate from my tents and my supplies. My troops must be well kept and well supplied in camp, if order and discipline are to be maintained. It is better that I should arrive two days later in Paris, than that discipline should be relaxed.'[2]

Grouchy was now in command of a considerable army and fought Blücher at Compiègne on the 27th and engaged again on the 28th; both fights were indecisive. The Prussians, however, forced the French back into Paris on the 29th and encamped all across the northern side of the city which had been fortified.

Even though Napoleon had abdicated and left Paris at the insistence of the French Chamber of Deputies, France was a long way from being willing to surrender unconditionally. A French army which numbered at least 70,000 including some National Guard units was in or near the capital. Wellington and Blücher now had not much over 100,000 men between them, but their quality was high. Storming the fortifications

[1] *Müffling's Passages*, 252.
[2] Ibid., 251.

of Paris on the north would be hazardous, but the south side of the city was unprotected.[1]

Blücher moved his forces west, crossed the Seine and moved east again south of Paris. Wellington's army took over the northern approaches to the city. The Prussians ran into some severe fighting at Issy on 1 and 2 July.[2] They were in a position, however, to fight their way into the French capital; Wellington was ready to storm the northern earthworks. A British pontoon bridge linked the two Allied armies. The French realised that for them resistance was hopeless. The vast power of the French nation could not be brought into action soon enough to save the capital which was already cut off. A city taken by storm has often suffered horribly.

Besides, France now could not long resist the forces already on her soil. It was known in Paris that an enormous Austrian army had crossed the eastern frontier on 23 June, beaten a French army under General Rapp on the 28th and shut it up in Strasbourg. An Austro-Sardinian army from Italy had crossed the Alps and attacked Suchet, who, on hearing the news of Waterloo, had asked for and obtained an armistice. The Spanish border was once again aflame; about 150,000 Russians were in France, or soon would be. Paris surrendered on 4 July 1815 even though it was not actually entered by the Allied armies until two or three days later. Louis XVIII was called back to the throne by the Chamber of Deputies and entered the capital on the 8th.

For a period of more than three months, France was in a state between peace and war. A number of small fortresses had to be taken by storm even as late as September.[3] The Treaty of Paris was finally signed on 20 November 1815. It returned small bits of territory along the frontier to neighbouring countries, including a strip below Charleroi to Belgium.[4] France had also to pay an indemnity of staggering proportions for that time, about 29,400,000 pounds sterling, and had to restore all the works of art plundered from Europe under Napoleon.

---

[1] *Dispatches*, XII, 526.

[2] *Henderson's Blücher*, 317, quotes Blücher as saying that he 'lost nearly 3,000 men' on these two days.

[3] Ibid., 320, says, 'There were still garrisons in numerous small French forts, and these were to hold out for several months. Eleven of them had been conquered by the Prussians alone before the end of September. On the 4th of October, Blücher himself writes that peace is as good as concluded though not yet publicly announced.'

[4] This changed frontier near where the French attacked on the 15th has already been noted in Chapter IV.

Finally, she had to support an Allied occupation force of 150,000 troops to be quartered in northern France for a period of five years. All the expenses of these troops including pay of officers and men were to be borne by France. Wellington was to be Commander-in-Chief at a salary of 30,000 pounds a year.

The Duke was now the most powerful man in Europe; his military reputation soared. He was made a prince in the Netherlands, and received many more foreign honours, but there was little more that Britain could do other than grant him another 200,000 pounds. He had received almost everything there was to give at home in 1814. He handled his duties as Allied Commander-in-Chief with care, diplomacy and forbearance without in any way weakening the efficiency of his forces. He actually concluded the occupation more than a year ahead of time, mainly because he saw how cruelly the burden of supporting the army hurt the French people and their economy. His justice and common sense not only during this period, but from the time his army crossed the border into France on 21 June 1815, probably had a great deal to do with the remarkable era of peace which followed Waterloo. For nearly a century, Europe saw only three short wars between major powers; Britain and France became at first friends and later staunch Allies.

In point of time the Waterloo campaign was perhaps the shortest major campaign in military history. The really important fighting occurred on 16 and 18 June. From the time that Napoleon crossed the Belgian border early on 15 June until the Allies held Paris firmly on 7 July was only twenty-three days. But if the Allies had not taken the initiative and moved fast after Waterloo, the war could have lasted far longer. Paris has fallen several times to British and German Armies operating together or separately, but no one has ever occupied the capital so quickly after crossing that frontier as Blücher and Wellington did in 1815.

XV

Analysis of Victory

A major military victory depends upon many factors. First, there are imponderables such as spirit, eagerness for victory, experience and discipline. The armies of France in 1815 were strong in all these, except perhaps the last. Napoleon's soldiers in the Waterloo campaign were not all veterans, but probably had on the average more combat experience than any army since Roman times. In some units and positions their opponents were stronger in these qualities than many realise. Both Wellington's and Blücher's armies contained veteran officers, NCOs and enlisted men who had spent years in war, wanted to win as much as the French did, and were better disciplined. The French had the edge in the matter of average quality, but not as regards the maximum efficiency of some units. Their command structure was better in that they had a common language and single line of responsibility, but this may have been counter-balanced to some extent by jealousy among French field and general officers and a well developed ability to err and then conceal their faults.

Second, there are the tangibles such as weapons, organisation and tactics. There was little to choose between the two sides in weapons and equipment; all contending armies were fairly well provided with ordnance according to their own ideas. Wellington had more and better infantry rifles, but his artillery was less powerful and less numerous.[1] Both these conditions were of his own choosing. The organisation and tactics of the contending armies also varied widely as already discussed in Chapter II, but in the Duke's case this

[1] The ordnance of the contending armies will be discussed in some detail in Part Two, Chapter I.

factor was modified by his decision, probably made finally on the morning of the 18th, to scrap his corps organisation and break up some divisions.

Third, an ever-present element in war is numerical strength. This was the dominant single material factor in this campaign, as it usually is in war between similar troops. The main objective of manœuvres and strategy is to obtain more strength at critical points at the right time. Napoleon's offensive plans were based on his ability to defeat either Blücher or Wellington separately; he could not expect to win against both together because they would outnumber him about 210,000 to 125,000. Taking advantage of surprise and the necessarily wide dispersion of both Allied armies, the Emperor managed to defeat the Prussians at Ligny, but was not able to make that victory complete because the troops he required for the final crippling stroke were involved with Wellington at Quatre Bras. Two days later at Waterloo he might have won against the Duke, if he could have used Lobau, the 'Young Guard' and the two cavalry divisions which were deployed against Blücher. Neither Wellington nor Blücher had the strength to fight Bonaparte's Grand Army unassisted; neither would have thought of doing so. They had to depend upon each other, or unite beforehand; their wide strategic, political and logistic responsibilities prevented their taking the latter course. Once the campaign started, their salvation lay in supporting each other.

Napoleon was taking a considerable risk in attacking two armies which together were more powerful than his own. If he could not win quickly and completely against one or the other, his whole offensive was likely to be disastrous. Wellington's modest victory at Quatre Bras was of extreme importance because it prevented Napoleon from defeating the Prussians sufficiently heavily for them to be forced to retreat towards the Rhine. Similarly, Prussian help at Waterloo was absolutely essential. Once Wellington and Blücher were united on a single battlefield against the Emperor, only a miracle could save the French.

Another factor related to numerical superiority at critical points was Napoleon's choice of battle tactics. He could manœuvre, or he could attack straight ahead. Against all logic, he did the latter. Waterloo was the most congested battle he ever fought; it was diametrically opposed to the advice of his subordinate commanders. Reille said, 'Well posted, as Wellington knows how to post it, and attacked from the front, I consider the English Infantry to be impregnable. But the English Army is less agile, less supple, less expert in manœuvring than ours. If we cannot beat it by a direct attack, we may do so by manœuvring.'[1] Napoleon ignored this comment as he did essentially the same advice from Foy and Soult; he fought exactly the kind of battle best suited to the Anglo-Dutch Army and Wellington's own unusual military abilities.

Too much has been written about the Prussians and the lateness of their arrival. They did not really press their advance until the cannonade at Waterloo was announcing to all Brabant that Wellington was determined to fight to a finish. Blücher did bring his Prussians to the Waterloo area as he promised. Even though they did not start to fight until about 4.30 p.m., they drew some 14,000 Frenchmen to the east where they never fired a shot at the Duke's army.

The Prussians did not perform with startling efficiency, but they tried wholeheartedly once they were committed. Blücher's loss of 6,998 men at Waterloo alone – there were 2,467 more casualties at Wavre – is irrefutable evidence of the courage and patriotism of the Prussian army and its old commander. We should realise, however, that the French still held Plancenoit after the 52nd had broken the reorganised battalions of the Imperial Guard north of La Belle Alliance. Even though Prussian cannon balls were occasionally ploughing across the Genappe road from 5 p.m. on, Blücher's troops did not actually reach this road until it had been cleared by the Duke of organised French resistance as far back as Decosta's house.

On the other hand, the Prussians probably aided in the final overthrow of the fresh battalions of the Imperial Guard under the Emperor's personal command. The Prussian pursuit after the battle was over was of extreme value in the disruption of the already defeated French forces. Even though the number of prisoners taken was small, Gneisenau's noisy activities during the night following the battle greatly contributed by creating chaos in French morale.

So much for the larger picture. All this would have meant nothing, if Napoleon had been able to beat Wellington by 4.30 p.m. on the 18th. Why did he fail to accomplish this? The odds appear to have favoured him.[2] There were, of course, many factors which led finally to Wellington's victory. We will analyse some of those of lesser importance first.

[1] *Houssaye*, 178.
[2] In the morning Napoleon thought them to be nine to one in his favour.

Prince Bernhard of Saxe-Weimar and Nassau troops in the pay of the Netherlands performed moderately well at PLHS. Detmer's Brigade of Chassé's Division and the van der Smissen-Krahmer battery probably deserve the highest acclaim of any soldiers who fought under the colours of the House of Orange. The Nassau infantry and the Brunswickers who fought directly under Wellington were exposed to many trials and, on the whole, came through them creditably. They were not quite up to the British and KGL standard, but far superior, for instance, to Bylandt's and D'Aubreme's Dutch-Belgians who either ran away before the enemy was within effective range, or were seized by panic without even seeing the French. The Dutch-Belgian cavalry was particularly bad; they refused to charge the French and could only with difficulty be persuaded to maintain a position, even though shielded from all direct fire.[1]

The four Hanoverian infantry brigades at Waterloo which included cadres of KGL officers and NCOs certainly behaved well. Best's and Vincke's Brigades stood shoulder to shoulder with Picton's veterans. Kielmansegge's men of Alten's Division remained at their post just west of the Genappe road where the French attacked so often with infantry, cavalry and artillery. Hew Halkett's Brigade had an easier time during most of the day, but took its part in the final shattering of the fresh reserve battalions of the Imperial Guard.[2]

We now come to a difficult problem in evaluation. The British heavy cavalry must have been an extreme, although perhaps not unexpected, disappointment to Wellington. Somerset's Household Brigade and Ponsonby's Union Brigade were individually the finest mounted soldiers in the world. The horses were superb and the men powerful, well drilled and skilful with their weapons. They smashed a French cavalry force and three full divisions of French infantry in the

---

[1] The Hanoverian cavalry brigade (von Estorff's) was probably as bad as the Dutch-Belgians. The Cumberland Hussars, the only Hanoverian cavalry unit actually at Waterloo, were the worst behaved troops in the Duke's army.

[2] Halkett, who took forward the Osnabrück battalion under his personal command, captured the notorious Cambronne: *Cotton*, 126, says, 'Halkett himself marked our Cambronne, and was on the point of cutting down the French general, when the latter cried out for quarter and received it. This fact does not well agree with the words popularly ascribed to Cambronne, "The Guard dies; it never surrenders!" Cambronne tried to escape from Halkett, whose horse fell wounded to the ground. But in a few seconds Halkett overtook his prisoner, and seizing him by the aiguillette, hurried him back to the Osnabrückers, and sent him in charge of a sergeant to the duke of Wellington.'

course of a few minutes. As has earlier been said, their contribution here was magnificent. But then they went out of control and destroyed themselves. Thereafter, they were so reduced in numbers and perhaps morale that they were unable to control the area directly behind Wellington's centre. The Duke's battle plan called for his artillery and infantry to hold tight to the crest. He expected his cavalry to defeat any French cavalry which had endured successively the close range Allied artillery fire and the musketry of his infantry. Somerset and Ponsonby at full strength could have defeated with ease the disordered masses of Napoleonic cavalry which penetrated between the Allied infantry squares. They did do it on more than one occasion to a limited extent, but were prevented by their earlier losses from being able to carry out their responsibilities to the full.

The other British and KGL cavalry in the centre and right performed creditably. The brigades of Dörnberg, Grant and Arentschildt never achieved so brilliant a success as Ponsonby and Somerset, but fought far longer at near full strength and were handled with more skill, perhaps because 57 per cent of the troopers and two of the three brigade commanders were from the KGL.[1] On the other hand, the light cavalry brigades of Vivian and Vandeleur were 80 per cent British, performed a rescue mission following the heavy cavalry fiasco with reasonable efficiency and were brilliant at the end of the battle.

Wellington's artillery did more for him at Waterloo than in any other of his battles. He had arranged it carefully in accordance with a preconceived plan already explained. After the gunners learned their jobs, they performed superbly, keeping their pieces in action until the last moment and returning to them as soon as they were clear of the enemy. Every single gun and howitzer seems to have continued in action so long as it remained serviceable. Napoleon has been widely acclaimed as the greatest artilleryman of all time, yet his guns did less for him at Waterloo than at most of his other major battles.[2] The Duke had fewer and smaller pieces, but used them to cause at least three times as many casualties.

The contribution of the British and KGL infantry was greatest of all. No men who ever fought were more effective than Byng's Guards

---

[1] See 'Strengths of the Contending Forces', p. 242, for details of individual regiments in these brigades. Dörnberg and Arentschildt were the German brigade commanders.

[2] *Becke*, 168, says, 'In no other battle of this era did artillery, so numerically superior, fail to produce a far greater effect than the French guns obtained in the battle against Wellington.'

in Hougoumont, Maitland's Brigade on the crest and Adam's Light Infantry Brigade which included the 52nd from 6 p.m. on. But the brigades of Pack, Kempt, Ompteda, Lambert and Colin Halkett suffered higher percentage casualties. Without these infantrymen, not even Wellington could have won Waterloo. So much has been written and said of these gallant men by those with a professional facility with words, but perhaps the praise they would like best came from Napoleon and Wellington. The Emperor said, 'The English infantry was firm and sound; their cavalry could have done better.'[1] Wellington wrote to his brother on the 19th, certainly not for publication, 'Our loss is immense, particularly in that best of all instruments, British infantry. I never saw the infantry behave so well.'[2] We should realise, however, that the superb bravery, bottom and discipline under fire of this infantry, which won so completely for Wellington at Waterloo, had led in the past under lesser British commanders only to magnificent casualties, Pyrrhic victories, or even battles lost through attrition.[3]

We come now to Wellington's personal contribution to his victory. Let us discuss this in two parts: first, his pre-battle plans and decisions; second, his actions after the fighting commenced. The Duke has been criticised for the Waterloo position. It was not perfect, less perfect in fact than any he defended in the Peninsula save Talavera. But his dispositions made the most of what he had. His resolution to defend the position to the last extremity was the fundamental turning-point of the entire campaign. He had carefully evolved his Waterloo tactics not only on the basis of his own triumphant experience in the Peninsula and in southern France, but also after a careful study of what Napoleon had done to gain his more recent victories in northern and central Europe. Throughout the battle, these tactics were remarkably successful in spite of a ridge which did not always protect, Allies who refused to fight, artillerymen who did not at first understand their orders, and British heavy cavalry that wasted itself uselessly before it could be employed as intended.

The Duke, after carefully evaluating Napoleon's use of artillery, came to some conclusions of his own, radically different from those of the French and the other Continental armies which tried to follow the

---

[1] *Napoleon*, 158.

[2] *Brett-James*, 183.

[3] Bunker Hill, Saratoga and Guilford Court House were still in the living memory of the British Army. Corunna and Albuera were less than seven years before.

Emperor in everything. Wellington realised long before Waterloo that the number of rounds that a battery of artillery could fire in one day was limited. He not only held some of his batteries in reserve, so that when they did come up, they were fresh and had undamaged pieces, but he also prohibited counter-battery fire. He refused to copy Napoleon's artillery concentrations and distributed the Anglo-Dutch pieces along his entire front. Even more important to the final outcome of the battle, the Duke ordered his gunners to desert their pieces when forced to do so, but to return to them as soon as possible. The French were forced to incur casualties for 'taking' the same guns time and time again.

Wellington's pre-battle plan for infantry consisted of the same set of tactics as was used so successfully in the Peninsula: a sheltering crest, covered lateral communications, a line against French infantry columns, and a square against cavalry with the entire formation protected by skirmishers well in front. The overall scheme of this plan worked well, but the Allied skirmishers could not hold back whole battalions and even brigades deployed in masses of tirailleurs. How the French happened to employ these tactics is a mystery; they had not used them to any considerable extent for many years. But they would have been suicidal, if the British heavy cavalry had been still available in near full strength and under control.

Historians have emphasised too much the passive part of Wellington's defence. They have told and retold the story of squares rooted in the ground and battalions dying where they stood. This is actually true for only one unit, Lambert's gallant 27th (Inniskillings) which suffered 478 casualties out of a total strength of 750.[1] The 27th was the only battalion in the army which lacked any cover at all; it was stationed across the principal defect in the Duke's position, but the post had to be held. Most of the rest manœuvred and suffered fairly lightly considering what they accomplished. The sobriquet 'Iron Duke' may be apropos of his mental disciplines, but not of his tactics.

The genius of Wellington's system of defence was its articulation. There were no earthworks and no positions which could not be temporarily lost. The infantry squares and oblongs could all suddenly become regular or double-thickness lines when required to do so; for a good portion of the day most battalions remained in column at half or quarter distance. The Duke's infantry did not hold any position firmly, save for the buildings at Hougoumont. The squares were not

[1] *Cotton*, 244.

only able to inflict maximum damage on the French cavalry at close range, but also to protect themselves and serve as a refuge for Allied gunners. The same battalions could retire behind crests and lie down, and then stand up in lines, advance and defeat French infantry with superior firepower. As had been demonstrated in the Peninsula, a British line directed by Wellington could always defeat a French column.

The Duke was personally responsible for this articulation because of the intensive training all his battalions received. In the battle, he ordered an astonishing number of battalion and brigade manœuvres himself. He often acted in a dual capacity as Commander-in-Chief of the army and also, when a crisis required it, as the temporary commander of smaller units. His army operated with maximum efficiency in this way. But he did not limit himself to what had been done before. He appears to have revived four-deep lines late in the day because they were superior to French infantry columns and gave security against French cavalry which might appear unexpectedly, but we should remember that he had the 92nd in this formation at Quatre Bras. The Duke had a truly remarkable ability to improvise and demonstrated it forcefully at Waterloo.

Wellington used his reserves as required, but never squandered them. Throughout the entire action, he brought up only what he needed and retained to the end an effectiveness of troops already engaged and reserves not yet committed superior to that of Napoleon. He had men able and ready for his grand counter-stroke because he had taken care of them throughout eight hours of combat.

In addition to instructing his troops in person, Wellington was a continuous source of inspiration to his entire army. No man was so much exposed as the Duke himself. He rode along the top of the ridge, which sheltered his troops, not for theatrical display, but because, after carefully balancing in his mind the advantages and disadvantages, he considered that it was better for him to do so. He felt that everything depended upon himself, and that the loss of his life might be the loss of his army. On the other hand, he knew that he had to deal with troops, many of whom had never been engaged and had had no opportunity of seeing him win a battle. He felt that his first object must be to inspire confidence in his soldiers. His calmness of demeanour, his methodical way of dealing with the various regiments during the day, all of which was visible to his men, gave them unbounded confidence in the success of his orders. 'Not a private in the ranks but felt that the

Duke of Wellington – the man of Wealth, Rank, and Success with the World at his feet – was jeopardising his life to at least the same degree as the poor outcast who had become a soldier from starvation.'[1]

Wellington personally rallied troops which had broken on at least four occasions. He brought forward du Plat's Brigade at a critical point when Hougoumont was in danger of being surrounded. During d'Erlon's attack, he almost certainly set into motion Somerset's heavy cavalry and was himself involved with Picton's infantry during its darkest hour. Throughout the French cavalry attacks, he was continuously going from place to place giving orders where necessary and encouragement everywhere. His presence was always a stimulant to his soldiers. Many felt defeat was not possible so long as the Duke was safe.[2]

Wellington carried his team through the tirailleur period, when he and they were closest to defeat, by doing the right thing at the right time almost too quickly for conscious thought. He restored the area above Hougoumont and then had to do the same thing in Alten's sector by sending fresh troops and personally rallying them almost immediately when they broke. Throughout the battle, he went to each point of maximum stress and did what was required to win, save only at La Haye Sainte. He himself commanded and inspired Maitland's Guards when they won the proud name that they have carried ever since. Then, with his unerring battle insight, he was off immediately to restore the damage done by the lesser Imperial French Guard attack farther to his left.

Once the situation was saved there too, Wellington carried his whole team from defence to offence. After making his famous gesture ordering forward his entire army, he gave Vivian and Vandeleur specific instructions. As we have seen, he galloped to where Colborne was in an uncharacteristic and brief period of indecision. The counter-attack which swept Napoleon's Grand Army from the crest of the Waterloo position into oblivion was largely the result of the professional military ability of the Allied Commander-in-Chief at battalion and brigade level and his intuitive grasp of where he was most needed throughout eight long hours of combat.

Many military historians do not consider Wellington in the same

---

[1] *Fraser*, 252–3.

[2] *Davies*, 36, says, 'Sir Andrew Barnard, asked if he had had any anxiety about the result of the battle, replied: "Oh no, except for the Duke. We had a notion that while he was there nothing could go wrong."'

class as Napoleon as a general. The Duke was not idolised by his soldiers, but did not send them to their deaths to accomplish selfish personal aims. He did not gamble with the lives and happiness of families, provinces and nations, nor did he fritter away enormous armies and then look to his country for another and another and another. He evolved no magnificent code of law; he did not change the fate of Europe by campaigns involving armies numbering hundreds of thousands.

It is fortunate for England and for Europe, however, that on the day that counted most, Wellington positioned his army flawlessly, handled it without a serious error, and personally directed it to victory. He was perhaps not so proficient in grand strategy, but he made less mistakes.[1] He was tactically successful because he was in superb physical and mental condition and had a professional competence which allowed him to do good work at many different levels. History can hardly fail to confirm his own estimate when he said, 'By God, I don't think it would have done if I had not been there.'[2] On 18 June 1815, at least, the Duke was a stronger man, a better soldier and a more resourceful commander. If any other man had directed the Anglo-Dutch Army, Napoleon would probably have ended his days as Emperor of the French.

[1] *Creasy*, 416–17, says, 'The great German writer, Niebuhr, whose accurate acquaintance with every important scene of modern as well as ancient history was unparalleled, after referring to the military "blunders" of Mithridates, Frederick the Great, Napoleon, Pyrrhus and Hannibal, uses these remarkable words, "The Duke of Wellington is, I believe, the only general in whose conduct of war we cannot discover any important mistake."' The quotation is from *Roman History*, V, 17.

[2] *Creevey*, I, 237.

PART TWO

I

Ordnance used at Waterloo

Military weapons in use in Western Europe in 1815 were simple compared to those of today, or even those of a couple of centuries before Waterloo. There were, of course, variations between the arms of the different nations and even in the weapons of the same country, but in most instances these were of relatively small importance. We will review briefly the matériel used by different arms (infantry, cavalry and artillery) and then by nationalities, if necessary.

INFANTRY

All infantries that fought at Waterloo in the main used muzzle-loading smoothbore flintlock muskets and angular sleeve bayonets, or muzzle-loading flintlock rifles which also usually took sword-bayonets. Muskets and rifles were missile weapons; bayonets could be used for shock either by actually stabbing the enemy, or by threatening to do so, as in the advance of a French column.

The choice between muskets and rifles depended upon a number of factors, all understood in the armies of Europe at that time. Rifles increased accuracy, but also increased the time that it took to load. Further, a rifle could not fire as many times before cleaning became absolutely necessary. In general, a rifle allowed a fairly skilled soldier to hit a life-size target more often than he missed it at 150 yards. A smoothbore musket could be used to get approximately the same accuracy at seventy-five yards. This increase in accuracy was counterbalanced by a reduction in the number of rounds that could be fired in a given time. A musket could probably be loaded and discharged about thirty times in ten minutes, while a normal rifle was good for no more than ten shots in the same time.[1] Furthermore, rifles were not usually so durable.

The French Army issued rifled arms experimentally during the wars of the Republic, but finally recalled them all. The only rifles used by Frenchmen at Waterloo were a few special non-standard weapons, mostly captured or the private property of officers. The Prussian, Hanoverian, Brunswick and Nassau armies all contained riflemen but, these were usually armed with non-standard Jaeger-type hunting rifles, often brought by young gamekeepers into the army with them. They generally did not take bayonets and often required extra heavy rammers and/or mallets for loading. These were special purpose arms only; infantry so armed could not fight and manœuvre in the normal way.

British and KGL riflemen had a weapon which was quite different from those made on the Continent. The Baker rifle could deliver both accurate slow fire and also musket-type, relatively fast fire. If a bullet was carefully patched and forced down the bore, it could be shot precisely. If a regular paper cartridge, 'carbine' size, was used with the bullet unpatched, loading was almost as fast as with a musket. The 95th, the KGL light battalions and the light companies of KGL line battalions were armed with these rifles at Waterloo. They were effective with both types of loading, depending upon whether speed or accuracy was required.

A word about the different muskets. All were basically the same, but the British Brown Bess was undoubtedly the sturdiest.[2] The French muskets were lighter and slightly smaller in calibre, ·69 to ·75. The Prussians and other Germans usually had Potsdam or similar muskets which were as heavy as British weapons, but not so reliable.

What other arms did the Waterloo infantry have? Quite a variety, but taken all together they were of almost negligible importance in the fighting compared to muskets and bayonets. Officers and most sergeants had swords of several different types; some had pistols also.

[1] Rough approximations only, and for all troops. British and KGL line infantry and riflemen could both do considerably better.

[2] Battlefield relics indicate three similar models of this British musket: the Model II with 42-inch barrel, the Model III with 39-inch barrel, and the East India Pattern with 39-inch barrel. There may have been a few muskets of the 'New Land' type with both barrel lengths; see *Blackmore*, 139 and *passim*.

Sergeants and some officers in the British Army carried halberds and spontoons of a standardised, not very effective type. Perhaps other armies had these too. All these minor weapons were for men not primarily fighting themselves, but directing others. It did not make much difference what they had, or even if they were armed at all, save of course psychologically to the individuals themselves.

CAVALRY

The most important cavalry weapon during the Napoleonic wars was the sabre. The lance was also employed effectively by the Poles and, after about 1809, by the French and other Continental armies also. But lances were not used until after 1815 in the British Army. The only lancers in the Anglo-Dutch Army at Waterloo appear to have been the Uhlans of the Duke of Brunswick's contingent (Uhlan is said to be a Polish word). A discussion of the relative value of sabres and lances can be involved and technical. It would seem that lancers who had to face a charge by sabre-armed troopers had often thrown away their lances before contact, because of the defensive inferiority of the lance, and drawn their sabres. For some purposes, however, a lancer had an advantage. He was probably more effective against formed infantry because of the length of his weapon. A lance was also valuable against disordered enemy cavalry, broken infantry and soldiers lying on the ground. As I have already stated, however, sabres were more important.

Waterloo sabres were of two general types. The curved sword used exclusively for cutting was issued in all armies, usually to light cavalry. The longer and straighter sabre which could also be used for thrusting – it usually was not so employed – was for heavy cavalry. There were some variations and even intermediate types, as well as some scimitars from the East, but these were basically light cavalry sabres.

The cavalry of all armies during the Napoleonic wars was also regularly issued with firearms. Pistols and short carbines predominated, types which could be used while mounted. These were valuable for guard duty, and for certain special missions, but were surprisingly ineffective when used by horsemen in regular combat. Some rifled carbines were issued in the British Army which were manufactured in accordance with the general principles of the Baker rifle.[1] Creditable

[1] I found and photographed a rifled carbine of this type at a small Waterloo museum in 1953.

shooting can be done with a weapon of this type when carefully loaded, but this additional accuracy was probably wasted on cavalry who had neither the skill nor the stable firing position necessary for good shooting. Even though French dragoons had dismounted and fought on foot with their short muskets ten years before, no cavalry did this, I believe, at Waterloo. Battlefield relics indicate, however, that short muskets were used at Waterloo by the French, most of them of a type that did not take bayonets.

What about cavalry armour? The French cuirassiers have been mentioned frequently; they derived their name from their partial body armour consisting of a chest and back plate which protected their torso from the waist up. They also wore a helmet, heavy leather boots and gauntlets. Cavalry units from other armies had helmets, heavy boots and gauntlets. The effectiveness of these protective devices appears, however, to have been questionable. Neither the body armour nor the helmet would stop a musket bullet. In a mêlée, enemy swordsmen and bayonet wielders appear to have struck at unprotected portions of the cuirassiers. The extra weight was certainly a disadvantage: Wellington said of some bowled-over cuirassiers at Quatre Bras, 'Those that were not killed were so encumbered by their cuirasses and jackboots that they could not get up, but lay sprawling and kicking like so many turned turtles.'[1] Both the British and Dutch Armies adopted cuirasses after Waterloo, but may have done so more for appearance than for combat effectiveness.

ARTILLERY

Sweeping generalised statements about the artillery matériel employed by both sides at Waterloo have been made by some who understood as little of this specialised subject as most of us do today of intercontinental rockets. Napoleon was an artilleryman who used this arm with a greater relative effectiveness than any other commander throughout his whole career. At Waterloo, however, Wellington benefited more from his artillery than Napoleon did from his. This was the result of tactics rather than matériel, but even in matériel the two armies were to some extent different. The French pieces were heavier, more powerful and longer-ranged. (See the artillery table opposite.)

The guns and howitzers used by the French at Waterloo were made according to two different systems. The 4-pounder and 8-pounder

[1] *Croker*, I, 330.

DETAILS OF ARTILLERY USED AT WATERLOO

(In pounds or inches as appropriate)

Nation	Designation of piece	Weight of tube	Weight of carriage	Weight of charge (propellant)	Diameter of bore	Length of tube (no cascabel)	Horses required piece and limber	Ammunition
Britain	6-pounder gun	576	1,065	1·5	3·67	54·0	4	Solid shot, canister, shrapnel[1]
	9-pounder gun	1,510	1,760	3·0	4·2	72·0	6[2]	Solid shot, canister, shrapnel[1]
	5·5-inch howitzer	448	1,125	2·0	5·5	26·8	4	Canister, common shell, shrapnel
Prussia	6-pounder gun	962	1,210	2·31	3·71	64·0	6	Solid shot, canister
	12-pounder gun	2,100	1,675	4·12	4·66	80·5	8	Solid shot, canister
	5·8-inch[3] howitzer	792	1,340	1·28	5·8	37·0	6	Canister, common shell
	6·7-inch[3] howitzer	1,415	1,675	1·82	6·7	42·5	8	Canister, common shell
France	4-pounder gun (Model 1774)	645	860	1·61	3·23	57·5	8	Solid shot, canister
	8-pounder gun (Model 1774)	1,270	1,255	2·64	4·18	72·5	10	Solid shot, canister
	6-pounder gun (Model 1802-3)	880	1,130	3·19	3·78	65·5	8	Solid shot, canister
	12-pounder gun (Model 1802-3)	1,950	1,490	4·29	4·78	84·0	12	Solid shot, canister
	6·54-inch[3] howitzer (Gribeauval)	700	1,365	2·69	6·54	30·0	10	Canister, common shell

This information comes to me through Commandant Dehond from an article by Major W. Gohlke, 'Artillery 1800–1815', published in *Das Sponton*, III/IV (1963), 51. I suspect some errors in weights of carriages and do not understand why the French used such large teams.
[1] This was issued in limited quantities, but apparently not used much in guns; howitzer shrapnel was more effective.
[2] *Mercer, passim,* says the British Horse Artillery used 8 horses for each 9-pounder.
[3] I have designated these howitzers by their exact bore diameters in British inches.

guns and apparently the 6-inch howitzers were of the Gribeauval system and still effective, even though evolved originally in 1774. There were also 6-pounder and 12-pounder guns of the 1802–3 model. The newer pieces were relatively heavier than the old. The reason for this is that Napoleon wanted to concentrate artillery fire for effect and needed longer range and better accuracy. This required higher velocity which meant heavier tubes and carriages to absorb the recoil energy; there were no recoil mechanisms in those days, nor for about seventy-five years thereafter.

If long range, and accuracy at long range, were not necessary, lower projectile velocities were satisfactory. This meant lighter tubes and carriages and a quicker rate of fire. In general, British pieces were of this type, although the newly issued British 9-pounders were heavy for their projectile weight.[1] The handiest and most efficient gun at Waterloo was the British 6-pounder. It was 54 inches long and weighed less than 1,650 pounds including the carriage. Similarly, the British 5·5-inch howitzer was lighter, shorter, more easily handled and quicker firing than the French howitzers.

We should digress briefly to mention that the difference between field guns and field howitzers was much greater in 1815 than it was even fifty years later. By the middle of the nineteenth century, howitzers became heavier and longer and began to resemble field-guns. This was not so at Waterloo; howitzers were extremely short and light in proportion to bore. One instance will suffice. The French 6-inch howitzer and the British 5·5-inch howitzer were 30 inches and 26·8 inches long and weighed 700 pounds and 448 pounds respectively. A French 12-pounder field-gun tube and a British 9-pounder gun tube weighed 1,950 pounds and 1,760 pounds respectively. But these howitzers at close range were even more effective than the field-guns; they threw as much canister as a double-charged gun and threw it more evenly and in a larger pattern.

The Prussian artillery and presumably that of the minor Allied armies were similar to that of the French. The new models of 1812 Prussian field-pieces were in some cases heavier than the French, but were drawn by fewer horses. There were 6-pounder and 12-pounder guns as well as two different sizes of howitzers, all similar in design and

---

[1] As actually used at Waterloo, one wonders if the change from 6-pounders to 9-pounders was beneficial. The lighter pieces could have fired at least twice as fast, but they may not have been able to stand double charging so well.

manufacture to the heavy artillery of Napoleon, as can be seen from the artillery table.

Artillery projectiles at Waterloo were of three general types. The most important were solid round iron balls which fitted the bores fairly snugly;[1] these were called common shot. Next in importance came canister, a number of small cast iron spheres in a sheet metal can which disintegrated on discharge. These individual projectiles were of various sizes and known indiscriminately as grape and canister. I believe, however, that no true grape (three balls to a layer filling the bore precisely) was used in the battle; it was all canister, but sizes varied. This has been referred to briefly in Part I, Chapter II. Finally, explosive shells were fired from howitzers of all nationalities.

There was one special type of artillery projectile used only in the British Army – shrapnel or spherical case. These were introduced in 1803 and had been employed with varying results in the Peninsula. They were minimum thickness hollow spheres filled with balls and a minimum bursting charge; if a fuse exploded this shell when it was fifty yards up and 100 yards in front of a target, the balls and fragments of the shell would all come down in a fairly even pattern on the target. The problem was to get a uniform time of burning from one fuse to the next. Shrapnel shell was produced for both howitzers and guns, but gun shrapnel was ineffective because the entire shell was too small. The great virtue of shrapnel shell was that it allowed canister type fire up to ranges of 1,000 yards.

AMMUNITION

All ammunition used at Waterloo was in the form of cartridges. That for small arms consisted of a bullet and a powder charge wrapped in paper. French infantrymen had forty each, but British and KGL foot soldiers carried sixty in each cartridge box plus another sixty in the knapsack.[2] Extra small arms ammunition was carried in special carts, wagons, and tumbrils, in either boxes or barrels.

Artillery cartridges were made of stiff cloth cylinders of bore diameter to contain the powder charge secured to a wooden sabot which had the common shot, shell or canister attached to the other end. These were packed precisely into chests which were carried on the limber of

---

[1] This maximum shot diameter was always under minimum bore diameter by an amount called 'windage', usually about an eighth of an inch.

[2] *Leeke*, I, 12, and others.

each piece, usually two chests per limber. Some gun and howitzer carriages had smaller chests of ammunition attached to them. Extra chests were carried in wagons and perhaps carts. Caissons were new at that time, but are mentioned as having been used by Whinyates's Battery, R.H.A.[1]

[1] *Duncan*, II, 418.

II

Wellington's Mistakes

Some writers have criticised Wellington severely in connection with Waterloo, even though he won. The Duke may or may not have been popular with the majority of his army; there is evidence on both sides. There is no question, however, that he has been disliked by many British historians and by most of those from the Continent. Some have damned with faint praise; others have said the victory at Waterloo resulted from French blunders, superhuman Prussian exertions or astonishing freaks of fortune. The Duke's unconcealed personal dominance and self-reliance have been made to appear cold and selfish; his realism has not been confused with modesty. Consciously or unconsciously, historians have endeavoured to find faults, particularly those who glorify Napoleon.

The first mistake frequently attributed to Wellington is that he dispersed his army too widely before the campaign began. I believe this criticism to be in error. Napoleon could attack anywhere from the Meuse to the Channel. There might be little or no warning as to the actual point or points he chose. The Duke's dispositions as I have explained were not based on guesses, but on carefully considered probabilities. The Duke guarded all practical avenues of approach with forces appropriate to the damage that Napoleon might do quickly.[1] Wellington had three principal responsibilities: his communications with Britain, the Dutch-Belgian capital at Brussels and the temporary capital of Louis XVIII's French government-in-exile at Ghent.

---

[1] Allied field-army dispositions did not cover the eastern approaches to Ghent, nor the open coastal area. Wellington was taking a calculated risk west of the Lys, but had some secondary troops in field fortifications there.

The Duke was too sound a professional soldier to give up his best line of communications with Britain. The loss of either capital city would have caused a furore of Bonapartist sentiment throughout Europe. Wellington had studied what Napoleon had done in the past; the Emperor's greatest victories had come from doing the unexpected. The Anglo-Dutch dispositions made surprise difficult and proper reaction to an attack at any point relatively easy.

Wellington is said to have been caught at a disadvantage by the French on 15 June 1815. Since none of his troops were actually engaged that day, there was no tactical surprise. But what about strategic surprise? The Duke did not actually expect Napoleon to attack at all; if the French did attack, Wellington was prepared for them to come through Mons rather than Charleroi. But all this has been covered adequately in Part One. In spite of the unfortunate delays in the arrival of intelligence from the Prussians and certain internal failures, Wellington reacted to win at Quatre Bras and at Waterloo. Napoleon's attack achieved nothing significant against the Anglo-Dutch Army by surprise or otherwise.

The third 'major' criticism of Wellington appears to be his attending the Duchess of Richmond's ball. A commanding general in modern times would not do something like this. But it was in the British tradition. Drake finished his game of bowls before defeating the Armada. Wellington did not want to give the many supporters of Napoleon in Brussels the opportunity of spreading wild rumours about a sudden movement, even though it was towards the enemy.[1]

As a corollary to the above, Wellington has been criticised for not being at the front, perhaps at Frasnes, on the evening of the 15th. Even if he had been informed of the attack on the Prussians in time, he could not have galloped off with staff and some cavalry only. This would have been contrary to his established pattern of command. Besides, he commanded his Reserve Corps himself and had no one to take over for him.[2] Wellington was not needed at Frasnes on the night of 15–16 June. No man who ever commanded armies has had such an uncanny ability to be at the right place at the right time. He was at Quatre Bras the next day, when he was needed, to avert a tragedy for the Europe that was against Napoleon.

The fourth and more serious charge against Wellington is that he

[1] Rumours in Brussels could be started by far less. See particularly *Creevey Papers*, I, *passim*.

[2] See the discussion of the use of Picton and the Duke of Brunswick with the other hereditary commanders in the Allied army in Part I, Chapter III.

gave the Prussians false information about the position of his army in a letter written before noon on the 16th. The questionable short letter was in error about distant troops, but the mistake was unintentional.[1] The Duke may have rectified the mis-statements of this letter in his personal conference with Blücher near the Brye windmill. This false information did no irreparable damage, for the Prussians were going to fight at Ligny anyway. Wellington did not have so many men as he thought he would have at Quatre Bras, but he accomplished all that anyone could reasonably expect him to do. He held Ney's force in play all day and finally defeated it. The Prussians lost to a numerically inferior French Army at Ligny.

Fifth, Wellington is accused of wasting the 17,000 men he left at Hal and Tubize. Military historians who will accept no other major criticism of the Duke sometimes admit this to be a serious error. As the battle turned out, it most certainly was; these extra men would have been a real help at Waterloo. The battle would not have been such a 'close thing', if this detached force had been present.

But all this is wisdom after the event. Wellington made his dispositions to guard against all reasonably likely moves by Napoleon who could have shifted his axis of attack from the Charleroi to the Mons road. The Duke was always concerned about his right flank because of Brussels, Ghent and his communications with Ostend.[2] He certainly did not forget this force which had an extremely important job to do if Napoleon were to manœuvre to his left, as many French analyists thought afterwards he should have done.[3]

On the morning of the 18th Wellington did not know the exact position of all French forces. He could see by personal observation that Napoleon had detached a considerable portion of his entire army. There were about 38,000 Frenchmen unaccounted for; he knew of Grouchy's movements in general, but not his strength. If Grouchy had only half this force, the other half could have been moving to turn the Duke's right flank. Wellington did not underrate Napoleon. Even though fighting a critical battle at Waterloo, he wanted to prevent the Emperor from winning by really doing the unexpected. The

---

[1] De Lancey, Wellington's QMG, died of Waterloo wounds; his papers were lost. An acceptable explanation of his dispositions paper delivered to the Duke early on 16 June 1815 is difficult. See *Ropes*, 87 and 106 for the way in which this muddle came about.

[2] *Fortescue*, X, 346, says, 'Four letters from him, dated at three o'clock in the morning are preserved, in each of which he alludes to the possibility that his position might be turned by way of Hal, and that Brussels might thereby be uncovered . . .'

[3] *Jomini*, 209–10.

Hal-Tubize force was there not only to prevent Napoleon turning the Anglo-Dutch right flank, but also to act as a reserve in case of a catastrophe. If it had been necessary to retreat, Wellington probably would have done so by his right on Ostend.[1]

One can also point out in this connection that the Hal-Tubize force included only one British and one Hanoverian infantry brigade, a total of 5,445 men. None of the four British infantry battalions in this force had fought in the Peninsula; the best element of Colville's Division was Mitchell's all-veteran 4th British Brigade which was at Waterloo. Further, by keeping this force on his flank, Wellington did rid himself of the boy Frederick of Orange who could have caused additional troubles during the battle similar to those attributable to his elder brother. The force was adequate for a delaying action such as the Duke foresaw, but would not have been as useful in battle as its strength might indicate.

Sixth, Wellington has been criticised for his choice of the position at Waterloo. Picton certainly made an observation of this type on the morning of the 18th. Picton knew more than most division commanders about handling their units in battle. He was tough and brave; his heroic military life and death in front of the Ohain road place him in the front rank of British division commanders. But he was not perceptive about terrain. After years in the Peninsula, he expected bold, bare slopes; he did not realise that similar tactical advantages could be obtained from the less rugged, rounded ridges at Waterloo. Wellington's army was almost as well protected by these over most of the front as behind the crest of the Busaco mountains. Lateral communications were secure and shielded from enemy observation. The farm enclosures of Hougoumont, La Haye Sainte and Papelotte-La Haye added elements of strength. Picton's snap judgement appears to have justified Wellington's estimate of his unsuitability for independent command, rather than to be a valid criticism of the Duke's choice of position. We should point out, however, that Picton's particular area was the poorest section of the entire position.

Napoleon criticised Wellington for fighting at Waterloo. How can a defeated commander legitimately criticise the victor for fighting where he did? The more complete the defeat, the more ridiculous the

---

[1] The question of the direction of Wellington's retreat, if one had been necessary, has fascinated many writers. Wellington apparently never made up his mind at the time; he would probably have decided, if and when it became necessary, in accordance with the policy, 'I make my campaign plan like a harness of rope. If a break occurs, I tie a knot and go on.' See also *Petrie*, 204–5, *Roberts*, p. 166, and *Bain*, 169.

criticism. But Napoleon used his great energies after Waterloo to justify all his own military acts and hurt the reputations of all his opponents, particularly Wellington.

The Emperor claims that Wellington should have retired through the forest of Soignes and fought on the other side. He contended that a defeat in front of the forest would have been disastrous for the Duke. This just was not so. Even Jomini, who was usually pro-Napoleon, was against him here.[1] The forest was open and was traversed by several good roads. Wellington has had no superiors in handling an army in retreat; the trees would have helped rather than hindered.

Seventh, Wellington has been faulted for the loss of La Haye Sainte. The Duke would have certainly accepted complete responsibility for this since it occurred under his general command. He never blamed subordinates in any public writing or statements. We should remember, however, that this local success was the single French achievement of the entire day, a very minor one for Napoleon, numerous renowned marshals and generals, and more than 70,000 French troops, most of them veterans. The fact that the farm held out until around 6.15 p.m., even though attacked vigorously and by large forces, is sufficient justification for the local commander and its garrison. La Haye Sainte was smaller and defensively less strong than Hougoumont.

The final loss of this farm was principally due to a shortage of ammunition for the rifles of Baring's 2nd Light Battalion, KGL. Most Allied units were resupplied with cartridges as required, including those in Hougoumont, but the La Haye Sainte riflemen were not. There are conflicting accounts of why this happened. Wellington's own mention of the failure to pierce the rear wall of the farm enclosure for the intake of ammunition appears to be in error.[2] The reasons for this shortage have already been discussed in Part One, Chapter X; ammunition was lacking. But was this the responsibility of the Commander-in-Chief? The Duke often saw to matters of no great importance, but he obviously could not see to everything during a battle.

[1] *Jomini's Art*, p. 183. He says, 'Would an army with its rear resting upon a forest, and with a good road behind the centre and each wing, have its retreat compromised, as Napoleon imagined, if it should lose the battle? My own opinion is that such a position would be more favourable for a retreat than an entirely open field. A beaten army could not cross a plain without exposure to very great danger.

[2] *Chad*, 3, quotes Wellington as saying, 'I put it full of Troops, but the officer commanding them neglected to break a communication through the back wall. When their ammunition was expended, the French attacking the house kept up such a fire that they were obliged to surrender.' There was, and still is, a door in this north wall of the building; see *Beamish*, II, plate V, and recent photographs.

The final material criticism of Wellington at Waterloo concerns his failure to use his three batteries of iron 18-pounders. These pieces were required for sieges where walls had to be knocked down. At round-shot ranges against personnel, they would have been very little more effective per round than 9-pounders, but were approximately four times as heavy and took at least four times as long to load and fire. Below 400 yards, they would have been even less useful per discharge than standard field-pieces because there was no multiple-projectile ammunition – grape or canister – available for them. Even if there had been, 5·5-inch field-howitzers would have been preferable. These 18-pounders were as inappropriate for use in battle as a modern 120 mm recoilless rifle (the British Army's present 'Wombat') would be for deer stalking.[1]

It would appear that Lord Roberts may have been correct in his analysis of the Duke when he wrote:

In the Waterloo campaign, Wellington made no mistakes. His distribution of the Allied troops along the Belgian frontier, his rapid concentration at Quatre Bras in concert with the Prussian Army at Ligny, his success on June 16th, his subsequent withdrawal to Waterloo, the manner in which he handled his troops before and during the battle, and the arrangements he made with Blücher for the flank attack from Wavre and for the pursuit of the defeated enemy, prove him to have been a profound master of the art of war.[2]

In the case of almost any other military commander the above com-mendation would be ample, but Wellington's modern critics have another approach. Severities of speech and writing, often quoted out of context, have alienated writers who really must know little of the man or his work. Leonard Cooper has written of the Duke and his soldiers, 'To him, they were "the scum of the earth – they have enlisted for drink, that is the simple truth". Even after the triumph of Waterloo he could find nothing better to call them than "the most infamous army I ever commanded". He never praised them or thanked them, though they served him as few commanders have ever been served. When they deserted he shot them; when they looted he hanged them; and, perpetually and on the smallest excuse, he flogged them.'[3]

---

[1] Siege work required high velocity and solid shot only; no other ammunition was provided. In the days before high explosive bursting charges, a single projectile of large size was only slightly more effective than a small one against troops in the open.

[2] *Roberts*, 190.

[3] *Cooper*, ix. The author later rectifies to a great extent this sweeping denunciation, but the first impression is often the lasting one.

This is brilliant, effective prose, but untrue. The Duke's recorded speeches and his writings are full of praise for his soldiers, as has been shown throughout in this work. The famous 'scum of the earth' quotation was part of a confidential admonition to higher unit commanders issued after extreme misbehaviour following the Vitoria victory in June 1813. No commander ever took more pains over the well-being of the rank and file of his army, a fact which they appreciated.[1] The implication about his methods of imposing discipline is one of sadism; nothing could be further from the truth. Can one imagine the Duke, with all his problems, being even indirectly connected with flogging soldiers 'on the smallest excuse'?

Now for the 'most infamous army'. This was an 'off the record' comment and not directed at the British, KGL, and Hanoverian portions of his command. How would a commander describe units that he had to dispose so they could not desert? That fired on him personally? The Cumberland Hussars fled to Brussels; most of the Belgians would not remain under direct artillery fire, stay to receive infantry, or charge. How else would he refer to an organisation which gave him as important generals boys of eighteen and twenty-three without any virtues for command?

All men who lived and attained high station in the eighteenth and nineteenth centuries can be scathingly criticised according to modern ways of thought. Anyone who did, wrote and said as much as Wellington can be portrayed in almost any light a clever man may wish. The Duke was not a successful politician, but he was a remarkable soldier.

---

[1] *Wheeler*, 196, says, 'If England should require the service of her army again, and I should be with it, let me have "Old Nosey" to command. Our interests would be sure to be looked into, we should never have occasion to fear an enemy. There are two things we should be certain of. First, we should always be as well supplied with rations as the nature of the service would admit. The second is we should be sure to give the enemy a d—d good thrashing. What can a soldier desire more?'

III

French Mistakes

Mistakes made by French commanders during the five-day Waterloo campaign have been emphasised by the efforts of Napoleon and his supporters to place the blame for his ultimate total defeat on others, particularly on Grouchy, Ney and d'Erlon. Napoleon himself has been charged with serious errors, although these are often explained by ill-health, or unaccountable misfortune.[1] We will treat the more important of these more or less in chronological order.

Almost everyone agrees that the French concentration before their 15 June attack was admirable. Napoleon's general plan to attack Charleroi near the junction point of the armies commanded by Wellington and Blücher appears to have been sound and well conceived, if he was to attack at all.[2] The first criticism of the French execution of this general movement is that time was lost reaching and crossing the Sambre. Napoleon ordered the advance to begin at 3 a.m. D'Erlon did not start until 4.30; Vandamme did not receive his orders on time and was not on the way until 6 a.m. Gérard moved more slowly than had been anticipated. The bridges over the Sambre, particularly at Marcinelle, were not taken as soon as they might have been. Gérard finally had to cross the river to the east at Chatelet, not in accordance with the original plan.

[1] 'In French military works, the reader never finds a French army beaten in the field without some plausible reason, or, as Las Casas terms it, a concurrence of unheard of totalities to account for it.' *Ellesmere's Essays*, 154, who acknowledges Captain Pringle's words in Scott's *Life of Napoleon*.

[2] Wellington and Lord Roberts felt that Napoleon would have done better to await the Allied attack behind the formidable French border fortresses: *Stanhope*, 59–60; *Roberts*, 147. Militarily, there was much to be said in favour of a defensive war by Napoleon, but it may not have been advantageous politically: *Hamley*, 185.

All these things are usual in war; nothing ever goes exactly as conceived, especially an attack of this type against good soldiers ably commanded. The inescapable immediate result of the French advance was that they were over the Sambre with artillery on a broad front from Thuin to east of Charleroi by early afternoon. This is particularly remarkable because the roads here had been torn up early in the spring to prevent their use by the Allies. Even though the French Army was composed of veterans of the highest quality, the organisation was new. The staff was working together for the first time. They cannot be seriously faulted for slowness on the 15th.

The next criticism of Napoleon and/or his army seems to be founded upon pro-French hopes, rather than military probability. The Prussian corps under General Ziethen which was defending the line of the Sambre was allowed to retreat north of the river and concentrate on Fleurus without serious loss. There was some hard fighting, but casualties appear to have been about even.[1] The French subordinate commanders are said to have failed to inflict crippling losses on Ziethen's Corps. They can hardly be blamed for this. The Prussians were not surprised. Their field officers and above, as well as many of the men in the ranks, were experienced in war and fully capable of conducting efficient rear-guard actions without becoming too greatly involved in them.

We now come to the first of the personal criticisms of Ney; there will be several more. Some Bonapartists believe that he should have taken Quatre Bras on the evening of the 15th. This seems unreasonable.[2] Ney did not report to Napoleon until 3 a.m. and was then assigned to command the French left wing, the composition of which he now learned for the first time. The advance of this wing was stopped at Gosselies by a strong Prussian force which finally moved farther east, uncovering the Brussels road. Ney sent cavalry forward to Frasnes, but it was stopped by a superior number of Dutch–Belgians including infantry and artillery. French infantry did not come up until after sunset. Even had Ney been fully familiar with, and confident in, his command, could he be expected to push forward with both flanks in the air? He knew that a strong Prussian force was behind him to the east. He had no definite

[1] Probably between 1,500 and 2,000 on each side, although the Prussians may have suffered a bit more severely.

[2] See particularly *Pratt*, 42–43. *Jomini*, 123, inclines to the opinion that Ney was verbally ordered by Napoleon to take Quatre Bras, but the instructions were probably, 'Push forward in that direction.'

orders to expose his command in this manner, particularly in what would have amounted to a night attack on an unknown enemy in an unreconnoitred position.

On the whole, all the criticisms of the French for 15 June 1815 seem weak. The Emperor and his army accomplished about as much as could be reasonably expected of them. They did not cripple their enemy, but achieved all their immediate objectives. Napoleon was certainly not displeased with progress made so far.[1]

Criticisms of decisions and actions of the next day are more complicated and to some extent more justified. Napoleon has been blamed for allowing the Prussians to concentrate three full corps, roughly 90,000 men, in position for battle at Ligny. If the French had attacked early in the morning on the 16th rather than in the middle of the afternoon, some believe that they would have been overwhelmingly successful. Careful analysis, however, indicates that an early attack was out of the question because the French just were not in position for it; their rear elements were not yet north of the Sambre. Blücher had nearly 60,000 men in position before 7 a.m.; his third corps was up by 10 a.m. Napoleon could not possibly have begun his attack with anything approaching comparable numbers before noon.

Napoleon and historians who have glorified the Emperor have criticised Ney for his failure to drive the Allied forces from Quatre Bras early in the morning of the 16th. Napoleon most dishonestly claimed to have specifically ordered Ney to take Quatre Bras soon after dawn.[2] Ney was not ordered to take Quatre Bras early on the 16th; Napoleon did not conceive his dispositions for that day until 8 a.m., probably near Fleurus.[3] His actual orders to Ney arrived much later and envisaged no serious fighting on this wing.[4] Ney probably advanced as soon as he prudently could. He moved before d'Erlon's Corps had joined him, a technical breach of his instructions. The attack that he did make about 2.30 p.m. could have left him with both flanks in the air. If he had been able to penetrate north of the Nivelles – Namur road,

---

[1] But *Robinson*, III, 521–2, says, 'Many writers (Jomini and Charras among them) have held that Napoleon's success on June 15th was really incomplete because he failed to seize the Nivelles–Namur road.'

[2] *Chesney*, 112, says that Napoleon's statement 'would not have been published had the ex-Emperor known that his real orders of the morning would have seen the light, as they did nearly twenty years later, thanks to the interest of Ney's son in the matter'.

[3] Ibid., 99, based on 'overwhelming testimony' in Charras.

[4] *Ropes*, 120–4.

Blücher's forces would have been to the rear of his eastern flank, and the part of Wellington's army which was moving to Quatre Bras from Nivelles in the rear of his western flank. Besides, even at 2.30 p.m. the Marshal had only half his force in hand. That he began his battle as soon as he did is probably to his credit.[1]

We should also remember in this connection that Ney was in the immediate presence of Napoleon, not on a semi-independent command. He certainly carried out his first actual orders, which reached him only a little before noon, with reasonable dispatch considering the dispersion of his force. How far Ney could have concentrated his force beforehand is open to question. It may not have been advisable so early in the campaign, even if it was possible. Concentration usually limits manœuvre, which was what the French did best.

We now come to a criticism of the French which is valid and pertinent beyond question. D'Erlon's Corps was part of Ney's command and was ordered by him to move up so as to be available for use at Quatre Bras by 4.30 p.m. at the latest. When a few minutes before 4 p.m. these four divisions were marching north towards this battlefield and were about abreast of Frasnes, a messenger from Napoleon turned them about and had them march through Villers-Perwin for the Ligny battlefield.[2] When they were about to arrive there, a peremptory order from Ney caused d'Erlon to turn about and retrace his steps, save for one division which he left near Wagnelee. D'Erlon's Corps arrived south of Quatre Bras after Ney's battle was over, apparently about 9.30 p.m. It was marching forwards and backwards between battlefields for six hours without firing a shot at either of them.

French historians are right in their contention that this force of 20,000 men could have won at Quatre Bras or turned a limited victory for the French at Ligny into a resounding success. But these things happen in war. The men involved certainly all appear to have acted in good faith and with fair judgement. With the best of intentions, orders were misunderstood, or interpreted poorly.

Napoleon and various French subordinate commanders have been criticised for not following the Prussians after defeating them at Ligny late on the 16th. A routine cavalry pursuit that evening appears to have

[1] *Hamley*, 201. Remember also the reticence of French commanders who had served in Spain to attack positions which they thought were held by Wellington.

[2] The messenger, the message and the intended recipient are all subject to question. See *Ropes*, 193, for a weighing of contradictory evidence.

been impossible; French mounted units which tried it were quickly brought to a stand by Prussian forces of cavalry, infantry and artillery. Thielemann's entire Corps retained defensive positions practically on the battlefield of Ligny until long after dawn on the 17th. Really powerful efforts to pursue the slowly retreating Prussians would have brought on a night battle. Apart from other considerations, the French were too tired for this.

We now come to what I believe is another valid criticism. A strong movement in the direction of the retreating Prussians in the evening of 16 June was impractical, but not on the morning of the 17th. Grouchy could have been sent north hours before he was; a great deal might have been accomplished. The Prussians were still in good order and subject to discipline, but they had suffered severely on the afternoon of the 16th and were more demoralised than they admitted later.[1]

Why did this delay occur? It was partly unavoidable; the short night just was not sufficient time for rest and recuperation, especially with the French system of supply. But in addition to this necessary delay, Napoleon seems to have dawdled. A noted French historian's defence seems only to convict more completely.

Marshal Grouchy in asserting that Napoleon, on the morning of the 17th, was as little inclined to action as an Oriental prince, only shows that he did not comprehend the true position of affairs, and that he neither knew nor understood that Napoleon was obliged to wait, first, until Ney should have defiled at Quatre Bras with 40,000 men; secondly, until Lobau's troops should be en marche towards Quatre Bras; thirdly, until the Guard should have eaten their soup and left their bivouacs; fourthly, until some reports from Pajol's cavalry should inform him of the direction the Prussians had taken.[2]

Pajol's troopers did take prisoners and capture Prussian artillery on the Namur road, but the main Prussian retreat was towards Gembloux and Wavre. Grouchy and about 33,000 Frenchmen were sent after them, but did not get well on their way until early afternoon. The delay, however, was caused by the Emperor, not Grouchy.

Ney has been castigated for not attacking Wellington at Quatre Bras shortly after dawn on the 17th.[3] Napoleon with the main French

---

[1] *Cotton*, 65, says that the Prussian losses on the 15th and 16th were 18,000 and that '10,000 more, enlisted from what had been French provinces, retired to Liège without orders'.

[2] *Thiers*, XII, 83.

[3] *Becke*, 147–8, calls this an extremely costly error. 'Had Ney acted in this fashion [attacked early] there would have been no Waterloo.'

force was several miles away and did not begin to march towards Ney for nearly eight hours. The unfortunate Marshal could not have attacked Wellington successfully at 4, 6, or 8 a.m. because the Duke had an overwhelming superiority in all arms. No experienced subordinate commander would have undertaken such an attack with his nearest reinforcements nearly three hours away, unless he had specific instructions to do so. Napoleon certainly did not give them, although he claimed to have done so.[1] Here Ney appears to be blameless; as we have seen, he skirmished furiously to the point of bringing on a battle, but did not do so because he lacked the force to win.

Even though we clear Ney, should the French still be faulted for a missed opportunity? The answer appears to be in the affirmative. Wellington was certainly worried, and only stayed because he chose the lesser of two evils. Some historians who have carefully studied this phase of the action believe that if Napoleon had moved from Ligny towards Quatre Bras even as late as 9 a.m., rather than after midday, he would have caught and badly mauled the Duke's army, even crippled it. I doubt this conclusion; even though Wellington did not want to be forced backwards with his miscellaneous army, he might have managed an operation of this type without serious loss. He retreated hundreds of miles in Spain in the face of more numerous French Armies with no disproportionate casualties and without the loss of a field piece.[2] The French delay on the 17th certainly made the Allied retreat easier, but a start sufficiently early to win a decisive action on the 17th may not have been possible.

Now we come to the (for the French) tragic 18th. Napoleon has been severely criticised for not attacking Wellington at Waterloo earlier. As things worked out, every hour that the French could have gained would have been in their favour. But the French could not have attacked shortly after dawn because their entire force had not yet arrived north of Rossome. Further, the commissariat difficulties of Napoleon's armies were as bad as ever; in addition to three days of marching and fighting, the troops had to find most of their food. Finally, all weapons needed to be cleaned after the downpour of the

---

[1] *Chesney*, 146–7, quoting Napoleon's *Memoirs*.

[2] The longest of these retreats was in the autumn of 1812, from in front of Burgos back to the Salamanca position and then back to Ciudad Rodrigo, nearly 250 miles. But there were many others. Wellington's personal ability to direct rear-guard fighting was particularly well demonstrated at El Bodon on 25 September 1811: *Weller*, 191.

afternoon and night before. An attack by a poorly concentrated, tired, hungry and inadequately armed army would have been worse than a delay.

On the other hand, Napoleon and many who have followed his account give an excuse that appears unsound. They say the battlefield needed a few hours to dry so that the French artillery and cavalry could move more easily. Strong sun and wind would only slowly dry soaked Belgian soil; a few hours under ideal conditions would have helped slightly. There appears to have been no sun, negligible wind, and many showers.

Napoleon did use a part of his time on the morning of the 18th for a grand display of the French might. This demonstration may have caused some dismay in Allied ranks, perhaps in Bylandt's Brigade of Dutch–Belgians. The rest were mostly out of sight behind crests. A more valid consideration may have been that Napoleon realised the extreme length of daylight at this time of year, from about 3 a.m. until after 9 p.m., and believed that his army could only take about nine hours of this for combat. He may have chosen the second half of the day rather than the first half, but his chances would have been better if he had attacked just as soon as he could.

The most notorious of the French mistakes was Grouchy's in not marching towards the sound of the guns. Napoleon and his school place the major blame for the Waterloo defeat on Grouchy, not only for his failure to come to the battlefield but also on other accounts. Grouchy has been accused of moving too late on the 17th and stopping for the night too early. We have already disposed of the first charge; he began as soon as was reasonably possible after receiving Napoleon's orders. The second is equally unfounded; in spite of the weather, none of his units bivouacked until after nightfall. They were all on the march by 8 a.m., hours earlier than Napoleon himself.[1]

The much more serious charges involve Grouchy's positions on the 18th. As Waterloo was fought, Grouchy did Napoleon little or no good. His 33,000 men, or any significant part of them, would certainly have been of enormous assistance to the French at Waterloo. We will

---

[1] *Chesney*, 187, citing Clausewitz, 132, says, 'Clausewitz, who amid deep theory reverts constantly to the practical conditions and difficulties of the warfare he had witnessed, shed a plainer light here than any other critic. He points out that from the field of Ligny, by Gembloux to Wavre, is a march of more than twenty miles, and that the distance was accomplished by Grouchy in just twenty-four hours, under very unfavourable conditions of road and weather. In their best days, he finds that Napoleon's troops, under such circumstances, often did not make over ten miles.'

leave until later the larger issue of whether or not Grouchy should have been dispatched to Gembloux at all, but consider now whether he obeyed his orders and behaved with professional efficiency in his semi-independent command.

Grouchy cannot fairly be blamed until the time that he heard the boom of guns at Waterloo slightly before noon. Any movement except in pursuit of the Prussians, who on the morning of the 18th were positively known to be at Wavre, would have been contrary to his orders.[1] At the time Grouchy and most of his senior officers were at Walhain Saint-Paul having breakfast.[2] Here the famous discussion in which Corps Commander Gérard proposed 'marching toward the cannon' took place.[3] So much has been written about this apparently stormy informal council of war, but French historians do not agree either on what was said, or on what should have been done.

Grouchy's decision to continue as ordered appears to have been sound. Napoleon certainly knew he was going to fight a battle, yet in his orders to Grouchy sent off around 10 a.m., he said in substance, 'March on Wavre and draw closer to the main army.'[4] Those who would have Grouchy march to the sound of the guns would also have him not only disobey his orders, but anticipate by two hours Napoleon's own desire for his presence.[5]

There is another aspect of this hypothetical question as to whether Grouchy should have disobeyed his order. Would any movement begun at noon have done Napoleon any good? There appears to be no question that Grouchy would have accomplished nothing useful by moving directly on Plancenoit at noon. His force was almost twice as far from

---

[1] Against this, see *Pratt*, 148–50. But Grouchy was detached to follow the Prussians to Gembloux and Wavre. How could he move otherwise?

[2] *Wolseley*, 181; *Ropes*, 287.

[3] *Jomini*, 176–7, examines this maxim, but is not definite as to its application in this instance. *Thiers*, 141 ff., gives a vivid account of this discussion and believes Grouchy should have moved west through Ottignies. See also *Chesney*, 168–9, who is opposed to this view.

[4] These words are from *Pratt*, 153. The message in original French has survived in three slightly different versions; English translations and paraphrases are far more numerous. *Ropes*, 266, says, 'His majesty desires that you will direct your movements on Wavre, in order to approach us, to put yourself in the sphere of our operations, and to keep up your communications with us.' One realises that the twentieth century does not have a monopoly on vague, wordy orders, but the movement on Wavre is definitely indicated by all versions.

[5] *Maxwell*, II, 62, says that orders from Napoleon to Grouchy to join the main army were sent at 1.30 p.m. and were delivered at 5 p.m., far too late to be acted on effectively. There is no substantial disagreement with this, even among French historians.

that point as Bülow's Prussian Corps had been four hours earlier from La Haye Sainte. Grouchy's men would have had to negotiate the same sort of poor, sodden roads and defiles; their entire march would have been under Prussian observation. They would have had to fight all the way from the vicinity of Mont Saint Guibert.[1] The Dyle bridges around Ottignies would have been defended by the same Prussians who actually defended those a little farther downstream at Limale and Limelette. Grouchy would not have reached Waterloo no matter what he did unless he had changed the direction of his movements long before noon on the 18th.[2]

The logical advocates for a move contrary to orders by Grouchy at noon want him to move neither on Wavre, nor Plancenoit, but directly on Limale.

Grouchy need not, according to their view, have gone to Plancenoit at all. An intermediate march across the Dyle at Limale would have surprised the Prussians on the way, by taking them perpendicularly, in flank. This case, however, admits of simple treatment, and indeed has been fully considered by theorists favourable to Napoleon. Jomini stands at the head of these, and his decision is, 'Nevertheless, we must be allowed to believe that, in any event, the Prussian Marshal, after having observed Grouchy's force, would have judged the divisions of Pirch and Thielemann sufficient to hold it back, whilst with those of Bülow and Zieten he aided Wellington to decide the victory.'[3]

So much for grand strategy, movements and the like away from the main battlefield; now for manœuvres and tactics at Waterloo itself. The French have been criticised for their attacks on Hougoumont, which they made increasingly strong as they failed to achieve success. As we have seen, Napoleon, Ney and Reille finally used up two full divisions and part of a third to no useful purpose.[4] If Napoleon could have anticipated in the beginning that Hougoumont would not be taken, he could have used these troops to advantage elsewhere. But this can always be said when an attack fails. Had it succeeded, Wellington's entire right would have been subjected to the kind of punishment the centre received later in the battle after the fall of La Haye Sainte.

---

[1] *Müffling*, 39, says that Mont Saint Guibert was occupied by 'two battalions, two regiments of cavalry, and two pieces of horse artillery'. This force moved north to Wavre after they determined that Grouchy was moving north, not west, from Corbais.

[2] *Chesney*, 190–1, and many others.

[3] Ibid., 192, citing *Thiers*, XX, 265, and *Jomini*, 223.

[4] Jerome's and Foy's Divisions completely and part of Bachelu's, Reille's whole Corps save for Girard's Division which was at Quatre Bras and Ligny.

D'Erlon has been criticised for the special division columns he used in his attack. This has already been discussed in detail in Part One, Chapter VIII. The formation did prove faulty, but could have been advantageous under other circumstances. Ney and sometimes Napoleon have been blamed for attacking with infantry, but no cavalry and artillery, and then with cavalry, but no infantry and artillery. I fail to understand how critics can set themselves up as superior to Ney in battle tactics. He and Napoleon had been handling French troops in combat for more than twenty years and doing quite well with them. To say calmly that they blundered requires a courage and confidence that I lack. Fortunately, I do not have to do so.

The infantry attack made by Ney and d'Erlon was accompanied by cavalry on both flanks. Uxbridge's ill-fated counter-attack smashed the French west flank cavalry before it came in contact with infantry. Supporting cavalry which was in position, but did not share in the attack, finally defeated the British troopers who were so successful before they went out of hand. In addition to the famous grand battery of between 76 and 84 guns which prepared the way for the infantry and supported it with fire, field batteries certainly advanced with d'Erlon's infantry columns, and were destroyed with them. The infantry-artillery-cavalry teamwork which produced so many French victories during the Napoleonic period did not disappear from the battlefield, but each part of it was countered by an appropriate Allied move, save that nothing could save the British heavy cavalry after they went out of control.

The cavalry attacks made mainly under Ney's direction were on such a limited front – 1,000 yards maximum between Hougoumont and La Haye Sainte – and by such a mass of horsemen that infantry and short-range artillery support was necessarily limited. The space available was too small for the cavalry alone; infantry and artillery would have increased the congestion and decreased the efficiency of these attacks.[1] Some French guns did come forward towards the end of the period; tirailleurs did manage to operate on the flanks of the French cavalry. But in general there just was not sufficient space in which to move.[2]

---

[1] At normal intervals, 10,000 horsemen on a front of 800 yards would have formed a 'column' at least 800 yards deep. See p. 109, n. 3. To have introduced artillery and infantry into this in large quantities, perhaps in layers, would have produced chaos.

[2] *Becke*, 206, says, 'Had guns been galloped up in the wake of the cavalry and opened a case-shot attack of the squares, nothing could have saved the centre of Wellington's line.' Can one imagine even six guns coming forward in line at speed, swinging through 180°, unlimbering, and opening fire amid the press of French cavalry?

Ney and sometimes Napoleon are also criticised for launching the French cavalry at Wellington's line too early. Since those attacks failed, they are fair game for the 'second guessing' of critics. Ney certainly did order the cavalry under his command forward sooner than was Napoleon's custom. He believed, however, that they might succeed. He saw a lot of Allied soldiers leaving the field and knew that the intervention of the Prussians was only a matter of time. If Ney's cavalry had broken Wellington's line, the French might have destroyed the Allied army and had ample time to turn on the Prussians.

There is another criticism of Ney in connection with the cavalry attacks. He is said to have exceeded his authority in sending forward so much cavalry. It would appear that Ney ordered forward units which had actually been assigned to him and that others joined them without positive orders from either Ney or Napoleon. Ney cannot be held responsible for this, since he would logically assume that Napoleon had sent them. Even though Napoleon may not have ordered these units forward, he was certainly present and could have stopped them if he had been so inclined.

The attack of the Imperial Guard on Wellington's army, usually known as the 'crisis' of the battle, has been called both a strategic and a tactical mistake. Let us dispose of the strategic angle first. Some claim that this force might have been more profitably used to cover the retreat of the entire French Army. Since the attack did fail, the critics are right. But how was Napoleon to know? Two battalions only of the Old Guard had just pushed the Prussians out of Plancenoit. If Napoleon had not been a gambler, he would not have achieved his place in history. Besides, the opportunity for a successful retreat may already have passed. Imagine what the critical historians would have said if at the last minute Napoleon had endeavoured to retreat without risking the infantry of his Guard which was said never to have failed!

Now let us examine the tactics used in these attacks. The preparatory artillery fire was as heavy as the surviving French pieces would allow. Mobile artillery certainly accompanied the columns of the Guard, probably batteries of the light, powerful 8-pounders. The entire corps of Reille and d'Erlon pressed forward to support the Guard, either in the form of strong masses of tirailleurs, or in battalion columns. All the French cavalry still capable of combat appears to have come forward also. I fail to see any tactical errors, save in the columns of the Guard itself. These were beaten by British lines, but the Guard could not abandon the formation it had used so long and so successfully.

Napoleon has also been criticised for not sending the Guard forward sooner. Some say that the Emperor's only real chance to win Waterloo was to follow up immediately Ney's success in taking La Haye Sainte.[1] The French might have achieved a breakthrough if the Guard had attacked thirty minutes sooner. But this is 'second guessing' and not conclusive; a temporary penetration by the French of Wellington's line did not win Talavera, Busaco or Fuentes de Onoro. Besides, Napoleon could not send the Guard forward against Wellington with Plancenoit still in Prussian hands.

We should now mention three allegedly poor general decisions made by the French. Would Napoleon have been better off to have sent only 10,000 men under Grouchy as Thiers appears to have advocated? Perhaps Grouchy recommended this.[2] A force as small as this including cavalry, infantry, and artillery would have been, I believe, in grave danger of being slaughtered by the Prussians and to no purpose. A conjecture like this may be a profitable mental exercise for students in staff colleges, but such things have no place in history.

Would Napoleon have been better off to have manœuvred rather than attacking head on? Soult, Reille and Foy thought so; Wellington was also of that opinion when asked about it in Paris a few days later. 'I should have turned the flank – the right flank. I should have kept the English Army occupied by a demonstration to attack, or perhaps by slight attacks, while I was in fact moving the main body by Hal on Brussels.'[3] But all this is conjecture; the decision was made and the frontal attacks in mass defeated. If the French had used something different from the tactics by which they had won since about 1808, they would have been even more severely criticised, unless they had by some chance emerged victorious.

The French have also been criticised for not occupying and holding Paris wood farther east than Lobau actually advanced in his preparations to meet and hold the Prussians. By so doing he might have delayed Bülow's frontal attack on Plancenoit, but he would have

[1] Ibid., 216, says, 'Had the Guard been launched en masse at Wellington's centre directly La Haye Sainte fell, the crippled line might have yielded under this terrific impact.'

[2] *Chesney*, 244, says, 'If Grouchy's word be worth anything, that unfortunate officer, amid the remonstrances which he offered on the 17th against a regular pursuit of the Prussians, then far out of sight, did actually propose as an alternative, that a division of 10,000 strong only should be charged with their observation, and that he himself, with all the rest of the Ligny troops, should co-operate in the movement to be made by Ney's wing against Wellington.'

[3] *Robinson*, III, 684–5, citing Gleig, *The Life of Arthur Duke of Wellington*, 315.

dangerously exposed his own French force to an attack on flank and rear from the Ohain-Frischermont area to the north by either the Anglo-Dutch left or Ziethen's Prussians. Lobau surrounded and annihilated, or even fighting another Grouchy-like battle, was not what Bonaparte needed to defend his flank.

To sum up, the main French mistakes not inherent in their system of war or Napoleon's general campaign strategy were d'Erlon's wandering on the 16th, too much delay in beginning the battle on the 18th, the loss of Grouchy from the area of decision on the 18th with no accompanying advantage, and the deliberate choosing by the Emperor throughout the campaign of massive frontal attacks instead of manœuvres. There were also pieces of ill luck such as befell d'Erlon's new columns; they might have done well against British infantry in line. But every losing commander has misfortunes; most winning commanders have some too, like being blessed with the Prince of Orange. The Emperor in taking the offensive against superior forces well commanded needed not only a good plan, but nearly flawless execution at all levels unless Wellington and/or Blücher made serious errors. The French plan was good, but the execution was far from perfect.

IV

Prussian Mistakes

Critics have generally dealt more leniently with Blücher and his subordinates than with either Wellington or the French. The Prussians were beaten at Ligny on the 16th by the superior skill and fighting ability of the veteran French Army under Napoleon. Since Bülow's, Pirch's and Ziethen's Corps finally did fight at Waterloo on the 18th, they are not seriously blamed for their late arrival. This attitude appears to be sound; the Prussians tried hard and finally made their full contribution to the Allied victory. Blücher was not so well endowed by nature and training with military virtues as Napoleon and Wellington. His performance was far from perfect, but he was better than most people would have expected.

Fairly detailed treatment has already been given to the breakdown in transmission of intelligence from Prussian headquarters on the 14th and 15th of June. Gneisenau did not see fit to pass on to Wellington his reasons for concentrating the Prussian Army, nor the fact that this was in process. Ziethen, his colleagues and his superiors did not keep their Allies adequately informed of events at Charleroi on the 15th; the intelligence that was sent was incomplete and late.

We have also dealt with the lateness of the actual Prussian entry into the fighting at Waterloo. As it turned out, no harm was done. The victory may have been more complete because of it. But the Prussian staff work, the distrust of a commander who was meant to be co-operating with Wellington, and the relative immobility of their heavy corps might all have led to serious consequences.

There are a few additional aspects of the campaign which are worthy of review here. Even though the concentration of 75 per cent of the Prussian Army at Ligny early on the 16th was admirable, Bülow's Corps was not there. Gneisenau, Blücher's Chief of Staff, was senior to three of the corps commanders and told them what to do clearly and precisely. He was junior to Bülow and appears to have been in awe of him. 'Gneisenau worded his dispatch too politely'[1] so that the recipient misunderstood the instructions, took them as advisory only, and delayed marching until the next morning. But for this, Bülow's Corps could have been within supporting distance of the rest of the Prussian Army on the afternoon of the 16th. Conjecture as to what might have happened at Ligny had Bülow been present late in the afternoon, or even early on the 17th is, of course, futile.

Ziethen's rear-guard actions against the French on the 15th have been deservedly praised. He and his engineers did not destroy, however, the bridges over the Sambre at Marchienne, Charleroi and Chatelet.[2] But at that time Prussian engineers knew little of explosives and probably thought that since the bridges were of masonry, they were indestructible. Besides, the engineers present with the French forces could probably have repaired them quickly with materials close at hand.

Wellington's famous criticism of the Prussian Army for fighting the battle of Ligny exposed in columns, perhaps on the forward slope of a hill and within range of French artillery, sticks in one's mind. 'It was also most unfortunate that the Prussian reserves were carefully arranged so as to act as stop-butts to the enemy's "overs", thus preventing any stray French round-shot from being wasted.'[3] But as the Duke himself remarked, 'Everyone knows his own army best.' Besides, I can find no single hill in this area where the Prussian Army could have aligned itself in this manner. Probably the Duke saw some columns at quarter distance and instinctively wanted to order them to form into line and lie down.

Blücher and his subordinate commanders deployed their forces at Ligny in such a way that Thielemann's Corps on their left was held in check mainly by the French cavalry and was not seriously engaged all day. Had Blücher deployed this corps behind the other two, his battle line would have been stronger. During the battle, the Prussian commanders were forced to shift troops from the centre to their right. Napoleon observed this 'Gradual weakening of the Prussian centre for

---

[1] *Henderson's Blücher*, 286. See also *Müffling's Passages*, 227, and *Chesney*, 59–60.

[2] *Wolseley*, 151, says that Ziethen 'made one serious mistake, however, in not destroying the bridges over the Sambre'. See also Hooper's *Wellington*, 209.

[3] *Becke*, 97.

the purpose of reforcing the right' and 'took advantage of his opponent's designs by collecting in rear of the heights of Ligny that force which so suddenly assailed and broke the Centre of the Prussian line.'[1] The final and decisive French attack might have been defeated with a different initial Prussian deployment, but their left flank could have been turned by a French attack in that area. Conjectures of this type are too indefinite to be profitable.

The movements of the Prussian Army on the 17th appear to be beyond serious criticism. The preliminary arrangements for the march west to the Waterloo battlefield and the slowness in executing them have already been discussed. Once the actual fighting started between Bülow's Prussians and Lobau's French Corps, the former displayed definite combat weaknesses. When one is accustomed to the calm tenacity and military efficiency of Wellington's infantry, one is surprised at the erratic performance of these Germans. They attacked with fire and abandon, but could also be driven back with an ease that French troops who had fought in the Peninsula must have found as novel as it was pleasant.

The Old Guard attack on Plancenoit was magnificent, but what headway would it have made against Byng's British battalions in Hougoumont? In their fighting against Napoleon in 1813 and later the Prussians appear to have perfected a system of not defending anything to the last extremity, of giving way before they were destroyed, so they could recover quickly and go on fighting from another position fairly close by. At this time, the Prussian infantry did 'not possess the same bodily strength', did not have the experience and 'powers of endurance' of British foot soldiers.[2] But Blücher's men knew how to scatter, rally and come back for more, even though they could not hold so tenaciously. The Prussians, once they began their attacks, continued them regardless of temporary setbacks. Blücher brought into the fight a constant stream of fresh units and handled them well.

We have already discussed briefly the promise the Prussians made to support Wellington and the fact that Bülow's attack did not actually fulfil that promise. Pirch's Corps reinforced Bülow's and gave the Duke no direct support. In arriving in the PLHS area about 7 p.m. Ziethen's did give this, but with the best of intentions, he nearly marched away; as has been described, Müffling happened to see the whole thing and persuaded him to return. Once these Prussians finally

[1] *Siborne*, 213.
[2] *Müffling*, 216, already cited on p. 22, n. 2.

attacked, they fought their fellow-Germans, the Nassauers under Saxe-Weimar. Their subsequent attack on Durutte was not of great brilliance, nor particularly successful. Their artillery often fired on Wellington's army, but they kept trying like the rest of Blücher's men.

The Prussian pursuit under Gneisenau was earnestly pressed and certainly disrupted the beaten French Army. A great deal of equipment was taken, but not many prisoners. The operation could not, for valid military reasons, be pressed, after the example of the French Army following up their 'victory at Jena. Thielemann's Corps did a good job on the 18th at Wavre, Limale and Limelette, but was badly outmanoeuvred along with that of Pirch on the 19th and 20th by Grouchy. The Prussian advance into France was finally successful, but its individual actions were not indicative of the highest military proficiency in army or commander. As Wellington said, however, there was glory enough for all. He and Blücher accomplished together what neither could have done alone.

V

Cavalry Attacks on Infantry Squares

Pictures of fighting at Waterloo give a false idea of what actually took place. So do most battle diagrams. The infantry squares are much too big; French cavalry appears to be charging *en masse*. The average British, KGL and Hanoverian battalion had a strength of about 500 men and formed a square about 60 feet on a side. Here are the figures from the old drill books. In close order, a man occupied 21 inches of front; squares were formed four ranks deep. The front and rear faces of a square might have been composed of 136 men or 34 files; 34 × 21/12 = 59·5 feet. The open space inside, exclusive of file closers and mounted officers, would have measured about 39 feet wide. (See diagram, p. 206.)

Now let us look at one of these squares from the point of view of cavalry attacking a face. It could be charged by no more than twenty French horsemen at a time; a normal cavalryman was said to be 36 inches wide including his horse. If the French cuirassiers were wider, as seems probable because they were mounted on the biggest horses obtainable in France, there would have been less of them in 60 feet of front. A second rank may have been necessary to make good artillery and sharpshooter casualties in the first, but ranks beyond two added little power to a cavalry attack. If an infantry square could beat off the first charge, the dead and wounded horses and men in their front would give them considerable protection thereafter.

BRITISH INFANTRY

Some details of the organisation of a British infantry battalion have been given in Part One, Chapter II. We need to know more about it, however, in order to understand how a square was formed. Bear in

A TYPICAL BRITISH INFANTRY SQUARE
AT WATERLOO : Strength about 500 men.

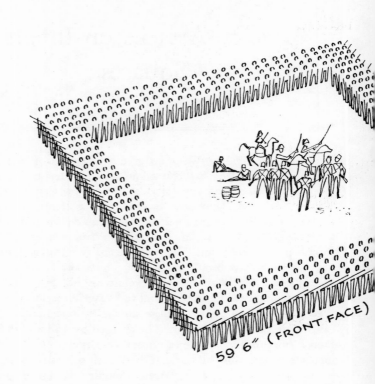

59′6″ (FRONT FACE)

Men in line:

Front and rear – *4 ranks of 34 in each* = 272

Sides   – *4 ranks of 26 in each* = 208

                               ———

                               480

They would form a square of about 60 feet on a side. The inside faces would measure about 39 feet (exclusive of file closers and any mounted officers).

A TYPICAL FRENCH CAVALRY ATTACK

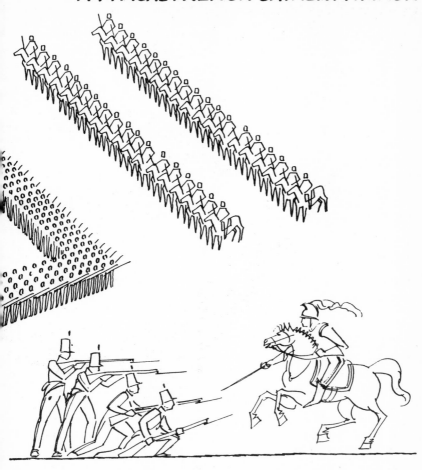

The square could be charged by no more than about 18 troopers at a time; French heavy cavalry occupied about 42 inches of front per horse and man.

This diagram is approximate and theoretical only. The problem lies in the formation of the corners. A man occupied a space 21 inches wide by 32 inches deep; this width-length discrepancy is not shown here. It would appear that infantry squares were never quite square. Three companies often formed the front and rear and two companies the sides, but there were other dispositions. Company division lines cannot be shown. Companies varied somewhat in strength and their placing differed from battalion to battalion.

mind that practically all battlefield manœuvres were accomplished by precise movements following standard, practised words of command, the equivalent of close order drill today.

The basic formation of a battalion of British infantry was a line two ranks deep; the Grenadier company was on the right, the eight line companies in the centre, and the light company on the left. The battalion could be formed into column by ordering all companies to swing 90 degrees pivoting on either their right or left flank, but not moving otherwise. A column so formed was known as an 'open' column. There were wide intervals between each company; the larger the battalion the more open the column. For a battalion of 500 men, this interval was about thirty-eight feet. Columns could also be formed at 'half' or 'quarter' distance which had respectively half and a quarter of the 'open' distance between companies. A 'close' column was formed when the companies were separated by no more than the distance between front and rear ranks of one company, a single pace of about thirty-two inches.

Columns formed on full company fronts were for drill and manœuvre in fairly open terrain. Large battalions, like those of the Guards and the 52nd, probably drilled mostly as wings with columns made up of half-companies (platoons). A full company, or a half-company for large battalions, appears to have been the standard 'drill section' of that time. Marches along narrow roads, however, had to be made in narrow columns of quarter companies or even less.

British infantry by the time of Waterloo always deployed against other infantry in lines two ranks deep. When cavalry appeared, a battalion formed a square; each face was four ranks deep.[1] When a battalion was in ranks, but not menaced by the enemy, it was normally in column of companies at quarter distance. It could form in line or into a square where it was in about thirty seconds, or move a short distance in any direction and then form. The square could be formed in several ways; if isolated from all other friendly infantry, it was probably as nearly perfect as it could be; it had equal sides and rounded corners. But where other battalion squares were present and a checkerboard alignment desirable, fronts and rears were more important than the sides. Many squares appear to have been composed of three companies in front and in the rear, with two for each side.[2]

---

[1] All other infantry also formed squares in the presence of hostile cavalry, but in Continental armies these were usually six ranks deep on each face.

[2] As we have seen and as *Kennedy* points out, 23, the battalion in Alten's 3rd Division formed rectangles with only one company on each side which left presumably four for the front and four more for the rear.

British squares were capable of opposing shock to shock, if cavalry charged home. The front rank which was kneeling, may have fired, but made no effort to reload. These men set the toes of their muskets into the ground and used their muskets and bayonets as pikes. The second rank men crouched low with their bayonet tips in line not far behind those of the first rank. These two together represented shock; each curassier's horse would have taken four bayonets in the chest, two of them resting firmly in the ground.

But the main reliance of the British infantry, even in square, was on the firepower of their muskets. In spite of many pictures to the contrary, it is unlikely that the third and fourth ranks had their bayonets fixed. They would have interfered with the proper and easy loading of their weapons. Bullets rather than bayonets caused most of the enemy casualties.

There were several means of delivering volleys from all ranks. Variations existed even between British battalions; KGL units appear to have had their own system. But both forces were more effective than any other infantry of that time. An entire battalion was able to fire one round per man at fifteen-second intervals.[1] It was, of course, possible for the whole side of the square to continue firing together, but this probably did not happen often. In the Peninsula, British infantry found that in the heat of battle half company volleys were more efficient, at least after the first discharge. The KGL battalions had several systems, but exactly which was used by them at Waterloo is now no longer known. File firing is said to have caused horses to become unmanageable and to have been used by Continental infantries, but was probably not employed by Wellington's own infantry units at Waterloo.[2]

During the great French cavalry attacks, many battalions appear to have hesitated to fire their muskets. A part of their reluctance came from a fear of using up their ammunition. But the presence of French cavalry within fifty yards may also have been important.[3] A square

[1] See particularly *Muller's Science*, II, 185–6. KGL units are said to have been able to fire even more quickly, but modern experiments indicate that it would have been difficult to sustain a faster rate for more than three or four rounds, due to the necessity of looking after the flint.

[2] File firing was when each file fired rapidly in turn, usually from right to left.

[3] *Chad*, 5, quotes Wellington as saying that one pause lasted fifteen minutes. 'Wellington, "Our People would not throw away their fire till the Cuirassiers charged, and they would not charge until we had thrown away our fire." Chad, "How long did this dreadful Pause continue?" Wellington, "A quarter of an hour without firing. It ended by our Squares advancing and driving off the Cuirassiers."'

with loaded weapons could not possibly be broken; a battalion un-
loaded might have been.

Now for the equipment, organisation and tactics of the French heavy
cavalry. Napoleon also had light cavalry and dragoons (an intermediate
type), but he used his cuirassiers and other similar heavy mounted
troops for shock in battle. These horsemen had pistols and carbines for
guard duty and harrying their opponents at close range, but their really
effective arm was the sabre.[1]

French squadrons usually numbered about 120 horsemen and occupied in the normal two-rank order a front of between 180 and 200 feet,
if they were closed up properly on the centre. Any irregularity would
have increased the width. A squadron was the basis of cavalry battlefield action. Larger units were composed of squadrons arranged either
in rough line with intervals, or in a series of these lines in echelon;
columns were tactically undesirable.[2]

In 1815 the way to use cavalry effectively was to take advantage of
both forms of shock, from moving men and horses and from the sabre
blows of the troopers. For maximum efficiency, the speed of the charge
was well under a gallop, not only to preserve a solid formation and
have the horses reasonably fresh at the time of impact, but also to allow
the men to use their arms precisely. A canter or fast trot was considered
best.

What happened when a French squadron of 120 men hit a British
square of about 500? As already mentioned, only about eighteen
men in the first cavalry rank could actually engage the square (see
diagram again). The rear rank can be disregarded; if the front rank
was defeated, subsequent ranks could do nothing. Some historians
and even Allied eyewitnesses had the idea that the French charged in
columns of several squadrons with no intervals between the ranks. This
view appears to be in error; if a 'close' column of French cavalry
had attacked, a single casualty in the front rank would have caused
many more farther back. The French were undoubtedly closer than

---

[1] Their other weapons and armour have already been discussed in Part Two, Chapter I.

[2] *Marmont*, 72, says, 'Cavalry, when about to attack the enemy, and the men to fight
hand to hand, should never fight in column. This formation will serve to facilitate its
march; but at the moment of its approach to the enemy, it must be deployed. A column
of cavalry surrounded, is soon destroyed; for there are very few of the soldiers who are
within reach to use their arms. Cavalry when deployed should be formed into two ranks,
so as to check the disorder which might occur in the first rank: it was formerly in three;
but it did not require much time to manifest the vice of that formation.'

their normal squadron-to-squadron distance, but were not arrayed in columns.[1]

As already mentioned, if even half of the eighteen horsemen and their mounts could have made 2,000-pound projectiles of themselves and carried through their charge in good order at controlled speed, they would have broken any square. This never happened; only a few isolated individual horsemen continued on into the bayonets.[2] Sergeant-Major Cotton, himself a Waterloo cavalryman and the confidant of more veterans from all armies in the post-war years than any other writer wrote:

Not a single individual set an example of soldier-like devotedness by rushing upon the bristling bayonets: certainly no agreeable task, nor to be attempted without imminent danger; but one, when required and gallantly done, that raises men to military rank and renown, and that may hasten the crisis and lead to victory. Of the fifteen thousand French horsemen, it is doubtful whether any perished on a British bayonet, or that any of our infantry in square fell by the French cavalry's sabres.[3]

It is rash to disagree with Cotton. Yet his statement is difficult to believe, and not altogether relevant. The point is that some action of these squares caused the cavalry not to charge home. What did they do? Apparently, two things. First, they fired a lot of bullets at the eighteen horsemen in the front rank of the section of the squadron which was coming at them. Second, with their two glittering rows of bayonets they exerted extreme psychological shock power. Every horse would have instantly been killed and its rider too perhaps impaled on the bayonets, had the charge been carried through. The squares would have been broken, but most of the men and all the horses who had done the damage would have been dead.

The psychological element appears to have been more important than the physical in these Waterloo infantry-cavalry duels. A square of steady, well-formed British infantry which maintained its lines of bayonets and its fire discipline had a considerable advantage over even the finest French cavalry. The squares stood firm; the horsemen, or perhaps the horses, refused to go into the bayonets and either stopped or swerved off past one corner or the other. No cuirassier charging at

---

[1] *Muller's Science*, II, 194–212. The normal interval between lines was 200 to 300 paces.

[2] *Robinson*, III, 604, carefully referenced.

[3] *Cotton*, 81.

Waterloo was much more than thirty feet away from the wide intervals which separated the infantry squares from one another.[1]

This psychological battle was not resolved until the cavalry was close, perhaps within a few strides. The sight of the steady lines of gleaming bayonets held by calm, resolute men in formation was always too much for the horsemen en masse. No square at Waterloo was actually tested by the combined shock attack of several cuirassiers going headlong into it.

One naturally wonders why the Emperor and his marshals sent forward cavalry in this manner. The answer is that good infantry was beaten by cavalry in the Napoleonic wars. If a battalion was caught in line, or while forming square, it could be destroyed quickly. The Prince of Orange caused the loss of one battalion at Quatre Bras and two more at Waterloo, as well as damage to a total of four others, by giving improper orders. Once infantry was broken, it could be ridden down and almost annihilated.[2]

We should also remember that the psychological element could have worked the other way round. On many Napoleonic battlefields, the sight of charging French heavy cavalry struck terror into infantry formations so that they broke before they met the charge. The resolution of Wellington's infantry to stay where it was and kill any horse and man who actually careered into it won the day against the determination of the French troopers and their horses to complete their charge. If a single horseman had penetrated a square, others might have followed. If the infantry had appeared in any way nervous, the French would have carried through their charge.

[1] Even when British infantry formed rectangles, the distance was not greater than about sixty feet. The large battalions, such as the Guards and the 52nd, formed into two squares to receive cavalry.

[2] Stewart suffered about 73 per cent casualties at Albuera in about three minutes when three of his battalions were caught in line by French (actually Polish) cavalry: *Weller*, 176–7.

VI

Waterloo Campaign Topography

The Waterloo campaign was fought in a surprisingly small area. The three major battlefields and some of the country are easily accessible. People from many nations continue to visit Waterloo and other places in the area every year. Both the campaign and the battle are easy to study and extremely rewarding. An actual visit will amply repay your effort, regardless of the level of your military and historical experience. Two days will suffice to fix indelibly in your mind accurate terrain pictures of where various actions took place 150 years ago. But two months can be used profitably by an expert who wants a high overall level of comprehension.

The battlefields of Waterloo, Quatre Bras and parts of Ligny are still much as they were in 1815. Most of the villages and practically all the enclosed Belgian farms have changed relatively little. Streams such as the Gemioncourt brook, the Ligny, Dyle and Lasne 'rivers' still flow in the courses of 1815, but are probably smaller now and have stronger banks. The Sambre was and is a real river and is unchanged. Farming methods and crops are not the same as they were, but this is not important. Mining and new canals have changed Belgium considerably, but have done little to confuse one in this particular area.

The changes that have occurred over the last 150 years must also be noted. The greatest lies in the growth of some cities, towns and villages. A chart at the end of this chapter shows approximate population in 1815 and in 1965. In general, but not invariably, the smaller places have grown much less than the larger. The enormous growth in population and in area covered is nowhere more apparent than in Brussels. The central square of the old town is much as it was in 1815, but most of the buildings and streets surrounding it are completely different. The vast metropolis spreads over an area that was mostly countryside 150 years ago.

The little town of Charleroi on the Sambre contained less than 2,600 people when Napoleon attacked early in the morning of 15 June 1815. The area known as Charleroi today comprises many square miles of dwellings, stores and industrial plants. The Sambre has all but disappeared; the points where the French forced a passage across the stream are unrecognisable. In a few years Charleroi will have grown to the north so as to include both Frasnes and Fleurus; it was not far away in the spring of 1965.

Another general dissimilarity which has come with time lies in the modern road systems. In the course of World War II, the old roads were widened and sometimes straightened. Since then, motorways have begun to criss-cross this part of Belgium. Some old roads have disappeared; new straight, wide ones have disrupted the country in some places.

Now for specific sites. First, the Ligny battlefield. The villages here have not increased astonishingly in size, but there still is not much to see even from the air. This is a confusing battle to read about and even more confusing to walk and ride over. One trouble is that the heights discussed in accounts of the battle do not now, and never did, really exist. The country is remarkably flat and now irregularly wooded; the villages called by various but similar names are easily confused. The Ligny river was supposed to be a military obstacle in 1815, but is now an insignificant brook, in places a bit of water in the bottom of a ditch.

Next, Quatre Bras. This is one of the most suitable battlefields in existence for thorough and easy topographical research. The crossroads where the Genappe – Charleroi road intersects that from Nivelles to Namur can be fixed quickly and precisely; here the modern roads still follow those of 150 years ago. The petrol station and the new small inn south of the Nivelles road are later additions, but the large farm on the north-east corner is mostly original. Orientation from the crossroads is easy, but have another look at Map 3, 'Quatre Bras'. The Duke of Brunswick monument just east of the Charleroi road stands about where he was mortally wounded. The enclosed farm of Gemioncourt is a bit farther south and farther away from the road. The similar farms of the Grand and Petit Pierreponts and Lairalle are all still operating, but only the last is on a good road. Bossu wood was cut down soon after the battle.

You will want to go down the Namur road. The Materne lake is now obvious, but is not exactly as it was in 1815. It had disappeared in 1953, but the dam was restored about 1957; the lake is probably now slightly larger than it was 150 years ago. The manor house just to the north of the lake has also been built since 1953. The Bois de Cherris is gone, but the hamlets of Thyle and Piraumont are still much as they were when fought over. About the only major change is the Namur road itself. In 1815, this road was probably wide enough for a single Volkswagen and had deep ditches and perhaps hedges on both sides. It is now a wide modern highway without ditches or hedges.

You should have a look at the Roman road here; it divided the cantonment areas occupied by Wellington and Blücher. Everything to the north-west was Anglo-Dutch; everything to the south-east was Prussian. This road in its entirety was still in use even seventy-five years ago; it ran from Bavay in France to Maastricht on the Rhine. Parts of it have been improved and are still in operation, but not the portion between the Ligny and Quatre Bras battlefields. You will need a Michelin or similar map to find it. You can drive roughly south-west along it for perhaps 150 yards towards Bry, but then it practically disappears into ploughed fields.

You may want to visit Maubeuge, Beaumont and Philippeville, the three towns from which Napoleon launched his offensives in 1815. As mentioned, Beaumont and Philippeville were then French. In spite of damage from both world wars in this century, something of the old Maubeuge survives, but Philippeville and Beaumont give no idea at all of what they may have been 150 years ago. Moving northward from any one of these three towards the Sambre is not particularly enlightening. Before you get to the area where combat took place, you run into the new suburbs of Charleroi. The Sambre can still be found unobscured by industrial plants and the like only to the west; you can drive from Lobbes to Binche, but specific points of interest are lacking.

After the battlefields of Ligny and Quatre Bras, and perhaps the French concentration areas, you will want to see something of where the Allied armies retreated. The country between Ligny and Wavre is filled with a maze of old and new roads which pass through, or by-pass, villages some of which appear to have the same names they had in 1815. Useful study in this area is extremely difficult. Unless you have a particular interest in Grouchy's movements, you will probably not want to spend much time here. If you do, by all means get and study *Ropes* and his remarkable Atlas (a separate volume).

The area through which Wellington's army retreated is a little more interesting, but not much. The Anglo-Dutch crossed the Dyle in the vicinity of Genappe. The old road passing through this village still follows a rather tortuous and congested course, but is wider now than 150 years ago, even though it is no longer a main thoroughfare. If you are so inclined, you can find an old bridge in a pasture downstream from Genappe, but between the town and the new road. This will demonstrate forcibly the changes in transportation over the past century and a half. The old road was standard width for that era and explains why artillery and other military vehicles were no more than fifty-seven inches wide.

From Genappe north towards Brussels, you will find monuments and buildings hallowed to the French. Le Caillou was Napoleon's place of residence on the night of 17 June 1815 and is now a museum staunchly loyal to the Emperor. The hamlets of Maison du Roi and Rossome are where the Old Guard neither surrendered nor died, but took to its heels. La Belle Alliance, or rather a bit of high ground seventy-five yards south-east of it, was where Bonaparte sat on his chair masterminding the battle so he could spend the rest of his life blaming others for the defeat. The monuments to Victor Hugo and the Imperial Guard are here.

If this is your first trip to Waterloo, you will begin to wonder if you have come to the right place. There is so much about Napoleon and so little to indicate that Britain and Wellington, or Prussia and Blücher, were involved. There is nothing you can do about this, save accept it. Waterloo has been for many years a kind of commercial memorial to Napoleon and the Grand Army of France. But the Belgian Government has regulations which prevent further encroachment on the battlefield itself. The terrain, the events and the final result appear to be reasonably safe in spite of a mass of still-continuing Napoleonic propaganda to alter history.

Before describing the battlefield of Waterloo, I should say a few words about the area between Wavre, Ohain and Plancenoit. A motor vehicle is not absolutely necessary here, but it will save many, many hours of walking. Initially, I suggest you just ride around in the area between these three towns. You will soon find out the topographical research problems for yourself. The Wavre of today is difficult to fit into the situation of the Prussian army on 17–18 June 1815. The place has grown greatly and is surrounded by a modern network of motorways which have done much to change the old topography. The Dyle, once you have found it, is a fair-sized stream, but it now flows between strong masonry banks. I have been able to find nothing of the old bridge and little of the old town.

But your troubles are just beginning. West of Wavre, you will have found two villages on either side of a trickling brook – one is on a hill to the east – sometimes, but not always, known collectively as Lasne-Chapelle Saint Lambert. The network of roads radiating from these villages towards Mont Saint Jean, Ohain, Plancenoit, Braine l'Alleud and Wavre are most confusing. I am indebted to Commandant Dehond as I have said not only for his personal, on the spot guidance in this area, but also for an old Ordnance map with a scale of 1 : 20,000 which is based on conditions as they were from 1865 to 1908. All I have been able to prove, however, is that the roads by which the Prussians moved 150 years ago are, in part at least, no longer traceable. In some sections, and for stretches of various lengths, the old roads have been improved and are now the new ones. In other places, they are no longer public thoroughfares, but exist for farm purposes and can be traced on foot. Finally, some sections have disappeared entirely into ploughed fields or meadows. The road down which Blücher and Bülow attacked towards Plancenoit can be determined definitely, but other Prussian routes are less clear.

Now for the Waterloo battlefield itself. Climb first to the top of the Lion monument, if you can negotiate 226 tall steps in a row. From here on a clear day you can get a first-class elevated view of the entire area. You must bear in mind, however, that your altitude tends to flatten terrain. Small ridges, hollows and knolls which were of considerable importance during the battle will not be apparent to an observer from the top of the Lion.

Fix firmly in mind the positions of Hougoumont, La Haye Sainte and the groups of buildings known in this work as PLHS. Fix also the village and farm of Mont Saint Jean to the north and the modern town of Braine l'Alleud to the west. See how the Nivelles and the Genappe roads come together in Mont Saint Jean to the north next to the Château Chevalle – not built in 1815 – and slowly separate to the south. Note also the Ohain road to the east, but the large convent school less than a mile away was not there at the time of the battle. Finally fix in your mind La Belle Alliance and Plancenoit. If you can get a battle-field map with a 1:8,000 scale – it cost when last available about five shillings – by all means buy it. If not, my Map 5, 'Waterloo', will have to do; you can also use some of the other maps for specific locations.

Once oriented, have a look right around the base of the monument itself. This area is the most important of all, but was greatly disturbed when the Netherlanders dragged up all the earth necessary for the mound. Note particularly the hardly passable road which runs just north of the monument out to the Nivelles road past the new manor-house standing in wooded grounds. The road is all that remains of the positions of Maitland's Guards, the Nassau battalions supported by Mercer's battery and the 23rd, and other units in the area. The two attacks of the Imperial Guard hit the Duke's line east and west of the base of the monument.

You are now ready to come down and visit individual points of interest. I would suggest first that you walk along the road just mentioned west towards the new manor-house, but turn south before reaching it so you come into what remains of the protected way above Hougoumont. Remember as you proceed that both sides of this now impassable road, and perhaps the roadway itself, have been lowered from two to six feet. The entire area was probably smoothed out in the process. You must also visualise the wooded garden and manor-house as bare slopes protected to some extent by greater Hougoumont.

Have a look now at Map 6, 'Hougoumont'. Try to walk south towards where the banked-up eastern orchard hedge ended. Have a look at the relevant aerial photographs also. The orientation problem here is that you will tend to see Hougoumont as it is now, rather than as it was. The north-south section of the garden wall appears to be the eastern limit of the place. The original Hougoumont enclosure was twice as wide as indicated by this wall; the orchard lay to the east of the garden with stout ditched hedges all round. You can find some of these even today, but they are weathered almost flat. The modern Hougoumont has lost the woods and hedged pasture which stretched for 400 yards south of the buildings, garden and orchard. You will find indications only of the extent of the old hedges and the ditches which protected them. In the days when labour was cheap and iron wire expensive, cattle-proof boundaries were constructed in this way.

You will want to go into the building enclosure at Hougoumont; visitors are welcome in the courtyard, the ruins of the chapel, the garden and through the passage to the south beneath the first floor of the farmer's dwelling. You will find a number of memorials here, mostly British. There are two graves in the garden covered by stone slabs;

one is where Captain J. K. Blackman of the Coldstreamers was buried on the day after the battle; the other is for Sergeant-Major Edward Cotton of the 7th Hussars who died at Waterloo in 1849, a wealthy man after many years of professional battlefield guiding and collecting of relics. There is also a monument to the French who died at Hougoumont inside the garden enclosure; there were certainly many French casualties in the general area, but I believe no French soldiers entered the garden, save possibly as prisoners.

The area immediately to the west of the Nivelles road has not changed much since the battle. The road which continues the Hougoumont lane on the other side was occupied by part of Mitchell's Brigade, but no great amount of fighting occurred there. You are now ready to retrace your steps past the Lion monument towards where the Ohain and the Genappe roads intersect. The three inns just north and west of the crossroads were all erected since the battle and occupy about the same area as Alten's Division less Colin Halkett's Brigade and Kruse's Nassauers who were closer to the Lion. There is a recently planted small sycamore on the spot where Wellington's elm originally stood, suitably marked.

You can now walk down the Genappe road to La Haye Sainte. You are welcome to go in the courtyard, and even through the passages in the south barn and under the west barn or stables by which the French finally entered the courtyard. Much of La Haye Sainte is still as it was 150 years ago. The owners have retained the dovecote over the main gate and one wooden partition showing more than a dozen musket-ball holes. The orchard and pasture south of the farm and the kitchen garden area north of it have, however, changed considerably.

Across from the north end of the La Haye Sainte buildings is what remains of the sandpit. Not a great deal is left, for an electric railway from Brussels to Plancenoit and elsewhere once ran close to this. You can still see, however, the knoll to the north and the fairly deep small valley that cuts in behind it. The Ohain road to the north is in front of instead of behind the crest here, particularly to the east of the Genappe road. This was where the 1/27th took such cruel punishment because it was exposed. Imagine infantry in square in this area; only by going much too far north could they be protected by the crest. This was the weakest spot in the Duke's entire position. You can figure out for yourself what went on here, but remember there was a stout hedge parallel to the Ohain road, but some forty yards south of it, which extended approximately 140 yards east from the Genappe road.

Now turn east along the Ohain road towards the group of modern buildings. These have nothing to do with the battle, but are situated to the north and to the west of the old fork in the road here; both branches lead to Ohain. The southern way is now the better road and passes the farms of Papelotte and La Haye and the hamlet of Smohain. Some, but not all, of the buildings in this area were here at the time of the battle. The original château of Frischermont which stood south-east of Smohain today survives only in fragments: a strong outer wall, the original well and well-house, and some heavy foundations are about all that is left.

If you have gone down to Frischermont, retrace your steps to a point on the lower Ohain road below Papelotte where another road comes in from the south. If you walk south on this, you will come to the most imposing defile to be found in the entire campaign area. This is why I believe that Durutte's Division could not possibly have attacked PLHS in the same formation used by the rest of d'Erlon's Division, a column of battalions each deployed into a three-deep line. To make such a formation even less desirable here, Craan's map shows thick hedges on the borders of the fields high above these sunken roads.

Depending on your time and personal interests, you can see a lot more of the Waterloo battlefield. A visit to Plancenoit is particularly desirable, but it's a long walk. The village church and cemetery were the focal point of the fighting here late in the afternoon of 18 June 1815. Many of the houses have been erected since the battle. The Prussian monument to the east is well worth seeing. If you climb up behind this monument onto a hillock only fifteen yards away, you will quickly discover what remains of the road down which the Prussians attacked after crossing the Lasne. They were deployed on both sides, initially in about equal strength on each, and forced back Lobau's troops right across where you are standing, into and through the village.

Having come so far, you are now on your own. You will know what you want to see and be able to find it. A word of caution, however, for a serious student who wishes to go farther afield than the three actual battlefields and into the cantonment area. Don't expect too much. The towns fortified by Wellington in the spring of 1815 were largely destroyed 100 years later during World War I. Ypres is now but a name hallowed by another, worse-led British Army. The new city retains nothing of its 1815 identity.

Following the Allied advance to Paris is also less rewarding than you might think. Cambrai was almost totally destroyed in the 1914–18 war. The outwork at Péronne taken by the light companies of the Guard and the gate and wall behind it appear to have survived, but most of the remaining city defences are gone. Great changes are, of course, to be expected around Paris.

A word about timing your visit. The exact season of a campaign is always a desirable time to do terrain and other local research. The Lion monument and some other places will be crowded with summer vacationers, but the weather could be clear. Autumn, winter and spring all have advantages and disadvantages, particularly if you want good photographs.

For accommodation, Brussels is too far away, but is the only answer if you must have full modern conveniences. The places close by usually have good food, fair beds and insufficient plumbing facilities for a stay in summer. If you want to get the most out of your day, be in the field early when the light is best and other battlefield visitors are still in bed.

CITIES, TOWNS AND VILLAGES IMPORTANT IN THE WATERLOO CAMPAIGN

Name	Approximate Population in 1815	Approximate Population in 1965	Remarks
Antwerp	60,000	600,000	Deep water supply port for British army.
Ath	8,000	12,000	HQ of Hill's Anglo-Dutch Corps.
Beaumont	1,500	2,000	French concentration point before 15 June 1815.
Binche	3,900	11,000	Border control centre near Roman road.
Braine l'Alleud	2,770	13,000	Town just west of Waterloo battlefield, occupied but not fought over.
Braine le Comte	3,300	11,500	HQ of Prince of Orange's Anglo-Dutch Corps.
Brussels	75,000	1,000,000	Belgian Capital.

Name	Approximate Population in 1815	Approximate Population in 1965	Remarks
Brye	250	350	Village near which Wellington and Blücher met late in morning 16 June 1815.
Charleroi	2,516	275,000	HQ of Prussian 1st Corps and focal point of French attack.
Fleurus	2,160	7,800	Important in Quatre Bras manœuvres.
Genappe	1,075	1,850	Important in Waterloo manœuvres.
Ghent	60,775	250,000	Capital of Bourbon French Government in exile.
Hal	4,612	20,000	Centre of Wellington's West Flank Force.
Lasne-Chapelle St Lambert	1,200 in all	2,000 in all	Two separate villages united in 1828 which were important in the movements of the Prussian Army on 18 June 1815.
Ligny	443	2,200	Centre of Ligny battlefield which also includes other villages.
Limale	973	3,000	Village near Wavre fought over 18 June 1815.
Marbais	1,217	2,200	Between Ligny and Quatre Bras battlefields.
Mons	19,830	30,000	Near frontier and on main road from Paris to Brussels.
Mont Saint Jean	300	2,500	Village where Nivelles and Genappe roads join.
Mont Saint Guibert	286	1,800	Occupied in force by Prussians 17–18 June 1815.

Name	Approximate Population in 1815	Approximate Populatiocn in 1965	Remarks
Ninove	3,365	13,000	HQ of British and KGL cavalry.
Nivelles	7,000	15,000	HQ of 2nd Dutch-Belgian Division, possible concentration centre.
Ohain	1,600	2,300	Large village on Wavre road.
Ostend	10,554	60,000	Main supply port for British Army.
Philippeville	1,115	1,700	French concentration point before 15 June 1815.
Plancenoit	520	650	The focal point of Franco–Prussian fighting 18 June 1815.
Quatre Bras	50	75	Crossroads which the Anglo–Dutch Army defended 15 June 1815.
Sombreffe	980	2,700	Prussian concentration point 16 June 1815.
Saint Amand	200	1,100	A village important in the Ligny battle.
Wagnelee	300	850	A village important in the Ligny battle.
Wavre	4,067	10,000	The Prussian concentration point 17 June 1815.
Waterloo	1,879	11,000	Wellington's HQ, 17–18 June 1815.

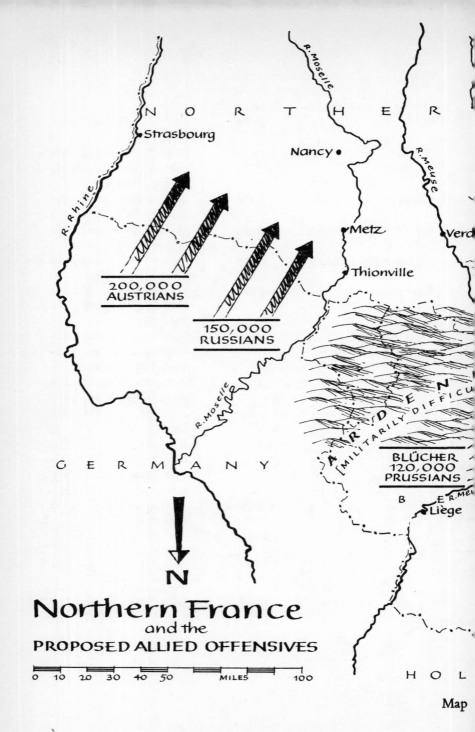

N O R T H E R

Strasbourg

Nancy •

R. Moselle

R. Meuse

Metz

Verd

Thionville

R. Rhine

200,000
AUSTRIANS

150,000
RUSSIANS

R. Moselle

A R D E N
[MILITARILY DIFFICU

BLÜCHER
120,000
PRUSSIANS

G E R M A N Y

B   E R. Me

Liège

N

Northern France
and the
PROPOSED ALLIED OFFENSIVES

0 10 20 30 40 50   MILES   100

H O L

Map

R. Seine

F R A N C E

R. Marne

Paris

R. Seine

Château Thierry

•Rheims

Soissons

R. Aisne

Compiègne

•Laon

R. Oise

Charleville

E S

[1815]

R. Somme

Péronne•

•Amiens

•Avesnes

Philippeville•

•Beaumont

Cambrai

Abbeville

Maubeuge

R. Sambre

Charleroi

Valenciennes

•Douai

Namur

•Mons

G I U M

Tournai

•Lille

R. Lys

WELLINGTON
90,000 ANGLO-DUTCH

Menin

Boulogne

•Brussels

R. Scheldt

Courtrai

•Ypres

Ghent

Calais

ntwerp

Dunkirk

STRAITS OF DOVER

Nieuwpoort

Dover

Ostend

A N D

N O R T H   S E A

I

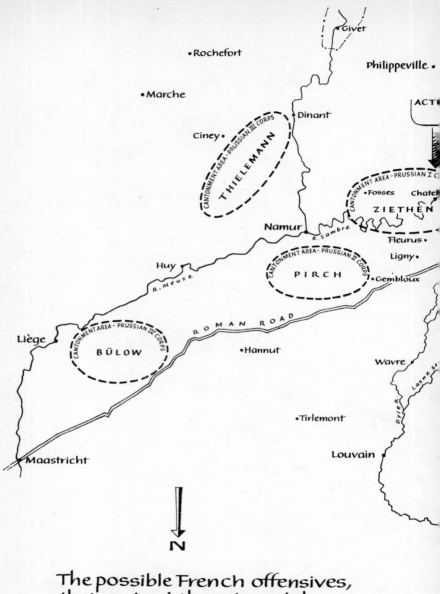

The possible French offensives,
their actual thrust and the
Allied Cantonments

0	5	10	15	20	25	

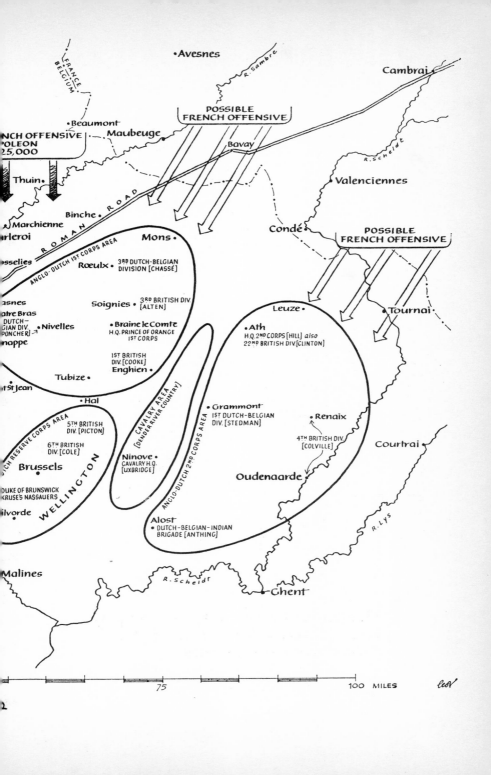

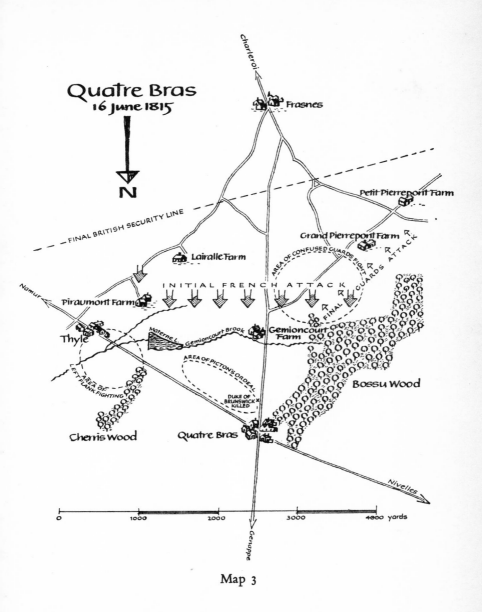

Quatre Bras
16 June 1815

N

Charleroi

Frasnes

FINAL BRITISH SECURITY LINE

Petit Pierrepont Farm

Lairalle Farm

Grand Pierrepont Farm

AREA OF CONFUSED GUARDS FIGHT

INITIAL FRENCH ATTACK

FINAL GUARDS ATTACK

Namur

Piraumont Farm

Thyle

Materne L. Gemioncourt Brook

Gemioncourt Farm

Bossu Wood

AREA OF PICTON'S ORDEAL

AREA OF LEFT FLANK FIGHTING

DUKE OF BRUNSWICK KILLED

Cherris Wood

Quatre Bras

Nivelles

0   1000   2000   3000   4000 yards

Genappe

Map 3

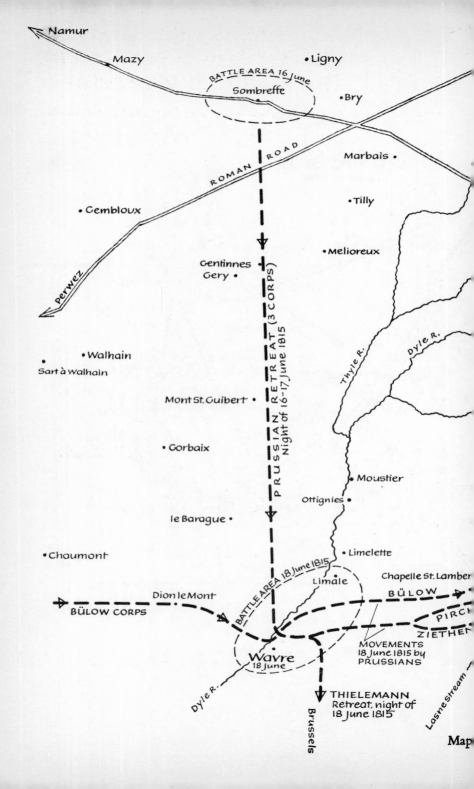

Map

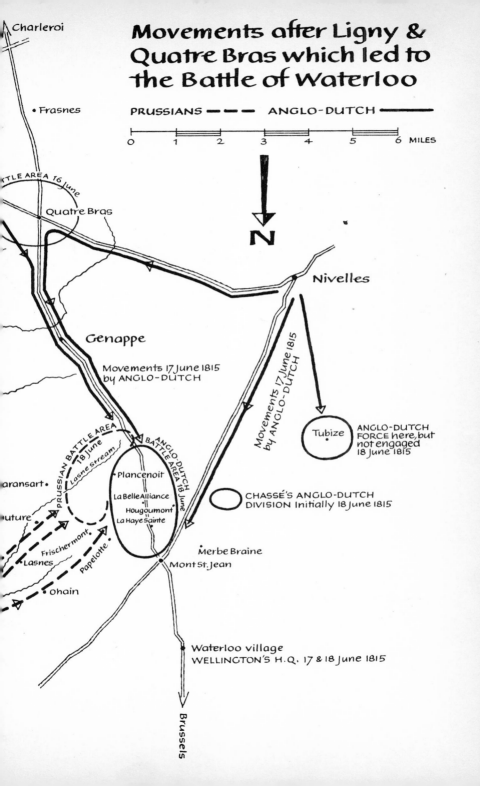

Movements after Ligny & Quatre Bras which led to the Battle of Waterloo

Charleroi

PRUSSIANS ━ ━ ━ ANGLO-DUTCH ━━━

0   1   2   3   4   5   6   MILES

N

• Frasnes

TTLE AREA 16 June

Quatre Bras

Nivelles

Genappe

Movements 17 June 1815
by ANGLO-DUTCH

Movements 17 June 1815
by ANGLO-DUTCH

Tubize

ANGLO-DUTCH
FORCE here, but
not engaged
18 June 1815

PRUSSIAN BATTLE AREA
18 June

Lasne stream

aransart •

Plancenoit

ANGLO-DUTCH
BATTLE AREA 18 June

CHASSÉ'S ANGLO-DUTCH
DIVISION Initially 18 June 1815

uture

La Belle Alliance

Hougoumont

La Haye Sainte

Frischermont •

Lasnes •

Papelotte

• Merbe Braine

Mont St. Jean

• Ohain

Waterloo village
WELLINGTON'S H.Q. 17 & 18 June 1815

Brussels

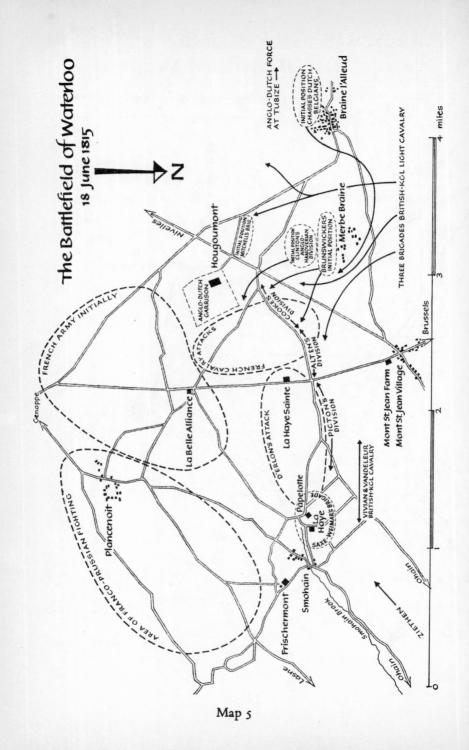

The Battlefield of Waterloo
18 June 1815

N

ANGLO-DUTCH FORCE AT TUBIZE →

INITIAL POSITION CHASSES DUTCH BELGIANS

Braine l'Alleud

ANGLO-DUTCH FORCE →

Merbe Braine

INITIAL POSITION MITCHELL'S BRIG.

INITIAL POSITION CLINTON'S ANGLO-HANOVERIAN DIVISION

BRUNSWICKERS' INITIAL POSITION

THREE BRIGADES BRITISH-KGL LIGHT CAVALRY

Nivelles

Hougoumont

ANGLO-DUTCH GARRISON

COOKE'S DIVISION

ALTEN'S DIVISION

Brussels

FRENCH ARMY INITIALLY

FRENCH CAVALRY ATTACKS

Genappe

La Belle Alliance

La Haye Sainte

Mont St Jean Farm

Mont St Jean Village

D'ERLON'S ATTACK

PICTON'S DIVISION

VIVIAN & VANDELEUR BRITISH-KGL CAVALRY

Papelotte

La Haye

SAXE-WEIMAR'S BRIGADE

AREA OF FRANCO-PRUSSIAN FIGHTING

Plancenoit

Smohain

Frischermont

Smohain Brook

Lasne

ZIETHEN

BULOW

Ohain

Ohain

0   1   2   3   4 miles

Map 5

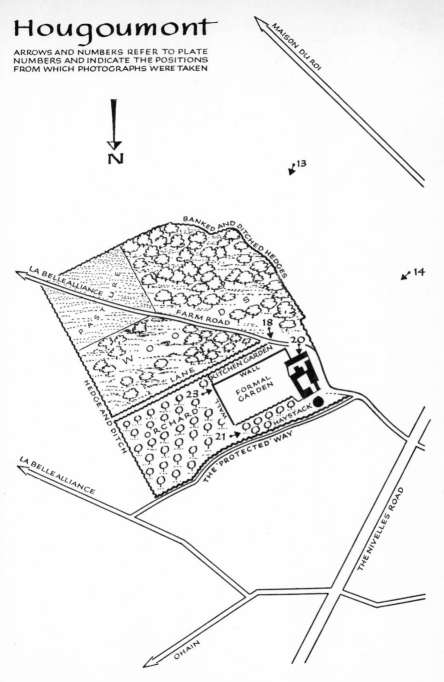

Hougoumont

ARROWS AND NUMBERS REFER TO PLATE
NUMBERS AND INDICATE THE POSITIONS
FROM WHICH PHOTOGRAPHS WERE TAKEN

N

MAISON DU ROI

13

BANKED AND DITCHED HEDGES

LA BELLE ALLIANCE

14

FARM ROAD

18

20

PASTURE WOODS

LANE

KITCHEN GARDEN

WALL

FORMAL GARDEN

23

ORCHARD

HEDGE AND DITCH

WALL

HAYSTACK

21

THE PROTECTED WAY

LA BELLE ALLIANCE

THE NIVELLES ROAD

OHAIN

Map 6

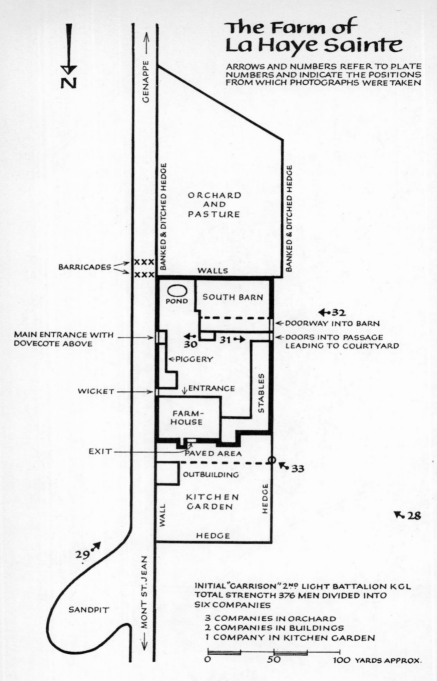

The Farm of La Haye Sainte

ARROWS AND NUMBERS REFER TO PLATE
NUMBERS AND INDICATE THE POSITIONS
FROM WHICH PHOTOGRAPHS WERE TAKEN

N

GENAPPE →

ORCHARD AND PASTURE

BANKED & DITCHED HEDGE

BANKED & DITCHED HEDGE

BARRICADES → XXX
XXX

WALLS

POND

SOUTH BARN

←•32

← DOORWAY INTO BARN

MAIN ENTRANCE WITH DOVECOTE ABOVE

30 ← 31 →

← DOORS INTO PASSAGE LEADING TO COURTYARD

← PIGGERY

WICKET →

↓ ENTRANCE

STABLES

FARM-HOUSE

EXIT →

↑ PAVED AREA

← 33

OUTBUILDING

HEDGE

↖ 28

KITCHEN GARDEN

WALL

HEDGE

29 ↗

MONT ST. JEAN

SANDPIT

INITIAL "GARRISON" 2ND LIGHT BATTALION KGL
TOTAL STRENGTH 376 MEN DIVIDED INTO
SIX COMPANIES

3 COMPANIES IN ORCHARD
2 COMPANIES IN BUILDINGS
1 COMPANY IN KITCHEN GARDEN

0   50   100 YARDS APPROX.

Map 7

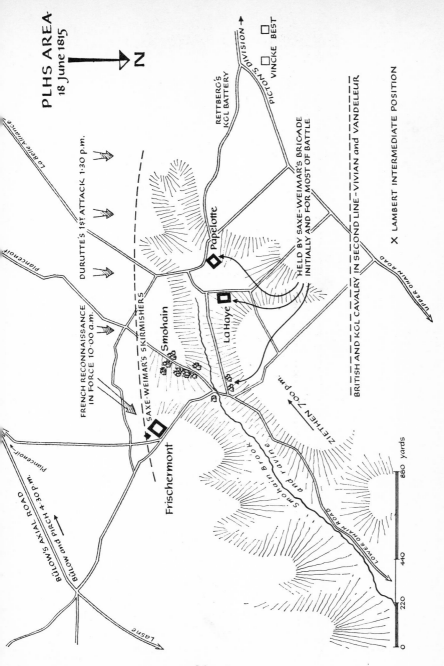

Map 8

Appendix
Strengths of the Contending Forces

I: Wellington's Field Army[1]

FIRST CORPS — THE PRINCE OF ORANGE
25,233 infantry, 56 guns
First British Division – Lt-Gen. Sir George Cooke –
4,061 infantry, 12 guns
1st British Brigade – Maj.-Gen. Sir Peregrine Maitland – 1,997 infantry
2/1st Guards (G) 976
3/1st Guards (P) 1,021
2nd British Brigade – Maj.-Gen. Sir John Byng – 2,064 infantry
2/2nd Guards (G) 1,003
2/3rd Guards (G) 1,061
Sandham's British and Kuhlmann's KGL Field Batteries[2] – 12 guns
Third British Division – Lt-Gen. Sir Charles Alten
6,970 infantry, 12 guns
5th British Brigade – Maj.-Gen. Sir Colin Halkett – 2,254 infantry
2/30th (G) 615
33rd (G) 561

---

[1] The Composition shown has been arrived at after a careful comparison of *James, Fortescue, Siborne, Hooper, Ropes* and *Becke*. No two of these agree in all details, but the only substantial disagreement is on the inclusion of garrison forces in the field army. I have not listed the 5th British Brigade, three British garrison battalions, nor the Hanoverian reserves since none took any active part in the campaign. These remained in or near fortifications as did some similar French regulars and National Guards.

(G) indicates one of Graham's units; (P) a Peninsular unit.

[2] The term 'field batteries' is used rather than the then correct 'foot brigades' because it is more meaningful today. A group of guns and one howitzer was then known as a brigade. If the gunners marched, it was a foot brigade; if they rode, it was a horse brigade.

2/69th (G) 516
2/73rd (G) 562
2nd KGL Brigade – Colonel C. Ompteda – 1,527 infantry
  1st Light Battalion 423
  2nd Light Battalion 337
  5th Line Battalion 379
  8th Line Battalion 388
1st Hanoverian Brigade – Maj.-Gen. Count Kielmansegge – 3,189 infantry
  Bremen Battalion 512
  Verden Battalion 533
  York Battalion 607
  Lüneburg Battalion 595
  Grubenhagen Battalion 621
  Jaeger Corps 321
Lloyd's British and Cleeve's KGL Field Batteries – 12 guns

Second Dutch-Belgian Division – Lt-Gen. Baron de Perponcher
  7,533 infantry, 16 guns
1st Brigade – Maj.-Gen. Count de Bylandt – 3,233 infantry
  7th Line 701
  27th Jaegers 809
  5th Militia 482
  7th Militia 675
  8th Militia 566
2nd Brigade – H.S.H. the Prince Bernhard of Saxe-Weimar – 4,300 infantry
  2nd Nassau (3 batts) 2,709
  Regt. of Orange-Nassau (2 batts) 1,591
Byleveld's Horse and Stievenaar's Field Batteries – 16 guns

Third Dutch-Belgian Division – Lt-Gen. Baron Chassé
  6,669 infantry, 16 guns
1st Brigade – Maj.-Gen. Ditmers – 3,088 infantry
  2nd Line 471
  35th Jaegers 605
  4th Militia 519
  6th Militia 492
  19th Militia 467
2nd Brigade – Maj.-Gen. D'Aubreme – 3,581 infantry
  3rd Line 629

12th Line 431
13th Line 664
36th Jaegers 633
3rd Militia 592
10th Militia 632
Krahmer's Horse and Lux's Foot Batteries – 16 guns

SECOND CORPS – LT-GEN. LORD HILL
    24,033 infantry, 40 guns
Second British Division – Lt-Gen. Sir Henry Clinton
    6,833 infantry, 12 guns
3rd British Brigade – Maj.-Gen. Adam – 2,621 infantry
   1/52nd (P) 1,038
   1/71st (P) 810
   2/95th (6 companies) (P) 585
   3/95th (2 companies) (P) 188
1st KGL Brigade – Col. G. C. A. du Plat – 1,758 infantry
   1st Line Battalion 411
   2nd Line Battalion 437
   3rd Line Battalion 494
   4th Line Battalion 416
3rd Hanoverian Brigade – Col. Hew Halkett – 2,454 infantry
   Bremervorde Landwehr Battalion 632
   Osnabrück Landwehr Battalion 612
   Quackenbruck Landwehr Battalion 588
   Salzgitter Landwehr Battalion 622
Sympher's KGL Horse and Bolton's British Field Batteries – 12 guns

Fourth British Division – Lt-Gen. Sir Charles Colville
    7,212 infantry, 12 guns
4th British Brigade – Col. Mitchell – 1,767 infantry
   3/14th 571
   1/23rd (P) 647
   51st (P) 549
6th British Brigade – Maj.-Gen. Johnstone – 2,396 infantry
   2/35th (G) 570
   1/54th (G) 541
   2/59th 461
   1/91st (G) 824
6th Hanoverian Brigade – Maj.-Gen. Sir James Lyon – 3,049 infantry
   Lauenburg Battalion 553

Calenberg Battalion 634
Nienburg Landwehr Battalion 625
Hoya Landwehr Battalion 629
Bentheim Landwehr Battalion 608
Brome's British and Rettberg's Hanoverian Field Batteries – 12 guns

First Dutch-Belgian Division – Lt-Gen. Stedman
  6,389 infantry, 8 guns
1st Brigade – Maj.-Gen. Hauw
  4th Line, 6th Line, 16th Jaegers, 9th Militia, 14th Militia, 15th Militia
2nd Brigade – Maj.-Gen. Eerens
  1st Line, 18th Jaegers, 1st Militia, 2nd Militia, 18th Militia
  Wynand's Field Battery

Lt-Gen. Anthing's Dutch-Belgian 'Indian' Brigade
  3,599 Infantry, 8 Guns
This force was organised for the Dutch East Indies and appears to have
been composed in part of men recruited there. Riesz's Field Battery
was a part of this command. Both Stedman and Anthing were nominally under the command of Prince Frederick of the Netherlands, who
was eighteen years old at this time. The whole unit is sometimes called
'Prince Frederick's Corps', but it was definitely a part of Hill's Command.

WELLINGTON'S RESERVE
  20,563 infantry, 912 cavalry and 52 guns
Fifth British Division – Lt-Gen. Sir Thomas Picton
  7,158 infantry, 12 guns
8th British Brigade – Maj.-Gen. Sir James Kempt – 2,471 infantry
  1/28th (P) 557
  1/32nd (P) 662
  1/79th (P) 703
  1/95th (P) 549
9th British Brigade – Maj.-Gen. Sir Denis Pack – 2,173 infantry
  3/1st (P) 604
  1/42nd (P) 526
  2/44th (P) 455
  1/92nd (P) 588
5th Hanoverian Brigade – Col. Vincke – 2,514 infantry
  Hameln Landwehr Battalion 669
  Gifhorn Landwehr Battalion 617
  Hildesheim Landwehr Battalion 617

Peine Landwehr Battalion 611
Roger's British and Braun's Hanoverian Field Batteries – 12 guns

Sixth British Division – Lt-Gen. Sir Lowry Cole[1]
    5,149 infantry, 12 guns
10th British Brigade – Maj.-Gen. Sir John Lambert – 2,567 infantry
    1/4th (P) 669
    1/27th (P) 698
    1/40th (P) 761
    2/81st (P) 439
4th Hanoverian Brigade – Col. Best – 2,582 infantry
    Verden Landwehr Battalion 621
    Luneburg Landwehr Battalion 624
    Osterode Landwehr Battalion 677
    Munden Landwehr Battalion 660
Unett's and Sinclair's British Field Batteries – 12 guns
Brunswick Corps – H.S.H. Duke of Brunswick
    5,376 infantry, 912 cavalry, 16 guns
A special command consisting of 8 battalions of infantry, a regiment of
Hussars, a squadron of Uhlans (Lancers), and 2 batteries of artillery.
Nassau Contingent – General Kruse
    2,880 infantry
1st Regiment consisting of 3 battalions
Unattached Artillery – Beane's and Ross's British Horse Batteries
    12 guns[2]

BRITISH AND HANOVERIAN CAVALRY – LT-GEN. THE EARL OF
UXBRIDGE
    10,155 troopers, 36 guns
First British Brigade – Maj.-Gen. Lord Edward Somerset – 1,226
    1st Life Guards 228, 2nd Life Guards 231, Royal Horse Guards 237,
    1st Dragoon Guards 530
Second British Brigade – Maj.-Gen. Sir William Ponsonby – 1,181
    1st Dragoons (Royals) 394, 2nd Dragoons (Scots Greys) 391,
    6th Dragoons (Inniskillings) 396

---

[1] Sir Lowry Cole had leave of absence to get married; the event took place on 15 June 1815 so that he missed Waterloo.

[2] Three batteries of British artillery which were provided with long iron 18-pounders are not included. These were not in the field; they were for siege purposes only. Their weight, slowness of fire and ineffectiveness against personnel would have made them extremely inefficient in battle.

Third British Brigade – Maj.-Gen. Sir William Dörnberg – 1,268
    1st Lt Dragoons KGL 462, 2nd Lt Dragoons KGL 419,
    23rd Lt Dragoons 387
Fourth British Brigade – Maj. Gen. Sir John Vandeleur – 1,171
    11th Lt Dragoons 390, 12th Lt Dragoons 388, 16th Lt Dragoons 393
Fifth British Brigade – Maj.-Gen. Sir Colquhoun Grant – 1,336
    2nd Hussars KGL 564, 7th Hussars 380, 15th Hussars 392
Sixth British Brigade – Maj.-Gen. Sir Hussey Vivian – 1,279
    1st Hussars KGL 493, 10th Hussars 390, 18th Hussars 396
Seventh British Brigade – Col. Sir F. Arentschildt – 1,012
    3rd Hussars KGL 622, 13th Light Dragoons 390
First Hanoverian Brigade – Col. Estorff – 1,682
    Cumberland Hussars 497, Prince Regent's Hussars 596,
    Bremen and Verden Hussars 589
Each of the first 6 brigades above had a British horse battery attached to it. They were Bull's (Howitzers), Webber Smith's, Gardiner's, Whinyates's (also some rockets), Mercer's, and Ramsay's. A total of 36 guns.
Dutch–Belgian Cavalry (placed under the command of the Earl of Uxbridge before the campaign opened) – 3,405 men, 8 guns.
First Brigade – Maj.-Gen. Trip – 1,237
    1st Dutch Carabiniers 446, 2nd Belgian Carabiniers 399,
    3rd Dutch Carabiniers 392
Second Brigade – Maj.-Gen de Ghigny – 1,086
    4th Dutch Lt Dragoons 647, 8th Belgian Hussars 439
Third Brigade – Maj.-Gen. van Merlen – 1,082
    5th Belgian Lt Dragoons 441, 6th Dutch Hussars 641
Petter's and Gey's 'half batteries' of horse artillery – 8 guns

RECAPITULATION OF ENTIRE FIELD ARMY:

	Infantry		Cavalry		Artillery	
	Brigades	Rank & File[1]	Brigades[2]	Rank & File[1]	Pieces	Rank & File
British	9	20,310	3	5,913	90	4,630
K.G.L.	2	3,285	4	2,560	18	526
Hanoverian	5	13,788	1	1,682	12	465
Total Directly Under British Control	16	37,383	8	10,155	120	5,621

		All Ranks		All Ranks		All Ranks
Dutch-Belgians	8	23,190[3]	3	3,405[2]	56	1,635[2]
Brunswickers	2	5,376	1	912	16	510
Nassauers	1	2,880[3]	—	—	—	—
Total Allies	11	32,446	4	4,317	72	2,145
Total of All	27	68,829[1]	12	14,474[1]	192	7,766[1]

Infantry	68,829
Cavalry	14,474
Artillery	7,766
Engineers, Train, Staff Corps	1,240
Grand Total	92,309[1]

II: Prussian Field Army in the Waterloo Campaign

Field-Marshal Prince Blücher von Wahlstadt, Commander-in-Chief; Lt-Gen. Count Gneisenau, Chief of Staff; Maj.-Gen. Grolman, Quartermaster-General.

	Infantry	Cavalry	Artillery, Engineers, etc.	Guns	Total Personnel
First Corps – Lt-Gen. Ziethen	27,887	1,925	4,880	96	32,692
Second Corps – Lt-Gen. Pirch I	25,836	4,468	2,400	80	32,704
Third Corps – Lt-Gen. Thielemann	20,611	2,405	1,440	48	24,456
Fourth Corps – Gen. Count Bülow Dennewitz	25,381	3,081	2,640	88	31,102
Totals	99,715	11,879	9,360	312	120,954

[1] There is a serious irregularity here in that the British and subordinate services kept their records on the basis of rank and file only and did not include officers and some other personnel in their total strengths. The Dutch-Belgian, Brunswick and Nassau figures include all ranks. An addition of 5 to 7 per cent to British, KGL and perhaps Hanoverian totals would make them comparable with those of other forces.

[2] The brigading of British and KGL cavalry was unusual. Three were composed entirely of British units (Somerset's, Ponsonby's and Vandeleur's); the other four contained both British and KGL regiments.

[3] The Nassau troops in the Waterloo campaign fall into two categories. The 2nd Brigade of the 2nd Dutch-Belgian Division under Lt-Gen. Perponcher was commanded by Prince Bernhard of Saxe-Weimar and consisted of five battalions of 3,300 Nassau infantry in the pay and organisation of the Netherlands Army. A separate Nassau contingent commanded by Col. Kruse and consisting of 2,880 infantry was directly under Wellington.

Each Corps had four infantry brigades which varied in strength from 6 to $9\frac{1}{2}$ battalions, from 3,980 to 9,069 men. These would have been called divisions in other armies. At least one battery of artillery was attached to each infantry brigade. All cavalry was assigned to the four Corps; there was no independent cavalry reserve. There were in all 136 battalions, 137 squadrons, and 39 batteries. These statistics are from *James, Fortescue, Siborne* and *Ropes*; there are only minor inconsistences between them. *James* and *Fortescue* list a total of only 296 pieces of artillery, but show 56 guns in the Third Corps.

III: French Field Army in the Waterloo Campaign

Emperor Napoleon, Commander-in-Chief; Marshal Soult, Duke of Dalmatia, Chief of Staff.

	1st Corps	2nd Corps	3rd Corps	4th Corps	6th Corps	Imperial Guard
Commander	d'Erlon	Reille	Vandamme	Gérard	Lobau	Drouot
Divisions of Infantry	4	4	3	3	3	3
Brigades of Infantry	8	8	6	6	6	22 battalions
Number of Infantry	16,885	20,635	15,130	13,101	8,573	13,026
Divisions of Cavalry	1	1	1	1	None	Not so organised
Brigades of Cavalry	2	2	2	2	None	2
Number of Cavalry	1,706	2,064	1,017	1,500	None	4,100
Artillery Foot Batteries	5	5	4	4	4	13
Horse Batteries	1	1	1	1	None	3
Total Guns	46	46	38	38	32	122
Total Personnel, Engineers, etc.	2,140	2,480	1,958	1,618	1,448	3,758
Total Men	20,731	25,179	18,105	16,219	10,021	20,884

APPENDIX

Cavalry Reserve – Four Corps of two divisions each with a horse
battery to each division. Each division composed of two brigades of two
regiments each, with some exceptions. Total cavalry in this reserve was
11,849 with 48 guns. The Guard was organised into regiments as
follows: 8 dragoons, 6 lancers, 8 mounted chasseurs, 11 cuirassiers,
5 hussars and 2 carabiniers.

The Guard Infantry was organised into 3 divisions[1] –

Four Regiments of Grenadiers	Seven Battalions	4,140
Four Regiments of Chasseurs	Seven Battalions	4,603
Two Regiments of Voltigeurs and two Tirailleurs	Eight Battalions	4,283

Total—13,026

The Guard Cavalry consisted of 2 divisions under Lefebvre-Des-
nouettes (19 squadrons of lancers and mounted chasseurs) and Guyot
(14 squadrons of dragoons, mounted grenadiers, and gendarmes
d'élite).

Grand Total

Infantry	87,350
Cavalry	22,236
Artillery, Engineers, etc.	14,553

Grand Total   124,139[2]

The above details, save for Imperial Guard Infantry, are from *James* and
Fortescue, but check closely with *Charras*, *Houssaye* and other reliable
French sources. Guard Infantry organisation is mainly from *Anatomy of
Glory*.

[1] The organisation of the Guard Infantry is given in several different ways. The principal
problem is the Middle Guard (*La Garde Moyenne*). *Charras*, I, 67, and La Tour d'Auvergne,
48, believe this to be the four regiments of Chasseurs. *Houssaye*, says that the Middle
Guard was the 3rd and 4th Grenadiers and the 3rd and 4th Chasseurs which were all
created in April and May of 1815 from suitable material. The 'Young Guard' probably
comprised the Voltigeurs and Tirailleurs, but even here there is inconsistency in regimental
designations.

[2] Enumerating a large army down to the last man is, of course, practically impossible;
however, this total checks closely with others. *Fuller's Decisive Battles*, II, 496, says
'89,405 infantry, 23,595 cavalry, and 11,578 artillery with 344 guns', a total of 124,578
without engineers, staff and train. Hooper says 'a total of 128,088, that is 89,415 infantry,
22,302 cavalry, and 15,871 artillery with 344 guns'. Both based their calculations on
Charras.

Bibliography

An enormous number of books and articles have been written about Waterloo. The British Museum 'Wellington and Waterloo' classification contain 315 titles. There are hundreds more about Napoleon and others who participated in the battle; many works of the first half of the nineteenth century contain some reference either to the battle, or to people who were there. French and German writers have been as concerned with this campaign as those who have written in English. There are a few important books in other languages also. Previously unpublished manuscripts, reports and letters are still appearing, and are sometimes of value.

The abundance of source material is at first disconcerting, but does not lead to lasting confusion. Original records which include the writings of all eyewitnesses tend to sort themselves into categories. The most valuable for my purposes are Wellington's *Dispatches* as originally selected and published by Colonel Gurwood,[1] *Supplementary Dispatches* edited by the second Duke of Wellington, and Colonel Gurwood's *General Orders* which appeared in a separate volume.

The mass of other writings by eyewitnesses has been extremely helpful, but varies greatly in value. Some accounts by important figures in the conflict who were also literate are the best evidence of what actually happened at various places and times. Others are personal observations of limited scope which give the 'feel' of the battle, but no new facts. There are also intermediate accounts which give a bit of both. Müffling's *Passages*, Cavalié Mercer's *Journal*, and

[1] These volumes began to appear in 1837, but were not completed until 1845: *D.N.B.* VIII, 813.

Shaw-Kennedy's *Notes* are of the first type. They were written by professional soldiers still in the full possession of their faculties recalling the happenings of the most important days of their lives.[1] Harry Smith, Tompkinson, Leach, Leeke, Wheeler, Robertson, various anonymous soldiers and many, many others give more limited accounts of what they did, saw, and remembered. Hundreds of personal letters written shortly after the battle are also important in one or both categories.

Early full-length accounts of Waterloo written by eyewitnesses are uneven in value. When they wrote from personal observation, they produced original records. When they based their accounts on what others told or wrote them, they laboured under handicaps. General Müffling, the author of the *Passages* mentioned above which was published after his death, also wrote an account of the entire campaign which appeared in 1816. Sergeant-Major Cotton of the 7th Hussars wrote his charming *Voice from Waterloo* not only as an eyewitness, but also as a resident in the area who studied all records which were then available and spent years guiding others, including general officers who participated in the fighting, over the battlefield.

Captain Siborne was not at Waterloo – he joined Wellington's army in Paris on 5 September 1815 – but wrote in many ways as an eyewitness. After living for eight months at La Haye Sainte, he constructed the model of the battlefield that was for so long in the Royal United Service Institution Museum in Whitehall. Lord Hill when Commander-in-Chief of the British Army allowed Siborne officially to circularise all surviving Waterloo officers. Siborne's history is based on the enormous quantity of letters which he received in reply, his conversations with these men, and his own topographical research. Siborne's son, General Siborne of the Royal Engineers, went through his father's letters and published those that were in his opinion the most interesting and significant. All Waterloo students are indebted to the two Sibornes.

Another form of semi-original source for Waterloo are conversations with important figures as set down by their contemporaries. Because of Wellington's long life, his quotability and his importance after Waterloo, we have a vast, but sometimes conflicting, lot of material based

---

[1] *Müffling's Passages* appear to have been completed in 1844, but were based on earlier notes. *Mercer* must also have used nearly contemporary notes, even though his *Journal* was not finished until about 1828. *Shaw-Kennedy* wrote his *Notes* not long before 1860.

upon what he is supposed to have said.[1] Gurwood's carefully recorded notes along these lines, which would have been so valuable militarily, were burned at the Duke's insistence, but Stanhope, Croker and other non-military friends of Wellington's later years have left volumes. A thin little book published in 1956 and edited by the seventh Duke of Wellington records what George William Chad put down of his conversations with the Duke. Greville, Creevey, Gronow and many more devote part of their works to what Wellington did, said and wrote. We must realise, however, that the Duke probably outlived his reliability as a military witness of what happened many years before.

The careful historian must also consider relics of the battle along with what has been written about it. So much survives in the little museums around Waterloo, in Brussels museums, at the Rotunda at Woolwich, in the Tower of London, at Les Invalides in Paris and in many other smaller collections. The best way to know exactly what one of Napoleon's favourite 12-pounders was like is to examine one that is still in its original carriage at Woolwich. First-hand information about Baker rifles can be gained most satisfactorily by firing them extensively.

True secondary sources which appeared before Siborne (1844) are not of much account; there just was not yet enough primary material available. Beginning with Creasy and Jones in 1851 and 1852, however, there have been many fine secondary studies of the battle and campaign. Wellington and Waterloo have also been discussed in greater or lesser length in many volumes devoted to groups of battles, the British Army, military science and tactics, and the like. In this whole field and in English, I have found Fortescue, Robinson, Hooper, Chesney, James, Hamley, and Pratt of real value; I was disappointed in Wood, Roberts, Griffiths, Wolseley, Fuller and Naylor. Oman deserves special mention. Although he wrote nothing on Waterloo so exhaustive as his *Peninsular War*, his Chapter XX of the *Cambridge Modern History*, IX, entitled 'The Hundred Days' is superb. His *Wellington's Army* and his *Studies* are occasionally of great value.

There have been many biographies of Wellington; the early ones have been of little value to me. Guedalla and to a lesser extent Aldington are important, although not military. Maxwell treats Waterloo

---

[1] Perhaps the most astonishing inconsistency is that according to *Chesney*, 186, Wellington told Gen. Zeigler, commandant of Namur in 1821, that he 'should have taken the direction to my left, that is towards Wavre' if he had to retreat on 18 June 1815. He said to Croker and others, as discussed in *Roberts*, 165–6, 'Had I been forced from my position, I should have retreated to my right, towards the coast.'

with extreme accuracy and care and at considerable length; Hooper is also good, but shorter.

For details of weapons and tactics, I have used a group of books too numerous to mention specifically; these are given in the bibliography below. I have also profited by a few regimental histories and special monographs, particularly Gardyne's *Life of a Regiment*, Cope, Aubrey-Fletcher, Beamish, Ward, Petrie, Vivian, Brett-James, and Anglesey. I bless the creators of *The Dictionary of National Biography* and have used the 1938 and 1965 Editions of the *Encyclopedia Britannica* often.

On the French side, Napoleon's two accounts of the Waterloo campaign are of value, even though prejudiced and despicable in places.[1] Jomini was in the French Army in 1815, but not at Waterloo. He had a real understanding of what actually happened and writes more clearly than his British contemporaries. I liked Charras and Marmont, but not Thiers. Of the later writers, Houssaye seems to be best. He uses references from the other side carefully and honestly. Belgians and Germans who have written about the campaign are too much interested in pleading their own causes.

Procuring this reference material has been easier than I feared; more than 90 per cent of the titles given in the bibliography were either already in my library or soon purchased. I am particularly indebted in this connection to Mr Charles Harris of Francis Edwards and Mr John Maggs of Maggs Brothers, London booksellers. For books not available by purchase, Mr Warren Kuhn, formerly of the Princeton University Library, has gone far beyond the call of duty and friendship to borrow material for me. When I have been *in extremis*, the British Museum has come to the rescue with microfilm.

The bibliography below is divided into two sections. Where a work has been referred to twice or more in footnotes to the text, or is referred to in this short essay, it will have been given a *short title* and is listed by this alphabetically in the first section. Others are listed by their authors in the second. It should not be concluded, however, that the first list is in every instance more valuable than the second.

SHORT TITLES USED IN FOOTNOTES

Aerts	AERTS, WINAND. *Waterloo*. Brussels, 1908.
Aldington	ALDINGTON, RICHARD. *The Duke*. New York, 1943.

---

[1] The efforts to shift the responsibility for the loss of Waterloo to Grouchy and Ney are as dishonest as they are ineffective with unprejudiced readers.

Alexander | ALEXANDER, SIR JAMES EDWARD. *The Life of Field-Marshal, His Grace The Duke of Wellington.* London, 1840.

Anatomy of Glory | LACHOUQUE, HENRY. *The Anatomy of Glory, Napoleon and His Guard.* London, 1961.

Anglesey | ANGLESEY, MARQUESS OF. *One-Leg, The Life and Letters of Henry William Paget.* London, 1961.

Aubrey-Fletcher | AUBREY-FLETCHER, MAJOR H. L. *A History of the Foot Guards to 1856.* London, 1927.

Bain | BAIN, NICOLSON. *A Detailed Account of the Battles Quatre Bras, Ligny, and Waterloo.* Edinburgh, 1819.

Batty | BATTY, CAPT. *An Historical Sketch of the Campaign of 1815.* London, 1820.

Beamish | BEAMISH, NORTH LUDLOW. *History of the King's German Legion.* London, 1832 and 1837.

Becke | BECKE, MAJOR A. F. *Napoleon and Waterloo.* London, 1936.

Blackmore | BLACKMORE, HOWARD L. *British Military Firearms 1650–1850.* London, 1961.

Boulger | BOULGER, DEMETRIUS C. *The Belgians at Waterloo.* London, 1901.

Brett-James | BRETT-JAMES, ANTONY. *The Hundred Days.* London, 1964.

Cambridge | *Cambridge Modern History.* Cambridge, 1906.

Chad | CHAD, GEORGE WILLIAM. *Conversations of the First Duke of Wellington.* Cambridge, 1956.

Charras | CHARRAS, LT-COL. *Histoire de la Campagne de 1815.* Paris, 1869.

Chesney | CHESNEY, COLONEL CHARLES C., R.E. *Waterloo Lectures: A Study of the Campaign of 1815.* London, 1907.

Clinton | CLINTON, H. R. *The War in the Peninsula and Wellington's Campaigns in France and Belgium.* London, 1878.

Cole | COLE, JOHN WILLIAM. *Memoirs of British Generals Distinguished during the Peninsular War.* London, 1856.

Cooper   COOPER, LEONARD. *The Age of Wellington: The Life and Times of the Duke of Wellington, 1769–1852.* London, 1964.

Cope   COPE, SIR WILLIAM H. *The History of the Rifle Brigade.* London, 1877.

Cotton   COTTON, SERGEANT-MAJOR EDWARD. *A Voice from Waterloo.* Mont Saint Jean, 1900.

Creasy   CREASY, SIR EDWARD S. *The Fifteen Decisive Battles of the World.* London, 1943.

Creevey Papers   CREEVEY, THOMAS. *The Creevey Papers.* London, 1904.

Croker   CROKER, JOHN WILSON. *Correspondence and Diaries.* London, 1885.

Dispatches   GURWOOD, LT-COL. *The Dispatches of the Field-Marshal the Duke of Wellington during his Various Campaigns in India, Denmark, Portugal, Spain, the Low Countries and France.* London, 1837–38.

Ellesmere's Essays   ELLESMERE, 1ST EARL OF (EGERTON, FRANCIS). *Essays on History, Biography, Geography, Engineering, etc.* London, 1858.

Fortescue   FORTESCUE, HON. J. W. *History of the British Army.* London, 1899–1930.

Fraser   FRASER, SIR WILLIAM. *Words on Wellington, the Duke, Waterloo, the Ball.* London, 1902.

Fuller's Decisive Battles   FULLER, MAJ.-GEN. J. F. C. *The Decisive Battles of the Western World.* London, 1957.

Fuller's Light Infantry   FULLER, COL. J. F. C. *British Light Infantry in the Eighteenth Century.* London, 1925.

Gardner   GARDNER, DORSEY. *Quatre Bras, Ligny, and Waterloo.* London, 1882.

General Orders   GURWOOD, LT-COL. JOHN. *The General Orders of Field-Marshal the Duke of Wellington, K.G., etc. In Portugal, Spain, and France.* London, 1832.

Gleig's Reminiscences   GLEIG, GEORGE ROBERT. *Personal Reminiscences of the First Duke of Wellington.* Edinburgh and London, 1904.

Glover   GLOVER, RICHARD. *Peninsular Preparation: The Reform of the British Army 1795–1809.* Cambridge, 1963.

Guedalla	GUEDALLA, PHILIP. *The Duke*. London, 1931.
Hamley	HAMLEY, SIR EDWARD BRUCE. *The Operations of War Explained and Illustrated*. Edinburgh and London, 1909.
Harry Smith	SMITH, SIR HARRY. *The Autobiography of Lieutenant-General Sir Harry Smith*. London, 1901.
Hart	HART, LIDDELL, *Ghost of Napoleon*. London, 1933.
Henderson's Blücher	HENDERSON, ERNEST F. *Blücher and the Uprising of Prussia against Napoleon*. London, 1911.
Hooper	HOOPER, GEORGE. *Waterloo: The Downfall of the First Napoleon: History of the Campaign of 1815*. London, 1862.
Houssaye	HOUSSAYE, HENRI. *Waterloo*. London, 1900.
James	JAMES, LT-COL. WALTER HAWEIS. *The Campaign of 1815*. Edinburgh and London, 1908.
Jomini	JOMINI, GENERAL BARON DE. *The Political and Military History of Waterloo*. New York, 1861.
Jomini's Art	JOMINI, BARON DE. *The Art of War*. Philadelphia, 1863.
Kennedy	KENNEDY, SIR JAMES SHAW. *Notes on the Battle of Waterloo*. London, 1865.
Leach	LEACH, LT-COL. J. *Rough Sketches of the Life of an Old Soldier*. London, 1831.
Leeke	LEEKE, REV. WILLIAM. *The History of Lord Seaton's Regiment (the 52nd Light Infantry) at the Battle of Waterloo*. London, 1866.
Life of a Regiment	GARDYNE, LT-COL. C. GREENHILL. *The Life of a Regiment*. London, 1929.
Life of a Soldier	ANON. *Life of a Soldier by a Field Officer*. London, 1834.
MacKinnon	MACKINNON, COL. *Origin and Services of the Coldstream Guards*. London, 1833.
Marbot	MARBOT. *The Memoirs of Baron de Marbot*. London, 1893.
Marmont	MARMONT, MARSHAL (DUKE OF RAGUSA). *The Spirit of Military Institutions or Essential Principles of the Art of War*. Philadelphia, 1862.
Maxwell	MAXWELL, SIR HERBERT. *The Life of Wellington*. London, 1907.

Mercer's Journal	MERCER, GEN. CAVALIÉ. *Journal of the Waterloo Campaign Kept Throughout the Campaign of 1815.* London, 1927.
Morris	MORRIS, SERGEANT THOMAS. *Recollections of Military Service in 1813, 1814, and 1815.* London, 1845.
Müffling	M., C. DE (i.e. Baron F. K. F. von Müffling). *History of the Campaign of the British, Dutch, Hanoverian and Brunswick Armies . . . in the Year 1815.* London, 1816.
Müffling's Passages	MÜFFLING, FRIEDRICH KARL FERDINAND, BARON VON. *Passages from my Life.* London, 1853.
Muller's Science	MULLER, WILLIAM. *Elements of the Science of War.* London, 1811.
Napoleon	BONAPARTE, NAPOLEON. *The Waterloo Campaign.* London, 1957.
Oman	OMAN, SIR CHARLES. *History of the Peninsular War.* Oxford, 1902–30.
Oman's Studies	OMAN, SIR CHARLES. *Studies in the Napoleonic Wars.* London, 1929.
Petrie	PETRIE, SIR CHARLES, BART. *Wellington: A Reassessment.* London, 1956.
Pratt	PRATT, LT-COL. SISSON C. *The Waterloo Campaign.* London, 1907.
Regulations for Riflemen	*Regulations for the Exercise of Riflemen and Light Infantry.* London, 1798.
Roberts	ROBERTS, GENERAL LORD. *The Rise of Wellington.* London, 1895.
Robinson	ROBINSON, MAJ.-GEN. SIR C. W. *Wellington's Campaigns 1808–15.* London, 1927.
Ropes	ROPES, JOHN CODMAN. *The Campaign of Waterloo.* New York, 1906.
Saunders	SAUNDERS, EDITH. *The Hundred Days.* London, 1964.
Siborne	SIBORNE, CAPTAIN WILLIAM. *The Waterloo Campaign, 1815.* Birmingham, 1894.
Siborne's Letters	WATERLOO LETTERS. Ed. Maj.-Gen. H. T. Siborne. London. 1891.

Sidney	SIDNEY, REV. EDWIN. *The Life of Lord Hill, G.C.B. Late Commander of the Forces.* London, 1845.
Stanhope	STANHOPE, PHILIP HENRY. *Notes of Conversations with the Duke of Wellington.* London 1888.
Supplementary Dispatches	WELLESLEY, ARTHUR, DUKE OF WELLINGTON. *Supplementary Dispatches and Memoranda of Field-Marshal Arthur, Duke of Wellington.* (Edited by his son, the Duke of Wellington.) London, 1858–72.
Surtees	SURTEES, WILLIAM. *Twenty-Five Years in the Rifle Brigade.* London, 1833.
Thiers	THIERS, M. A. *History of the Consulate and the Empire of France under Napoleon.* London, 1894.
Tomkinson	TOMKINSON, LT-COL. WILLIAM. *The Diary of a Cavalry Officer in the Peninsular and Waterloo Campaigns 1809–1815.* London, 1894.
Vivian	VIVIAN, CLAUD. *Richard Hussey Vivian First Baron Vivian, A Memoir.* London, 1897.
Weller	WELLER, JAC. *Wellington in the Peninsula.* London, 1962.
Wellington's Army	OMAN, C. W. C. *Wellington's Army 1809–1814.* London, 1913.
Wheeler	WHEELER, WILLIAM. *The Letters of Private Wheeler 1809–1828.* London, 1951.
Wolseley	WOLSELEY, FIELD-MARSHAL VISCOUNT. *The Decline and Fall of Napoleon.* London, 1895.
Wood	WOOD, GENERAL SIR EVELYN. *Cavalry in the Waterloo Campaign.* London, 1895.
Yonge	YONGE, CHARLES DUKE. *Life of Field-Marshal Arthur, Duke of Wellington.* London, 1860.

OTHER WORKS

ANON. *The Battle of Waterloo. . . . From a Variety of Authentic and Original Sources. . . . by a Near Observer.* Edinburgh, 1816.

—, *Character of the Armies of the Various European Powers.* London, 1802.

—, *Journal of T. S. of the 71st Highland Light Infantry, in Memorials of the Late Wars,* Edinburgh, 1828.

—, *Military Memoirs of an Infantry Officer 1809–1816.* Edinburgh, 1833.

—, *The Nineteen Movements as Ordered for the British Army*. Calcutta, 1809.

—, *Rules and Regulations for the Manual and Platoon Exercise Formation, Field Exercise, and Movement of His Majesty's Forces*. London, 1807.

ACTON, LORD. *Napoleon*. Cambridge, 1906.

ADYE, RALPH WILLETT, *The Bombardier, and Pocket Gunner*. London, 1827.

ALISON, SIR ARCHIBALD, *History of Europe from the Commencement of the French Revolution to the Restoration of the Bourbons*. 7th ed. 20 vols. Edinburgh and London, 1848.

BARNES, MAJ. R. MONEY, *A History of the Regiments and Uniforms of the British Army*. London, 1954.

BAS, FRANÇOIS DE, *La Campagne de 1815 aux Pays Bas*, Bruxelles: 1908–09.

—, *Prins Frederik der Nederlanden*. 4 vols. Schiedam, 1884–1914.

BEAMISH, NORTH LUDLOW, *Cavalry in War*. London, 1855.

BECKE, ARCHIBALD FRANK, *Introduction to the History of Tactics*. London, 1909.

BELL, DOUGLAS, *Wellington's Officers*. London and Glasgow, 1938.

BISMARK, F. W. VON, *Instructions for the Field Service of Cavalry*. Translated by Captain N. L. Beamish. London, 1825.

—, *Lectures on the Tactics of Cavalry*. Translated by Major N. L. Beamish. London 1827.

BRETT-JAMES, ANTONY, *Wellington at War 1794–1815*. London and New York, 1961.

BUNBURY, THOMAS, *Reminiscences of a Veteran. Being Personal and Military Adventures in Portugal, Spain, France, Malta . . . and India*. 3 vols. London, 1861.

BURGHCLERE, LADY, *The First Duke of Wellington, A Great Man's Friendships. Letters of the Duke of Wellington to Mary, Marchioness of Salisbury*. Edited by Lady Burghclere with a biographical sketch of Lady Salisbury. New York, 1927.

CARR-GOMM, FRANCIS CULLING, *Letters and Journals of Field-Marshal Sir William Maynard Gomm, G.C.B.* London, 1881.

COOKE, CAPT., MOODIE, LT T. W. D., and MUNSTER, THE EARL OF, *Memoirs of the Late War: Comprising the Personal Narrative of Capt. Cooke. A History of the Campaign of 1809 in Portugal of the Earl of Munster, and a Narrative of the Campaign in 1814 in Holland by Lt T. W. D. Moodie*. London, 1831.

COSTELLO, EDWARD, *The Adventures of a Soldier; or Memoirs of Edward Costello . . . Comprising Narratives of the Campaigns in the Peninsula under the Duke of Wellington*. London, 1841. 2nd Ed: London, 1852.

CUNINGHAME, JAMES, *The Tactics of the British Army.* London, 1804.

DALRYMPLE, LT-COL. WILLIAM, *Tactics.* Dublin, 1782.

DAMITZ, KARL VON, *Histoire de la Campagne de 1815 . . . d'apres Les Documents du General Grolman.* 2 vols. Paris, 1840.

DAVIES, GODFREY, *Wellington and His Army.* Oxford, 1954.

DE ROTTENBURG, COL., *Regulations for the Exercise of Riflemen and Light Infantry, and Instructions for their Conduct in the Field.* London, 1798.

DONKIN, SIR R. S., *A Parallel Between Wellington and Marlborough.* London, 1830.

DUNCAN, CAPT. FRANCIS, *History of the Royal Regiment of Artillery.* London, 1873.

DUNDAS, COL. DAVID, *Principles of Military Movements, Chiefly Applied to Infantry, etc.* London, 1788.

ERCKMANN-CHATRIAN, ÉMILE, *The History of a Conscript of 1813 and Waterloo.* Translated by Russell Davis Gillman. New York, 1909.

—, *Waterloo: A Sequel to the Conscript of 1813.* New York, 1889.

FITCHETT, W. H., *Wellington's Men – Some Soldier Autobiographies.* London, 1900.

FORBES, MAJ.-GEN. A., *A History of the Ordnance Services.* 3 vols. London, 1929.

FORTESCUE, HON. J. W., *Wellington.* London, 1925.

FOY, MAXIMILIEN, *Vie Militaire du Général Foy.* Paris, 1900.

FRASER, EDWARD, *The Soldiers Whom Wellington Led – Deeds of Daring, Chivalry, and Renown.* London, 1913.

FRAZER, SIR A. S., *Letters of Col. A. S. Frazer, K.C.B. Commanding the Royal Horse Artillery in the Army under the Duke of Wellington. Written during the Peninsular and Waterloo Campaigns.* Edited by E. Sabine. London, 1859.

—, *Remarks on the Organization of the Corps of Artillery in the British Service.* London, 1818.

GAWLER, *The Crisis and Close of the Action at Waterloo.* Dublin, 1833.

GLEIG, GEORGE ROBERT, *The Life of Arthur Duke of Wellington.* London, 1865.

—, *The Subaltern.* Edinburgh and London, 1825.

GORE, CAPT. ARTHUR, *An Historical Account of the Battle of Waterloo, etc.* London, 1817.

GOURGAUD, BARON GASPARD, *The Campaign of 1815; Or a Narrative of the Military Operations Which Took place in France and Belgium during the Hundred Days.* London, 1818.

GRAHAM, BRIG.-GEN. C. A. L., *Story of the Royal Regiment of the Artillery.* Woolwich, 1944.

GREVILLE, CHARLES CAVENDISH FULKE, *The Greville Memoirs.* Edited by Strachey, Lytton and Fulford. 8 vols. London, 1938.

GRIFFITHS, MAJ. ARTHUR, *Wellington at Waterloo.* London, 1898.

GROLMAN, see VON DAMITZ.

GRONOW, CAPT., *The Reminiscences and Recollections of Captain Gronow, 1810–1860.* 2 vols. London, 1900.

HARDMAN, F., *Peninsular Scenes and Sketches.* London, 1846.

HAY, CAPT. WILLIAM, *Reminiscences . . . 1808–1815 under Wellington.* London, 1901.

HEADLEY, J. T., *Napoleon and His Marshals.* New York, 1847.

HENDERSON, COL. G. F. R., *The Science of War.* London, 1905.

HIBBERT, CHRISTOPHER (ed.), *The Wheatley Diary.* London, 1964.

HICKS, JAMES ERNEST, *Notes on French Ordnance – 1717 to 1936.* New York, 1937.

HIME, LT-COL. HENRY W., *The Origin of Artillery.* London, 1915.

HOOPER, GEORGE, *Wellington.* London, 1893.

HOPE, LT JAMES, *Letters from Portugal, Spain and France. etc.* Edinburgh, 1819.

JARRY, GEN. JOHN, *Instructions Concerning the Duty of Light Infantry.* London, 1803.

JONES, GEORGE, *The Battle of Waterloo.* London, 1852.

KEITH, ADMIRAL VISCOUNT, *The Keith Papers.* London, 1927–55.

KELLY, CHRISTOPHER, *History of the French Revolution and of the Wars Produced by That Memorable Event.* London, 1817.

KINCAID, CAPT. J., *Adventures in the Rifle Brigade.* London, 1830.

—, *Random Shots from a Rifleman.* London, 1835.

LA TOUR D'AUVERGNE, E. L. J. M. DE, *Waterloo, Étude de la Campagne de 1815.* Paris, 1870.

LAWRENCE, W., *The Autobiography of Sergeant William Lawrence.* London, 1886.

LE MARCHANT, D., *Memoirs of Major-General J. G. Le Marchant.* London, 1841.

LESLIE, MAJ. JOHN H. (ed.) *The Dickson Manuscripts Being Diaries, Letters, Maps, Account Books, with various Other Papers of the Late Major-General Sir Alexander Dickson (Series C from 1809–1818).* Woolwich, 1905.

MALMESBURY, JAMES HARRIS, EARL OF, *A Series of Letters of the First Earl of Malmesbury, His Family, and Friends.* Edited by his Grandson. 2 vols. London, 1870.

MCGRIGOR, SIR J., *Autobiography and Services with Notes. etc.* London, 1861.

MULLER, JOHN, *Treatise on Artillery.* Philadelphia, 1779.

NAYLOR, JOHN, *Waterloo.* London, 1960.

ROBERTSON, D., *The Journal of Sergeant D. Robertson.* Perth, 1842.

ROBINSON, H. B., *Memoirs of Lieutenant-General Sir Thomas Picton, G.C.B.* London, 1836.

ROSE, J. HOLLAND, *Napoleonic Studies.* London, 1904.

SCHAUMANN, A. L. F., *On the Road with Wellington.* London, 1924.

SCOTT, SIR WALTER, *Life of Napoleon.* 9 vols. London, 1849.

SMIRKE, R. J., *Review of a Battalion of Infantry Including the Eighteen Manoeuvres.* London, 1799.

SMITH, CAPT. GEORGE, *An Universal Military Dictionary,* or, *A Copious Explanation of the Technical Terms,* etc. *Used in the Equipment, Machinery, Movements, and Military Operations of an Army.* London, 1779.

STEPHEN, SIR LESLIE and LEE, SIR SIDNEY (ed.) *Dictionary of National Biography.* 22 vols, 5 Supplements. Oxford, 1917.

STEVENSON, SERGEANT JOHN, *A Soldier in Time of War, 1841.* London, 1841.

TEMPLE, HENRY JOHN, 3RD VISCOUNT PALMERSTON, *Private Journals of Tours in France in 1815–1818.* London, 1871.

WARD, S. G. P., *Wellington's Headquarters. A Study of the Administrative Problems in the Peninsula 1809–1814.* Oxford, 1957.

—, *Wellington.* London, 1963.

WARTENBURG, COUNT YORCK VON, *Napoleon as a General.* London, 1902.

WELLESLEY, MURIEL, *The Man Wellington Through the Eyes of Those Who Knew Him.* London, 1937.

WILKINSON, SPENSER, *The French Army Before Napoleon.* Oxford, 1915.

—, *The Rise of General Bonaparte.* Oxford, 1930.

WILSON, LT A. W., *The Story of The Gun.* Woolwich, 1944.

WILSON, PHILIP WHITWELL, *The Greville Diary.* 2 vols. London, 1927.

General Index

Plate numbers are given in italics after the main entry.

259

Index of Places

THE NAPOLEONIC LIBRARY
New editions of classic works
on the Napoleonic Wars
Published by Greenhill Books

JOURNAL OF THE WATERLOO CAMPAIGN
by General Cavalié Mercer
ISBN 0-947898-04-2.
Napoleonic Library 1

THE NOTE-BOOKS OF CAPTAIN COIGNET
Soldier of the Empire, 1799–1816
by Captain Jean-Roch Coignet
ISBN 0-947898-13-1.
Napoleonic Library 2

A BRITISH RIFLEMAN
Journals and Correspondence during the Peninsular War
and the Campaign of Wellington
by Major George Simmons
ISBN 0-947898-33-6.
Napoleonic Library 3

WELLINGTON'S ARMY, 1808–1814
by Sir Charles Oman
ISBN 0-947898-41-7.
Napoleonic Library 4

THE CAMPAIGN OF WATERLOO
by the Hon. Sir John Fortescue
ISBN 0-947898-49-2.
Napoleonic Library 5

STUDIES IN THE NAPOLEONIC WARS
by Sir Charles Oman
ISBN 0-947898-63-8.
Napoleonic Library 6